John Carroll

My Boy Life

Presented in a Succession of true Stories

John Carroll

My Boy Life
Presented in a Succession of true Stories

ISBN/EAN: 9783337053857

Printed in Europe, USA, Canada, Australia, Japan

Cover: Foto ©ninafisch / pixelio.de

More available books at **www.hansebooks.com**

MY BOY LIFE.
By Rev. John Carroll, D.D.

BEN OWEN.
By Jennie Perrett.

MY BOY LIFE,

PRESENTED IN A SUCCESSION OF TRUE STORIES,

BY
JOHN CARROLL, D.D.

"The child is father to the man."
—*Wordsworth.*

A BOOK FOR OLD OR YOUNG.

TORONTO:
WILLIAM BRIGGS,
78 & 80 King Street East.

1882.

Entered, according to the Act of the Parliament of Canada, in the year one thousand eight hundred and eighty-one, by the REV. WILLIAM BRIGGS, in the Office of the Minister of Agriculture, Ottawa.

Dedication.

TO

ALL THE SELF-MADE MEN

(BOTH LAY AND CLERICAL,)

IN OUR WIDE CONNEXION;

AND TO ALL

THE NOBLE BOYS,

WHO INTEND TO BE

SUCH MEN AS ARE MEN

This Volume

IS INSCRIBED,

WITH

SENTIMENTS OF PROFOUND CONSIDERATION,

BY

THE HUMBLE AUTHOR.

Ramble Lodge, August 18, 1851.

INTRODUCTION.

I FEEL myself honoured in being asked to write an introduction to these autobiographic sketches of my beloved and venerated friend, the Rev. Dr. CARROLL. I have read these sketches with profoundest interest—often with moistened eyes, and often with an irrepressible smile. The greater number of them have undergone the practical test of publication in a periodical having a circulation of nearly twenty thousand copies, and have proved exceedingly attractive not only to juvenile but also to adult readers. By reading these "True Stories of Boy Life" sixty years ago, every Canadian boy and girl of to-day may learn invaluable lessons. And those who have left their youthful days far behind them will find here agreeable reminiscences of the past and a vivid insight into the social condition of the early years of this century in this province.

While thankful to God for the ameliorated circumstances of society at the present time, and the greater educational and religious advantages enjoyed by the youth of to-day, let us be thankful also to the grand old pioneers who, by their lives and labours, have made Canada what it is. Conspicuous among these have been the Methodist Missionaries of Canada, who, with Bible and saddle-bags, carried the glad message of the Gospel to the lonely cottages of the frontiersmen in the depths of the primeval forest; and conspicuous among these Missionary heroes has been the author of these sketches.

By thousands all over this land to whom he has ministered the bread of life, this record of the providential leadings of his early years will be read with intensest interest; and to many more of a younger generation, we trust, these pages will make known the circumstances under which were developed that genial character, earnest piety, and unwearying zeal, which we all so much admire in him whom all who know him love to call our revered and honoured FATHER CARROLL. Though having more than reached the allotted span of threescore years and ten, his heart is as young as when he was a boy. He still possesses more vivacity and more energy; he still reads more books, writes more pages, travels more miles and preaches more sermons than many a man not half his years. May he long flourish in his hale old age—full of years and full of honours—and still enrich the world with his ripe and mellow wisdom, and with still more of his racy and readable books, is the earnest prayer of his friend,

W. H. W.

CONTENTS.

		PAGE
I.—WHY THIS BOOK, AND WHAT ABOUT IT		1
II.—MY PARENTS AND NATIVITY		5
III.—MY LITTLE TWIN BROTHER		16
IV.—A LONG ROUGH JOURNEY PERFORMED IN UNCONSCIOUS INFANCY		27
V.—MY ELDEST BROTHER'S BEAUTIFUL LIFE AND TRAGIC DEATH		32
VI.—OUR INDIAN NEIGHBOURS		40
VII.—CHILD MEMORIES OF THE ALARMS AND HARDSHIPS OF WAR		49
VIII.—A THREE DAYS' COASTING VOYAGE		72
IX.—OUR FIRST PLACES OF ABODE IN YORK, AND HOW WE CAME TO OCCUPY THEM		75
X.—THE WAR SPIRIT AMONG THE YORK BOYS		78
XI.—NEDDIE, MY LITTLE PLAYMATE		83
XII.—RECOLLECTIONS OF THE LONG-LOG HOUSE		92
XIII.—FOND MEMORIES OF CERTAIN DOMESTIC ANIMALS		101
XIV.—THE GHOST LORE CURRENT DURING MY CHILDHOOD		109
XV.—HOW I EARNED MY FIRST FELT HAT		116
XVI.—THE "ELMSLEY FIELD," AND ITS ONE TRAGIC MEMORY		121

CONTENTS.

	PAGE
XVII.—THE RISE OF AN INSTITUTION WHICH INFLUENCED MY DESTINIES FOR GOOD	129
XVIII.—HOW I CHANCED TO GET THE FIRST PRIZE	134
XIX.—HOW I INVESTED MY FOUND MONEY	141
XX.—A TRAMP TO THE BUSH IN SUGAR TIME WITH YOUNG LADIES	147
XXI.—"OLD GRAY," THE MILL HORSE	157
XXII.—GOING ON A BUSH FARM	163
XXIII.—DRIVING AN OX TEAM	168
XXIV.—MORE WORK ON A BUSH FARM	176
XXV.—"OLD KATE," THE MARE, AND I	182
XXVI.—MY PETS AND PROPERTY IN THE BUSH, AND WHAT BECAME OF THEM	192
XXVII.—A CHRISTMAS WEEK THAT ENDED WRONG	204
XXVIII.—AN IMPULSIVE ACT—A SUDDEN DEPARTURE FROM THE BUSH	211
XXIX.—SOME ACCOUNT OF MY DEAR OLD "BOSS"	219
XXX.—BUTTERNUTTING ON SUNDAY AND ITS PUNISHMENT	229
XXXI.—A MIS-SPENT SUNDAY THAT ENDED WELL	235
XXXII.—MY LAST ACCEPTED DRAM	242
XXXIII.—HOW I CAME TO GO AMONG THE METHODISTS	246
XXXIV.—THE CRISIS I HAVE ALWAYS CALLED CONVERSION; AND WHEN, WHERE, AND HOW IT TOOK PLACE.	253
XXXV.—WHAT MODICUMS OF KNOWLEDGE I POSSESSED AT FIFTEEN; AND HOW I HAD STUMBLED INTO THEIR POSSESSION	260
XXXVI.—MY BOYISH THOUGHTS OF A BUSINESS FOR LIFE, AND THE ONE I FINALLY CHOSE	277
XXXVII.—A SUMMARY AND CONNECTION OF THE FOREGOING PAGES	285

MY BOY LIFE.

No. I.

WHY THIS BOOK, AND WHAT ABOUT IT?

IT will be perceived at a glance, that it is *autobiographical*—and many will say, "therefore, egotistical." If the word egotistical is used in the sense of "vain and self-conceited," then I trust all candid readers will exonerate me from the charge; but if it only means something about the writer's self, then I accept the characterization,—albeit, I think *egoistical* would be more appropriate. Besides, if I live to finish the whole work, of which this is an instalment, it will be much about other persons and things, as well as myself, namely, almost all the leading personages and events that have crossed my path in the course of my humble journey through a long, diversified life. These matters ought to be of some interest and importance, if I am of none. One word in defence of works of this character in the abstract: Some one has said, "Almost any one's autobiography would be valuable, if he only knew what to tell, and how to tell it." Yes, and the more commonplace his career, the more likely to come home to the business and bosoms of the many. Say that JOHN CARROLL is of no great account, and I will agree with you; but it is all the more likely that the story of his life will enlist the sympathies of the "common run."

A history of my own life and times is something which scores of persons have urged me to write, for years and years. And several years ago I commenced to write what I entitled, "THE LESSONS OF A LIFE-TIME," and had written five or six hundred pages of large foolscap, when other plans were suggested. In that work I divided my life into natural EPOCHS, and gave in each an account of the *outward and physical circumstances* of that period; *my mental or intellectual life* (including the development of my faculties from childhood, my schools and schoolmates, such as they were, and of my methods of inquiry and study); *my religious or spiritual life; my ministerial and official life; my literary life*, &c., &c., &c., as the epochs transpired, under separate headings, or departments, deducing the lessons the events had taught me and those which I thought others might learn from my blunders, which were many. But I found that after all the time, ink, and paper I had expended, I had not passed over a third of my career, and the unfinished part was the most crowded and important of my existence. With the many engagements I am constantly drawn into, I did not see how I was to find time and strength to finish it; I was not sure but that a plan of work so complex and unusual would prove tiresome; furthermore, I saw it was going to be a very expensive work to publish, and the question was, would the sales defray that expense?

At this juncture I was led to draw on some of the materials for an account of my early life in a series of "STORIES" for the amusement and instruction of the young readers of *Pleasant Hours*. These I found interested many of the old as well as the young who had read them. I rather anticipated they would engage the attention of adult minds as well as juvenile ones, for I myself had ever felt an interest in accounts of the boyhood and youth of any person who had attained to any measure of public attention, and I also found it was the same with other people. Besides the incidents I related, while they referred to matters which would naturally take the attention of young minds, were not told in nursery, but common phraseology, which would command the respect of adults, and which the well-schooled children of our country in this day understand as well, or better than grown people. Then, as to those particular reminicences, many of my friends wished to see them collected and preserved in an accessible and permanent form.

Therefore, after conversing with my scholarly and versatile literary friend, the Rev. W. H. Withrow, A.M., whose taste and judgment I very much confided in, I concluded to abandon the larger and more elaborate project, and to cover the ground embraced in my history by a series of sketchy volumes, each one complete in itself, and saleable as an independent book, yet an essential part of a greater whole; that if I did not live to finish that whole, what I had actually accomplished would not seem a mere fragment; while each one of the sections, in each volume, would be a microcosm—a little narrative by itself and making a complete reading for a sitting, yet bearing a relation to the other sections.

This, I imagine, will be particularly the case with the first volume, which is largely made up of the "True Stories," retouched, supplemented, and wrought into a somewhat homogeneous whole. I say "somewhat," because, from the way it has come into being, it will, perhaps, be found that some parts are rather discursive and others repetitious.

As it is, tho public have it. Take it, and make the most of it you can; for, on the subject of my BOY LIFE, it is all you will get—except my blessing, which you have already, and shall have. Amen.

Those who desire more of these lucubrations, relating to further stages of my humble life, will please indicate their wish to me, or to the authorities at our Publishing House, that I may know how to act in the future.

THE AUTHOR.

No. II.

MY PARENTS AND NATIVITY.

IN many biographies, whether written by the subjects themselves, or their friends, there seems a great effort to conceal any thing like obscurity or poverty, in their origin. This in my opinion, is weak and despicable, and hints and innuendoes about the nobleness of their ancestral line are still worse; both proceed from the silliest kind of affectation and vanity. I, therefore, entirely concur in the truth and manliness of the following from the poet Saxe:—

> "Of all the notable things on earth,
> The queerest one is pride of birth,
>   In this our fierce democracy :
> A bridge across a hundred years,
> Without a thing to save it from sneers
> (Not even a couple of rotten peers)
> A thing for laughter, flouts, and jeers,
>   Is American aristocracy.
>
> Depend upon it, my snobbish friend,
> Your family thread you can't ascend,
> Without good reason to apprehend,

> You may find it waxed at the farther end,
> By some plebeian vocation;
> Or worse than that, your boasted line
> May end in a loop of stronger twine,
> That plagued some worthy relation."

I never heard that any of my forefathers, either on the paternal or maternal line, had been hanged, but the "waxed end" might be found if looked after in my genealogy.

My father was a *saddler* and *harness-maker* by trade and understood well his handicraft; he was distinguished for substantial work, and excelled particularly in the department of *saddles* and *neck-draft collars*. In his time in America, people travelled two or three, if not four times, as much on horseback as in carriages; hence the demand for saddles. Some of my earliest recollections are of amusing myself among the litter and scraps of his shop, and of some of the tools he employed—such as his tack-hammer, his wooden mallets (one faced with shark skin), and his long iron "collar rods" employed in stuffing the rims of the draft collars with long straw, which were left as hard as wood and as polished as if made of marble. Another peculiarity was that the collars were left in an almost circular form, he never using any collar-block but the horse's neck, to which alone, he said, it must be fitted. Nothing would arouse his anger so quickly as for a visitor to his shop to squeeze a new collar into an oblong shape, as they often felt an impulse to do.

"Pox take it, you fool!" he would say, "Do you know the mischief you are doing?"

Of my father *physically*, I have this to say: he was an old man when I first remember him. He was full twenty years older than my mother; I and my twin brother were the last of twelve children; he must, therefore, have been close on to sixty years of age when I was born. But from what I saw and learned, he came of a strong, long-lived race of men. He was considerably above the medium stature—about five feet, eleven—he may have been six feet before he began to settle down. He was big-boned and muscular, not less than one hundred and eighty pounds in weight. Had great weight of arm and hand; and had he never ill-used himself, he would have been for many more years than is usual, a very hale and powerful man. All the encounters into which his convivial habits led him, were said to have issued in victory, but the particulars would edify no one. One I will mention because it shows how strength and daring may serve a man's safety in a rude and lawless state of society. When we lived at the Grand River in Canada, among the Six Nation Indians, and the still worse behaved white squatters on the Indian lands, just before the war of 1812, when he could not have been less than sixty years of age, occurred the following: He, having by his "Britisher" ways made himself unpopular with the disaffected around, of whom there were said to be many, was one day going to mill with a team of horses and grist of grain, accompanied only by a half-grown boy, and called at a tavern to rest his horses and warm himself. A well-to-do and purse-proud Canadian Dutchman (one Staatz) a younger and more vigorous man than himself, somewhat under the influence of liquor, came in, accompanied by several of a kindred character, and charged the old man with having stolen his whip, who, when father denied it and failed to produce it, began chasing the old gentleman about the room. Father, except when under the influence of liquor, was not particularly passionate—and never quarrelsome—but rather fair-spoken (though boastful and pretentious); and on this occasion at first made no resistance; but at length he disengaged himself, stepped back, and threw off his great-coat; and when his assailant approached again, father knocked him down, like a bullock felled by the butcher's axe; and when he arose, knocked him down again. This cooled the Dutchman's courage and awed the rest. Now Staatz suddenly discovered that Mr. Carroll was a most honourable and excellent man, and proffered to treat him. My brother William, who witnessed the scene, and twice related it in my hearing, did not say whether the treat was accepted or declined; but, judging from the old man's well-known belief in the potency of the social glass to feed, and clothe, and satisfy, and compose all difficulties, and assuage all evils to which flesh is heir, it is likely the glass was accepted.

Father was a native of Old Ireland (the North of it, the County Down, and Town of Ballynahinch) but came with his parents to America (the Old Colonies) when quite young, and learned his trade in the City of Philadelphia. The rest of the family lived near by, in the town of Reading—on land, I suspect. His father, who was a Roman Catholic, as far as he was anything (not bigotted) and who often received the prefix *O* or *Mac* to his name by countrymen, had been tossed about the world for many years as a sailor. Father said his mother was, as he pronounced it, "a Presbytayrean." If asked about his own religion, of which he had not much to spare, he would answer, "Protestant." Though far from being a truly religious man at any time of his life, I am bound to say, that though sometimes profane, he never treated sacred things with irreverence; but could so talk on religious subjects as to leave the impression on strangers, that he was a very religious man, especially if he had a glass in his head, which, he always maintained, used to "brighten his ideas."

He used to maintain that he was a blood relation of the celebrated Charles Carroll, of Carrollton, in Maryland, who, he boasted "owned a whole manor;" but, as he never liked to spoil a good story, I am inclined to suspect that with regard to his claim to anything like an intimate relationship to the celebrated signer of the Declaration of Independence, he must have drawn the long-bow somewhat. For, if a good tough yarn were wanted, commend me to old Joseph Carroll at any time. Father's oldest brother "*Jeems*" as he called him, however, was indeed a very respectable and influential man of large means; and like *Charles* Carroll, a great devotee of the American colonial cause. But my father early quarrelled with the colonists, and joined the British standard, and served to the end of the war. He must, however, have been committed to the revolutionary cause for a time, for he was afraid to return to the family upon the acknowledgement of the Independence of the United States. His brother James, however, wrote him word to come back, and he would "intercede with Congress in his behalf." But he had become so fierce a "Britisher" that he sent word he would "see him and Congress d—d before he would make any intercessions to them." The consequence was, he never saw his relatives after. Father never called the Americans anything but "rebels."

His department in the army was the artillery, and he ranked as a bombardier, wearing a sword by his side, one edge of which was a sword-blade, the other a saw. He had sometimes acted as a sapper, and used to show a scar from end to end of one of his fingers, which had been laid open by the point of a pike that he was parrying, which had been aimed at him while with a detachment he was storming a stockade. Some of his war stories would be thrilling, if there were space to register them.

He was disbanded along with his corps in the West Indies, where he had served some time. The discharged troops were destined for Nova Scotia and New Brunswick, but being embarked in an unseaworthy old hulk, (an East Indiaman), which had been repainted and insured for a fabulous sum, and then intentionally run upon rocks in the Bay of Fundy, they were wrecked. She became a total loss, and a vast number of the passengers perished, while the captain and crew, in collusion with the fraudulent underwriters, escaped in their boats. Those of the passengers who escaped, of whom my father was one, did so mostly by constructing a raft out of the broken timbers of the ship, after father personally had been "eight and forty hours on a spar." To tie their raft together they made cordage out of an old cable, the only means of cutting which was a dull razor, while they tore out the several strands with their teeth. Two men, one of whom my mother afterwards knew and esteemed, were wafted ashore on two puncheons lashed together. The raft was picked up and the suffering freight brought into port totally destitute, my father among the rest.

My parent selected New Brunswick as his place of residence, where he drew a small, poor lot of land—I think on the shores of the Nashwaak. He might have succeeded well in a worldly point of view, only for some defects; he had rather superior powers of mind; had education sufficient to transact business; his conversational powers were adapted to prepossess people in his favour; and he was almost the only person with a knowledge of his most necessary trade in a wide new country. So lately as 1853, almost a century after, I was visiting relations in that part of the Province, and met with those who told me of his celebrity for skill in his business, and said that specimens of harness he had made were still in preservation. But sad to say, he was a poor manager; changeable in his plans—trying, from time to time, hunting, fishing, lumbering, and farming, as well as his own proper vocation. Then his convivial proclivities, induced by his song-singing and story-telling gifts, with the love of liquor acquired in his seven years' soldiering experiences, during which he used to boast, that he sometimes drank a dozen glasses of liquor in a morning and passed muster on parade as a sober man. He was not, however, a lazy man, but quite disposed to labour, had not his work been often interrupted by the causes I have mentioned; and the avails of his labour squandered despite the industry, capability, and economy of the woman it is a wonder he ever gained.

My *mother* was in all respects the opposite of my father. The young and lovely *daughter*—for she was a most comely woman—of a grave Quaker man, of a singularly amiable disposition, only eighteen when she was induced, clandestinely (in the absence of a mother's guardianship, who had died a short time before) to marry a man of forty (claiming of course to be much younger). Oh! what poverty, privations, shifts and turns, neglect and abuse, that poor woman suffered by being "lured" by the songs, blandishments, and persuasive tongue of a man, vastly her inferior, "from her native home," a home of full and plenty. Heroically she struggled with insufficient supplies of provisions and covering for day and night, living in dilapidated houses in that severe climate, to provide for and raise her large family of boys, preparing the materials of which their clothes were woven, and making it up into garments herself when woven. The elder ones' garments were made of the new cloth, and the little ones' clothes of the cast-off coats and trousers of the older ones. The first thoroughly new suit I ever wore, at the age of eight or nine, was of striped homespun carded and spun by my tireless mother's hands, while doing for a family of ten or twelve, without any domestic help—something she never had. Oh! my precious mother! my soul is agonized by the remembrance of thy sorrows! And glad I am that I had the chance of doing something to soothe thy mind in thy later years!

Father's changeableness led to a great many wearisome moves, till at last, through my mother's persuasions, he resumed his own proper business in Fredericton, and a pretty home was bought, and through her economy money enough was saved to pay for it. During the time the family resided there was the one green spot in their domestic life, the only oasis in a wide, dreary desert. But, alas! that was not to last! From the Masonic lodge he and others would adjourn to the tavern. There, while mellowed into maudlin generosity, he was induced to become responsible to a large amount for a brother mason—that brother failed without securing father; father seeing the storm rising, under cover of coming to Upper Canada to look after securing the claims he had for services rendered to the British Government for land, stepped out of the way, and dear mother and her four eldest boys, the youngest only four years of age, were left to face the tornado, which swept all away. He was gone two years and five months, during which, though the second eldest boy lost his sight during the time, mother maintained herself and children in tidiness and comfort. Nor was her husband's return, though he vaunted a grant from Gov. Simcoe for a thousand acres of land in his pocket, anything but a source of anxiety to his wife and hapless boys. Oh! drink, thou art a demon, and thy name is legion! Several years longer residence in New Brunswick added two more boys to the family, and brought down our history to the spring of 1809.

Then it was resolved to remove to Upper Canada to locate and settle on their thousand-acre demesne. In a boat they descended the St. John River to the Bay of Fundy; but they must perforce remain in the fisheries in Passimaquody until the four eldest boys, *Joseph, James, William,* and *Thomas,* could earn money enough to enable the family to complete their journey to the much anticipated land of promise.

Father always located his hapless family in some out of the way place, and on this occasion he put them in one of the three only huts on the islet known as Saltkill's Island, so named after its owner, John Saltkill, a bachelor Quaker, who had obtained a grant of it for services during the Revolution, my mother in imminent nearness to a confinement. There twins were born, of which two I was the eldest. There was just one family on the island besides ourselves, a Mr. Isaac Clarke and his wife. The circumstances of our birth are described in the next section. I was named *John Saltkill* after the proprietor, who wished to keep me and make me his heir; and my mate was named *Isaac Clarke* after the other resident—christening there was none. None in the family were baptized till long after (which they all were, except poor Isaac and Joseph), one now, and another then. My brother did not live long enough to assert his middle name; and I threw *Saltkill* away, and kept to *John* alone, when I came to choose for myself.

No. III.

MY LITTLE TWIN BROTHER.

OF sisterly affection—that is, of a sister's love to a brother, or the tender attachment which the kind ways of a sister will awaken in the heart of a brother—I know nothing, having never set my eyes on my only sister, who was born and buried many years before I came into existence.

Of the attachment between brothers of different ages I know something. I know that the beauty and tenderness of little brothers will awaken a feeling of care and kindness in the heart of a "big brother" when rightly constituted. Of Joe, the oldest and best of brothers, who died at the age of twenty-two, when I was no more than two or three years old, I had long a dim recollection, probably stereotyped by the oft-recited traditions in the family of his sympathy for our weakly mother and her two last-born infants. Indeed poor Joe's beauty of person, nobleness of character, early piety, and early and almost tragic death, dwelt upon again and again, was an heir-loom and species of almost ancestor-worship in our rude household.

For the next oldest, Jim, I had a peculiar kind of affection, because he was very big and very strong, and would good-naturedly allow half a dozen little ones to cling to his legs and neck while he thus carried us about the house, and allow us to make a horse of his knees, while he trotted us up and down, and allowed us to belabour the imaginary horse with a stick from time to time. I am not under so great obligations to him for teaching me to box when a little older; but in time there was a better attachment between us. He loved books and reading; but about the age of manhood his sight became so impaired by a disease, which fell into his eyes from serving his King and country in the militia, during the war of 1812, that he could no longer read for himself. But I early became an expert reader and fond of a book, and being very small of my age, I could sit on his knee next to his best ear (for his hearing was also defective), and read to him by the hour. Our interviews were not only "readings," but discussions the while. I remember the questions and talk to which the perusal of the blessed Bible, the Pilgrim's Progress, and sundry histories we read gave rise.

The next oldest brother, Bill, and I were never so intimate; he was long absent in the army, and soon after returning from the wars he married, and lived apart from the rest of the family. There was an attachment between him and me, but it was distinct from any of the rest.

The next brother, Tom, was more among us, and we younger ones had occasion to feel for him as clients towards a patron, or preserver, if not of children to a parent. Dear Tom, thou wast noble and lovable; but in the end somewhat unfortunate, yet rest on in thy fifty years' sleep in the dust of the earth.

George was six years older than I, and somehow gave me a marked patronizing regard; but as he was peculiar and a little whimsical in his likes and dislikes, I had to treat him a little cannily.

Nat was the next one to me who survived for any length of time; and there being scarcely four years between us, gave us a greater community of feeling than between me and any of the others, excepting one. But when young, like all children and boys, we had our contentions as well as our social pleasures.

Of that *other one*, my mate, or twin brother, I set out with the intention more especially of writing. As he died before quite ten years of age, all I have to say will bear the impress of childhood, and will be more likely to interest children than older persons; although there is something to be learned by the old in recalling the experiences of childhood.

My parents said we were born within half an hour of each other—I the first, he the last—on a small island in the Bay of Fundy, on a very foggy night. We were unusually small—our traditional weight, or lightness, though often mentioned, I have forgotten; but this I remember to have heard them say, that one of the tiny teacups of that day, not more than a third as large as the smallest now in use, easily covered the entire of either one of our visages. We were born on the journey from New Brunswick to Canada, partly by water and partly by land, and resumed our wayfaring three weeks after our birth. We must have suffered great discomfort as well as our poor mother, for we cried almost every waking moment till our long journey was ended, and for long after. We were both weakly, but I was said to be the stronger of the two, and soon began, it was said, to help myself, learning to sit alone, by being placed in a horse's draft collar on the floor, at the age of six months, and took to my pins and stubbed about the floor at eight months.

Being largely cast on my own resources, I think my mental faculties must have been very precociously developed, especially observation and memory. I remember, almost consecutively, since, at my mother's knee, my nose and chin just overtopping it, I had to be fed by her with a spoon, when I could not have been more than two years old, if I was that. In all those visions of the past, my memory recalls a little white-headed child, rather less than myself, standing by my side, grovelling with me on the ground, or lying in the same cot, such as it was. Our attachment to each other became very great. We were inseparable in our little plays and amusements, which were mostly extemporized, our playthings being invented by ourselves, no money ever being spent on toys for us. Some of these may be particularized before I have done. Before we could speak plainly, our gibberish was understood by ourselves, when no others could interpret it. This gibberish at length crystallized into a kind of dialect, which was used, between ourselves, from choice when it was no longer a necessity. Thus *salt* was "sock," *crust* was "pick-pick," and *water* was "tubity." On one occasion I was not to be found, and great alarm was felt on my account. The adjacent premises were searched, and my name was pronounced by all the older members of the family without eliciting any answer, but when my little mate came near where I was seated and hidden in the growing grain, and called out in his piping little voice, "Donny! Donny!" I responded "No!" Whether I was thus refusing to disclose myself, or whether we used *no* for *yes*, I cannot say; but the noise I made revealed my hiding-place. I think we were both predisposed to solitary amusements; certain I am that we seldom asked or had more to join in the play than our two selves, for neither of us ever admitted that he had more than "one brother." Like all children's amusements, they were mimic occupations of men, in which imagination supplied the place of real resemblance. The stirring scenes of the war-time filled us with military ideas and occupations; by bestriding a rod of elder and putting a yellow, tassel-like wild flower in our caps, we imagined ourselves light horsemen, and galloped away on some important express; or square bits of leather, purloined from the regimental shop, arrayed in paralled rows, were opposing armies, while a bullet or marble rolled by each alternately won the battle for the General the fewest of whose soldiers were knocked down.

When, "wild war's deadly blast was blown, and gentle peace returning," we imitated the rural occupations to which the erstwhile soldiering family came back, suggesting the idea of fields and flocks. Compartments made by chalk-marks, on the floor or hearth, were the fields—parti-coloured beans were the various kinds of cattle, and downy willow buds were the sheep. Many a fort or farmstead, according to our fancy, rose among the bushes or elsewhere; and partial to the profession of the baker and pastry cook, we perpetrated the usual number of mud cakes and pies. We sometimes went a-fishing and caught chub, but we were seldom favoured with any more artistic tackle than a pin-hook tied to the end of a piece of thread.

We were very much alike, and neighbours with the confidence that they knew us apart, almost always called us wrong—John for Isaac, and Isaac for John. My mother also, once when we were stripped for bed, mistook us, and gave me a flogging she intended for him. We knew each other's thoughts almost instinctively, and our opinions almost always coincided.

His capacity, however, was slower than mine, and he was always one class behind me at school. As I was the eldest, I was invariably the spokesman when we were sent of an errand together; and although I am sure he had more physical courage than I (that is, he was not so cautious about boyish quarrels and fights), yet I seemed always to assume the position of patron and protector to my little brother. Our affection for each other was very great, and one uttered the most piteous pleadings when he saw the other about to receive a flogging. We seldom told tales on each other, but were very loyal to one another, concealing each other's faults and misfortunes, or anything which was likely to humiliate the other.

When we were between nine and ten years of age, we were introduced for the first time into a newly-formed Sunday-school, the first ever held in the Town of York, now the City of Toronto, and one of the first in the Province. We frequented it together from November, 1818, to the following June, when, unhappily, a Sunday night's play-spell led to his death. My mother had become a Methodist about a year before, and became exacting about the proper observance of the Sabbath; but there were neighbouring children and boys, not over well conducted, who sometimes lured us from the right way. One Sunday evening after supper, some of these congregated in the yard at the back of our house, and we all joined in a noisy play. Our mother came out and forbade its continuance; and from the quietness that followed, she thought we had returned to the house and gone to bed. But we had removed to a back street, out of the way of those in the house, and resumed our play. It was a very active one, called "Hunt the Bear." Isaac received some rough treatment from one of the boys, at which he took offence, and withdrew from the play, and threw his heated person, reeking with perspiration, on the wet grass under the falling dew. Neither he nor we had sense or reflection enough to rescue him from the peril. At a somewhat late hour we stole into the house and went to bed. In the middle of the night he awakened his mother by crying out for a drink, saying, " O mammy, I am burning up inside!" A blighting fever was upon him. In the morning the family physician was summoned, and did his best according to whatever skill he had; and our mother tried her simple remedies. His hip, where he had lain on the grass, was in violent pain and much swollen, and I was sent to the fields to gather wild herbs supposed to possess healing virtue (Oh! with what painful desire and hope I gathered them); and hemlock boughs were brought, and placed in tubs of hot water, over the steam of which he was fomented; but alas! after the lapse of eight days, during the most of which he raved in delirium, God released him from his sufferings. True, he had lucid intervals, when he confessed his sins and prayed earnestly for himself and for all his friends. For days he rejected food, but at length called for some and ate it with voracity, saying there was a hollow place in his stomach where he wanted to put the food to remove the distress. Oh! how tearfully did I watch his bed-side, agonized by his want of recognition and appreciation of me. What would I have done to save him, or to call him back when he was gone? Oh! it was a cruel blow and blight to my young heart.

The company present after death and at the funeral in some measure diverted me from my sorrow; but when the people were dispersed, and the current of affairs returned to its usual channel, the desolation and loneliness I felt no tongue can tell. It seemed more than I could possibly bear. I gathered up his little playthings—among others a tiny house-frame—and shed my tears over them. Long after his death, my desire for his company became so agonizing and unbearable that, although I knew it was vain, I went out by myself and called him aloud. Often I dreamed that he came to life: once, that he came up from the graveyard in his shroud to the potato-field where I was hoeing the potatoes we had planted together, looked through the fence to my unutterable joy, and said, "John, I will go up to the house, put on my clothes, and come back and help you." The ecstacy awoke me to the sad certainty that I was bereaved for ever of the dear, ever-present companion of my ten years' life.

I should have said earlier, that I followed his body to the grave, borne on young men's shoulders, walking next the coffin, hand in hand with my poor stricken mother, to whom he had always shown the doting affection of an infant (much more so than I ever did myself). We laid him in a grave dug in the corner of St. James' Cathedral Square, Toronto, where the parochial school-house now stands; but when the clods began to rattle on the coffin lid, it was more than I could bear to see my dear little brother Ike buried up in the earth, and I begged to leave. A kind-hearted neighbour boy, John Harper, about two years older than myself, kindly accompanied me the half mile or more which intervened between the churchyard and our house, and very considerately came over often to keep me company and assuage my grief and loneliness. He is still alive, a respectable old gentleman doing business in this city. We have been life-long friends.

A tender incident occurred soon after. The little grave never had a headstone; we never passed that way but we stopped to look through the fence, and sometimes to weep, but always to feel intensely. One of the first times a member of the family went that way after his burial, he beheld a pretty young rose-bush planted on his grave, about where his breast might be supposed to be. It surprised and delighted us much; but for a length of time we were kept in ignorance as to who had performed the graceful act of kindness. At length a widow lady informed my mother that her little son, about a year older than I and my brother, had returned weeping from the funeral (he had not been a playmate, but was one of the Methodist Sunday-School with us), and begged of his mother to allow him to dig up one of the only two rose bushes growing in their garden. She consented, and he loosened it from its place, and planted it on the dead Sunday scholar's grave. When I discovered who had performed this soothing act of kindness, I made his acquaintance, and ever felt an almost brotherly affection for dear, generous Nelson Reece. After the lapse of years many of our town boys became scattered like autumn leaves, and I lost sight of Nelson, but never forgot his kindness. If still living, I should like to see and thank him once more before I die. At least I pray that I may meet him in heaven, where I expect to join my brother.

> "Oh! that will be joyful,
> To meet and part no more!"

It will heal a wound that has been made to bleed afresh (though sixty years ought to have obliterated the scars), by recalling the companionship and loss of my TWIN BROTHER.

This story has its moral; but every child can and will moralize for himself, and I will not insult his intelligence by doing it for him.

No. IV.

A LONG ROUGH JOURNEY PERFORMED IN UNCONSCIOUS INFANCY.

AT least, so said my parents, for often and often I heard them dwell on the wearisome details. Some reference to those details is necessary as a connecting link between my first sketch and the second. When the infants were only three weeks old, as a necessary first stage of our intended removal to Upper Canada, father transferred his family in some sort of boat from Saltkill's Island, near the Province line, to Campo Bello Island, just beyond the American line; so that I barely escaped being born a citizen of the United States; but "a miss is as good as a mile," and with the Britisher sentiments in which I was brought up, I was exceedingly glad of that miss, and was none too well pleased, when I became old enough to know the facts, that I so early inhaled the air of Yankee-land—a land the inhabitants of which my Tory father persisted in calling "rebels." Knowing my sensitiveness to any aspersion on my loyalty, when my brothers wanted to teaze me, they need but call me "Yankee!" to put me in a rage. My next oldest brother had a trick of doing that, much to my annoyance. I had a way, however, of turning the tables upon him; he had one vulnerable spot: he was a seventh son, and his father used to call him "Doctor," of which the little fellow would have been very proud, but for an unlucky surname he involuntarily received. On our voyage he had the misfortune to fall down the hatchway into a large pan of batter ready prepared for a breakfast of pancakes, from which immersion he received the cognomen of "Dr. Batter;" and when he annoyed me beyond endurance by calling me "Yankee," I generally silenced his battery, by telling "*Dr. Batter*" to shut up—I might say, that the juvenile physician's invariable prescription, when asked for advice, was a "bread and milk poultice."

Our passage from Campobello to New York, in a small sailing vessel, heavily laden with plaster of Paris, was a very rough one. The waves ran mountains high, the decks were drenched with salt water, and the hold was flooded nearly all the time. The poor weak mother suffered much; and as to us infants, it was said the briny baths to which we were subject, chafed the skin off our tiny bodies, and made us as red as a couple of boiled lobsters, which we very much resembled in size and otherwise.

Friends found in New York solaced the family somewhat for a short stay; but we soon embarked in a sloop on the Hudson for Albany; which, though crowded, was a slight improvement on the first stage of our journey. At Albany, father hired the horses and waggon of a farmer, whom he met in the market, by the name of Canfield, a Methodist, who proved a good man, (who I surmise, for certain reasons, afterwards became a travelling preacher), to drive us forward, through the long length of the "Empire State," from its Capital to the Niagara River, the dividing line between New York State and Upper Canada. It was a terrible journey to a person in my mother's circumstances. The narrow box of the waggon was crowded with some effects, which mother had brought from her father's affluent home, when she left it first, and had not parted with, but which she clung to with tenacity to the end. The twins and the next two youngest boys rode in the waggon. Tom, always a good nurse, must have often ridden, to relieve his mother of the infants. Ever faithful and sympathising Joseph walked on one side of the waggon and William on the other. James, always a favourite of the old gentleman's accompanied his father, who walked on ahead, under pretence of pioneering and preparing the way which largely consisted in testing the liquors at all the dram shops on the road. It is but just, however, to say, that his story-telling and song-singing capabilities constituted the key which unlocked some hearts toward us. So also his knowledge of Low German which he spoke fluently, having learned it when a youth in Pennsylvania, stood us in good stead. Once the waggon had stopped for the night at a Dutch tavern in the Mohawk Valley; the babies were very cross and the people looked very glum; and mother, who had ridden all day in a springless waggon over logs and stones innumerable, was ready to faint with fatigue. A gloomy night seemed in store for her. But when father came in and accosted the people in Dutch, all was changed; the old Dutch landlady wore a pleasant smile; one stout Dutch girl took one baby, and another girl took the other; and mother was ensconsed in the rocking chair, received a good supper, got early into a soft bed, and had one good night's rest.

We passed through Schenectady, and the incipient villages of Auburn, Cayuga, Canendagua, Onendaga, Batavia, &c., now more cities than anything else; but the country as a whole was new, and a great part of it a howling wilderness. Mudholes were countless, and sometimes nearly bottomless; the family avowed that sometimes all that was visible of the horses were their heads. The greatest difficulties and sufferings were encountered in the Tondawanda Swamp, of far famed length and depth. Mother's memories of its holes and causeways were excruciating.

The Americans are proverbially inquisitive, and in their then ruder state they were especially so. With patriotic zeal to secure settlers, they were anxious for us to stop in the country, and wished to know "Where we were going?" Through all the earlier stages of the journey, father answered, "The Holland Purchase." This was true, for we were going there—though much farther. His answer served its purpose until we passed beyond the "Purchase," when something else had to be tried; what it was I never learned. At length, our almost interminable journey drew towards its close, and our American Cousins learned we were going to Canada to augment the number of King George's subjects. We infants were only six weeks old when we reached our journey's end.

We crossed the rapid Niagara with such facilities as the backward civilization of the day afforded, and spent the first winter in Queenstown. From there we removed to the Ten Mile Creek, living both at the "Lower Ten" and then at the "Upper Ten," consuming in all, I suspect, the best part of two years. Just as we were preparing to leave the place, the greatest possible affliction fell on our hapless family, which I assign to a section by itself.

No. V.

MY ELDEST BROTHER'S BEAUTIFUL LIFE AND TRAGIC DEATH.

JOSEPH, or simply "Joe," as we called him in the family, was my mother's first-born, given her before she was twenty years of age. Beautiful in mind and body was he in infancy, childhood, and youth. Before others followed and "poverty like an armed man" came on apace, he received more attention as to his dress and education than it was possible to bestow on the rest. He was reported by all who knew him to be sweet in his disposition and pleasing in his manners. His love for his mother was very great, and in the desperate out-post of humanity she was charged to defend, he was a great solace and help to her—her companion during her dreary nocturnal vigils. About the age of sixteen, an accident he suffered (cutting his foot with an axe) led him to serious reflection, and, his fond mother believed, issued in a thorough religious change, so serious, devout, and conscientious did he become. 'Tis true neither he nor his mother, up to the time of his death, had joined any Christian Church, nor was the thing practicable to any one of a family so circumstanced and with such a head as ours. But the son and mother held sweet religious communings; he was an impressive reader, and read to her out of the Sacred Volume and such few good books as were attainable to them; and employed his fine voice in singing such revival melodies as were in circulation among the "Newlight" Baptists of New Brunswick, who were the most demonstrative professors known to them. Mother had been brought up in Qaker sentiments, and she knew very little of the few Methodists who had found their way into our native Province. Our people could pronounce the names of Black, of Mann, of McColl, and a few other itinerant preachers, who made certain " angel visits" through the land, but that was nearly all. Joe amused his friends by humble attempts at verse-making.

When we arrived in the Niagara country, my precious maternal parent's strength and nervous system were in a pitiful state of prostration. At an untoward time she first heard the Methodists, then very high in their professions, boisterous in their announcements, and denunciatory in their addresses to the unconverted. She used to say their ministry stripped her of her self-righteousness, but did not inspire her with the Gospel hope. It was very inopportune that *she* heard only those "sons of thunder," she, whose bruised spirit so much required to meet with the ministrations of a Barnabas. She gave up hope of every kind, and sank into a complete state of despondency, indeed of settled religious melancholy. She, who had been so exemplary in the care of her family, now gave up all effort for time or eternity. We infants, suffered from the neglect to such an extent, that I cannot bring myself to repeat her after descriptions of our pitiful condition. She could only sit and weep, and nurse her sorrows. Poor Joe, the only one who understood her case, and tried, though vainly, to comfort her. "Be of good cheer, mammy!" he would say, "the more the ground is ploughed the deeper the seed will be sown; you will live to yet minister grace to the hearers"—a prophecy which was fulfilled; but which he himself did not live to see accomplished.

Perhaps I have somewhere else said in these diffusive sketches that father tramped around the lake to the Capital at York, to locate his thousand-acre grant of land from Governor Simcoe; but the system in the Land Department was bad; the state of the public mind was unsettled by coming events; and a new executive had arisen which "knew not Joseph" Carroll. The authorities advised him to defer the location of his land till matters became more settled (a time which never arrived to him) and that for the present he had better take a cleared farm, and train his eight boys big and little, in agricultural work against the time they went on land of their own. Acting on this advice, father, with his usual extraordinary judgment, made choice of the wild region about the Grand River; and we afterwards lived in two several places on those outskirts of civilization: namely, at Fairchild's Creek and in the Indian Reservation itself on the banks of the noble river.

Every arrangement was made for the journey. A team of horses and a waggon were purchased and our family effects were got together, and preparations were made for a start. In mother's unhappy prostration of mind, nearly all the little arrangements for domestic comfort were made by Brother Joseph. A few days before our sad catastrophe he was said to have fondled his tiny twin brothers upon his lap and expressed his solicitude lest they might not live to be men, such was our delicate appearance. Of some such caresses within the brawny arms of our sainted brother, is all the recollection of him that lingers from the morning twilight of my existence.

Alas! had brother known, he might have wept for his own early fate instead of ours. Nay, mother thought he had some premonition of that coming fate. A few days before his death, the family heard him pour from his melodious throat the hymn commencing:

> "The race appointed I have run,
> The combat's o'er, the prize is won,
> And now my record is on high,
> And all my treasure's in the sky.

> "I leave the world without a tear,
> Save for the friends I hold so dear;
> But in compassion, Lord, descend,
> And to the friendless prove a friend."

If there was any personal application made of the lines, his mother, no doubt was referred to in the latter ones. When he grew up to manhood a fierce spirit of severity and intolerance had sprung up towards him in our father's mind. There were several causes for this: the junior's moral superiority was a standing reproof to the senior; the latter may have been jealous that the reverence which he himself should have constrained was transferred to the eldest son and brother; that son loved his mother, and was passionately loved by her in return; although allowing himself only a fraction of his earnings, he dressed genteelly and was attentive to his person, which somebody else was not. Once when he came in with his hair fashionably cut like other young men, the senior with a ridiculous zeal for Christian plainness angrily pronounced it "the mark of the beast," and approached with shears in hand and haggled off, what he called the "cock's comb." It was pitiful to see a six-foot young man thus humiliated, and fain to slink away and weep like a child. Often did he say to his mother, "Dear mammy, only for your sake, before I would submit to what I do, I would go as far as the King has a foot of land!" Poor fellow! he did not say "to the utmost verge of this green earth," he had no idea, with the loyalty in his blood, of going anywhere but within the Dominion of the British King. The last winter we spent in our native Province the eldest boys were called to do militia duty, to be ready for threatened emergencies. They learned the manual exercise, and Joseph's activity of mind made him particularly expert. So much so that when he arrived in Canada, he was employed to drill the local militia. His fine personal appearance, pleasing manners, military bearing, musical voice, and versifying powers, joined to his pure and innocent social qualties, rendered him a general favourite. And had he thought of matrimony, no young man could have married more advantageously than he. Indeed, a wealthy yeoman pressed his comely daughter upon him, with the promise of a good settlement in life. But his answer was "I will never leave home so long as my mother lives."

But I must hasten to the close. The country was very subject to the ague, and Jossph had been rendered miserable by an attack of it for some weeks; and was very anxious to get it "broken," as it used to be termed, before the family's intended removal. An old Dutch quack recommended a decoction of prickly ash bark and whisky. The nostrum was prepared and made strong, and Joseph took a glass, and, upon the advice of his mother, he soon after took another, so anxious were they to be rid of the wearisome complaint. But the draught seemed too potent, he was seized with spasms. Seeing his deadly pallor, and his distorted features, his mother approached him; but he spent his last lucid moment and his failing powers of speech in striving to comfort and fortify her against her prospective bereavement. Soon he lost all consciousness, and struggled out of one convulsion into another for eight and forty hours. Six or eight strong men tried to restrain his throes (no doubt a foolish mode of treatment) till the skin was literally worn from his body. During this time the house was a scene of confusion and passionate lamentation. All felt relief, therefore, when his great vitality was exhausted, and his spirit passed away, relieving him from his bodily pain. When the shocking strife was over, his features returned to their placid expression. There he lay, a well proportioned young man of twenty-two, whose coffin measured six feet three inches. Profuse were the tears shed upon the extinguishing of this light of our household; and we never ceased to talk of our brother, or forgot to weep for him. His memory was an influence for good in the family.

He was laid in his grave among strangers, no stone telling where he lay. After the stupefaction which this stunning blow produced had somewhat passed off, we picked up our traps, and drove away up through the townships of Gratham, Clinton, Grimsby, Saltfleet, Barton, and Ancaster; on through the Grand River swamp, (in which they encountered great obstacles and hardships, aggravated by the passionate tyranny of one who should have soothed and sustained us all.) Alas! alas! alas! for depraved human nature, aggravated and demonized by drink! But the goal was reached at last. My child memories, and traditions of our experiences there will be detailed in the next section.

No. VI.

OUR INDIAN NEIGHBOURS.

I HAVE a good memory for things that I have seen and heard. I don't think I ever met a person who could remember so many things from so early a period of his life as I can. I remember a great many things, here and there, since I stood at my mother's knee along with my little twin brother, and was fed with a spoon, when we could not have been more than two years' old. From the age of two to three years and a half our family lived on a large Indian farm on the banks of a noble river of Canada—the "Grand River" —with more Indians than white people for neighbours. To begin with, I will tell some of the little incidents I remember of that period, which was immediately before the war of 1812, which may interest my readers, and will be the best introduction to what I will tell in the next section.

I remember having had the "dumb ague" very badly for a long time. I must have become very much attenuated—that is, very poor and thin. My arms are disproportionately long and slender at any time, but one day during that time I stripped down the sleeve of my slip, loose at all times, and held out my right arm, not thicker than a walking-stick, and cried out boastingly, "See what long arms I've got." A burst of laughter from the family revealed my simplicity in sporting my deformity. I remember, furthermore, how plenty the red plums were on the flats of the river, large baskets of which were brought in by the bigger boys and set on the floor, of which we little ones ate without stint. From that time the ague left me, and I got as fat as it was my nature ever to be. Perhaps the knowing ones would say that, in the absence of quinine, there was something in the bitter rinds of the plums of an antifebril tendency. Probably the bitter of the rind broke the fever, and the sweet pulp under the rind put the flesh on my bones.

Not far from the door there was a calf pasture, or pen, with a high fence around it, in which a calf was turned loose. We little ones loved to look through the fence and admire the bossy, and pat his meek little nose and head through the rails. But one morning we awoke to see a very sad sight; bossy lay stretched on the grass, with a great hole in his throat. The family had been awakened by a great bellowing from the old red cow, whose looks are stamped on my memory ever since. The wolves were devouring her darling; but she could not surmount the fence, or else I guess she would have given some of them a hoist with her horns. No one went to the rescue in time to save poor bossy from the ruthless destroyers. Many a tear we shed for our meek little pet, and much sorrow was felt and expressed for poor Old Red, which fed us with her milk, for the loss of her baby.

I remember the woods were full of pigs living on grass, acorns, wild plums, and whatever they could steal. They would be considered very unusual in appearance now; they were streaked from head to tail, somewhat like a chipmunk. One of them, a blue pig with dark stripes, I claimed as my own. Since I became older, I have learned that the colour and marks I have mentioned give place to more thorough domestication, they being the colour of the wild hog. I cannot remember what became of my pig.

The flats of the river, on the farther side, constituted a natural meadow, where the cattle were pastured. I remember seeing the oxen, when loosed from the yoke, driven into the river, followed by some one in a canoe, and swimming across to join the herd in the glades beyond the river. It was a picturesque sight.

Very near our house, at one part of the time, was the residence of a dignified Mohawk Chief, Thomas Davis. He and his wife were large people; and though Mrs. Davis had a copper-coloured skin, she had a kind, motherly heart, allowing us to take the eggs the hens laid in a box in the porch, and furnishing us liberally with maple sugar whenever we went to see her; the Indian name of which I learned and still remember—*Chick-ha-tah*. I may here say, that we used to play with the little Indian children, in their only garment of a printed calico shirt, and sometimes without even that, and learned to talk with them as readily in their language as we could in our own.

The old chief had a son, a growing youth, from fifteen to twenty, named Joseph. We all liked Joe very much, and he was a favourite companion of my three eldest brothers. He thought he could talk English very well, but he spoke it with the Indian idiom and accent—that is, what you might call "wrong end first." One day, one of the boys away from the house wanted to remind his next younger brother that the horses required to be watered; and he sent a message to him to that effect by Joe Davis, which he delivered thus: "Tom, drink de horses, Beel says!"

Sometimes our Indian experiences were not so good a joke. After war was proclaimed, the country became very much disturbed. There were a great many American people, disaffected to the Government, squatting here and there on the Indian Reservation, who hated my father, an old Loyalist soldier of the Revolution, and very demonstrative in his loyalty to the British Crown. They threw down his fences and turned in the cattle by night; and I have heard father and mother say, that of a hundred acres of wheat sown, they never reaped a handful. Perhaps those Yankees stirred up the Indians, too, to be unkind to father. I was going to tell of two ugly scares that we children received at that time. A young Indian man, perhaps a little intoxicated, came to the door of our house, which stood open, dressed in a blanket coat, with cap, or capote, of the same, forming part of the garment, furnished with projections like horns, dancing and brandishing a knife, which he stabbed or stuck into the door. You will not be surprised that I screamed and fled to the other side of my mother's chair for protection. What she could have done for us, poor woman, I know not, for she she was unarmed and alone; but to soothe us, and show her contempt of him, she evinced no signs of fear, whatever she may have felt; and after a time the foolish fellow went away. At the other time I refer to, mother was away at a neighbour's, some miles distant, and, as it turned out, lost her way coming back. The two eldest boys and father were a long distance from home; a brother about ten years' old was living with a neighbour; and the only one of any size—Tom, about fifteen, but very strong, and with the heart of a lion—being tenderly attached to his mother, became alarmed at her remaining quite into the gloaming, and went to seek her. This left the three youngest of us by ourselves. Nat. was eight years old, and we twins were scarcely more than three. The sticks of which the chimney was made took fire, and we became very much alarmed. Two Indians passed, to whom we made known our troubles, but they only laughed. We twins could only do what the little girl did, described by Dr. Newton, when a little brother fell into a stream and was nearly drowned, although he was eventually rescued and brought home. The father asked one of three boys, "What did you do towards saving your little brother?" "I plunged into the stream after him and brought him to the bank!" Turning to the other boy, he said, "What did you do?" "I carried him home on my back, sir!" And accosting the little girl he said, "Sissy, what did you do?" "Why, pa, I began to cry, and I cried as hard as I could all the time." Said the doctor, "Perhaps her crying did as much towards the rescue as the efforts of her brothers; it stimulated them to exert themselves to the utmost." So our cries stimulated Brother Nat. He was not big and strong enough to fetch a pail of water from the spring on the other side of the stile, but he went all the oftener with the tin cup. But alas! he had a bootless task. By throwing the water on the burning spot, he contrived to keep the flame from spreading for a time; but it did spread, and at length he became weary and discouraged, and gave up. His next idea was to save his mother's bed, and a chest with valuables in it, which he intended to drag out of the house. Just at that point deliverance came. Tom had found his mother, and they were returning. When they came near enough to hear our cries, he ran, and coming in and seeing us covered with sweat, and tears, and soot, and seeing the chimney on fire, caught a pail, ran to the spring, and returned with the pail running over—he mounted the ladder to the loft, where he could dash the water on the burning spot, which so effectually checked the flames that the fire was soon extinguished. This was a sad, but still useful occurrence; for it roused mother, who had been so sunk in religious melancholy that she scarcely took any interest in her family for several years. Our sufferings in the open log-house, without a stove, which few possessed in those days, had been very severe. Once I froze a finger so badly which had been sticking out of bed at night, that the nail came off, and the form of the new one has been noticeable ever since. I could show it to you now.

I have spoken about hens, and pigs, and cow, and calf, and oxen; I must say a word or two about our two horses. In those days the land was mostly tilled by oxen, but we had a span of horses for longer journeys. They were what might be called "little big horses;" the favourite was almost a pony, but strong. Their names were Jack and Pomp. Jack was as black as jet; Pomp, or "Pompey," as we usually called him out of fondness, was of a peculiar colour—I never saw exactly the like of him in all my long life. Pompey was a delicate mouse-colour, diversified by copper-coloured spots over all parts of his body, nearly the size of a copper, and quite as round. As his head, neck, ears, mane, body, legs, and tail were beautifully formed, he was very handsome. No wonder we all caressed and petted him very much. He was so gentle, they often hitched him to the back-log intended for the fire, and drew it into the house, he coming in at one door, and passing out at the opposite. After introducing you to Pompey, I will close this section. He will appear again. I have concluded to add to what was originally a "story" in a child's paper, an incident illustrative of the savagery in which we lived, which happened to my brother James, prepared for a more elaborate autobiography, which will not now, it is likely, see the light. Brother Jim was the eldest son living, now that dear Joseph had gone. He was a young man only about twenty-one, but very muscular and strong, though embarrassed by defective vision, which ended five or six years after in total blindness. He could yet see to work, and even to read and write —though the last two became impossible before the war was over, by the measles caught while doing militia duty on the lines, before any of the rest of the family became identified with the army, from the disease settling in his eyes; but what I have promised to relate belonged to a period somewhat earlier. War was declared, and a government proclamation required all the Indian warriors to make their appearance at Squire Hatt's, near Burlington Bay, within, I think, "three days." Some whites and some Indians were talking over the requirement at some place of meeting, my brother James and a great strapping Mohawk among the rest. Powless did not see how he could go

—he "had no moccasins." James, who was intimate with him, said playfully, "Powless, I guess you're afraid!" Perhaps this was too true; for Powless took it in dudgeon, and said angrily, "You go get your gun and see if me afraid!" Brother laughed it off, and thought no more of it; but the next morning, having occasion to pass the Indian's house, Powless opened the door and called him in; and when he had got him within the walls, he began to upbraid him for making the charge of cowardice, and commenced to stamp, and rage like a madman. Presently he sprang for his knife, which was run in a crack of the wall; James sprang towards him, and clapping his hand on the Indian's, just as it grasped the handle, the blade broke off in the log. Foiled in that, he sprang for his axe, in a corner of the room, and grasped the helve; but Jim was as quick as he, and stronger besides; he seized him by the shoulders—flung him on the floor—wrested the axe from his grasp, and threw it away. But as Mrs. Powless had fled so soon as the scuffle began, Brother did not know but she might soon have a pack of Indians on his back, and thought it prudent to make his escape. The next time they met, Powless, was unusually deferential. Nothing answers so well with an Indian as a thorough subjugation

No. VII.

CHILD MEMORIES OF THE ALARMS AND HARDSHIPS OF WAR.

I HAVE already given some recollections of events which affected my childish imagination and feelings, that must have taken place in the early part of the War of 1812-15, while our family was still living far from the "lines," as they were called. I heard at the time, and often afterwards, that father became disgusted with the lawlessness and insecurity which prevailed almost everywhere in the country, and especially among the savage and half-civilized peoples of our vicinity, and thought that he and his family would suffer less annoyance even where the danger might be supposed to be greater; rightly judging that martial law was better than no law at all. The result was, that in one of his visits to the frontier he had an interview with the military authorities; and owing to his demonstrative loyalty and his old-time memories of, and proclivities for, military life (for he belonged to the artillery through the "Revolutionary War"), he was induced to join the army again as a volunteer (he was too old for legal enlistment), and to enlist two of his sons, who, though men for strength, were yet minors. The department to which they all became attached was what has been sometimes called the "Flying Artillery," or Royal Artillery Drivers, *i.e.*, those who handled the moveable guns upon gun-carriages. My father was a skilled saddler, harness, and collar-maker, and he was put in charge of all the harness, etc., with the title of "Master Collar-maker;" his sons were enlisted as drivers and harness-makers: they learned the drill, and upon occasion rode the gun-horses and even served in action, but in the long run were mostly required in the regimental shops. William held the rank of "Collar-maker," about equivalent to that of sergeant.

As soon as the roads were sufficiently dry to travel, in the spring of 1813, our indispensables were packed into the double horse waggon, and mother and the children, incapable of walking, were placed in it also; and our faithful Pomp and Jack were the force which dragged us along. We must have taken our weary way from the Grand River (above where Brantford now flourishes), through the Indian Reservation till we reached the townships, passing through the sloughs of the "Grand River Swamp," till we sighted Burlington Bay, where Hamilton now spreads its ample breadth, at which point we must have descended the mountain, passing along under its shadow, and crossing "Stoney Creek," the "Fifty Mile Creek," the "Forty," the "Thirty," the "Twenty" (now called Jordan), the "Sixteen," the "Twelve," the "Ten," the "Four Mile Creek," and last of all the "Two Mile Creek," shortly beyond which we found ourselves in the old town of Niagara, at the military headquarters.

I have told my readers of my remembrance of many things which happened before that journey; but I must confess that of the journey itself I remember little or nothing, except the black coat of sturdy Jack, and the pretty spots of our soon-to-be-lamented Pompey. The causes of forgetfulness were, perhaps, my mind was not yet enough expanded to know what it was all about; and I rather guess that a good part of the journey was in the night, and that I and my twin brother must have slept a good deal of the way. Happily that refreshment comes to children at least.

But my attention was destined soon to be awakened and my consecutive or continuous memory was to commence its register of all passing events, thus connecting my childhood with my old age in a conscious identity throughout. The event which caused the awakening referred to was the BATTLE OF NIAGARA, which happened May 27th, 1813, when I lacked two months of being four years old.

We had been in the town about a fortnight; our team of horses were grazing on the commons; and the mother and the youngest children had found a temporary home or shelter, with a former acquaintance.

One morning my mind was attracted by a great bustle. The militiamen, with their muskets in hand, but in coloured clothes, were pouring into the house— each to receive a badge of white cotton, or linen (in those days it was mostly the latter, cotton not yet having come into such general use as now), which was tied around an arm by the women, many of whom were in tears. You will say, What was this for? Why, we were on the eve of the famous battle of Niagara. Our relatives, the Americans, were preparing to cross, or were in the act of crossing, the river. Unhappily, both sides employed Indians, and Indian warfare consists largely in massacre; and the Indians would naturally think that all persons found in arms, not dressed in red, were "Yankees," who wore dark uniforms. Therefore, our militiamen, whose clothes were mostly dark, were fain to have some badge to distinguish them from the enemy, lest an Indian's rifle, or fusee, should be levelled at them, with the certainty of being tomahawked and scalped when down.

Father and our boys were as bad off as the civilians, for they had too lately arrived to be, at least, "fitted" with their uniforms. What my father and eldest brother, who were in the action, did, I cannot exactly say; but I remember father's coming bustling in with a drummer's coat for Tom, to demonstrate by its scarlet and lace that he was British.

The next thing I noticed was ranks of red-coated soldiers drawn up in lines near the house, performing various movements; and anon I missed them. Then began sounds of bang, bang; pop, pop, pop. Mother said "the balls flew like handfuls of peas." Presently a crashing sound went through the house; it was a cannon-ball which passed through both walls of the room we were in, over our heads. Mother, who had been several years in a state of religious melancholy, so that she had largely omitted her old-time care for her family; now, to use her own words, "ceased caring for her soul, and commenced caring for her children." The war cured my mother. Her first measure was to take us out of the house, where she thought we were more exposed, because of splinters, than we would be in the open. She spread a blanket on the ground, to obviate the dampness, under a fence, with the road in front and a wheat field, green and bright, behind us, on which we all sat down. Just as we had begun to congratulate ourselves on our safety, a cannon-ball struck in the field behind us, ploughing up the ground, as they always do; next, another ball struck in the road before us, and covered us with dirt. I thought it all "very funny," but had not sense enough to be frightened, and cannot say whether the older children were or not. But I know that mother thought it "time to flit." We went back to the house, tied up a feather-bed and some bedding in a sheet, or blanket, and a brother ten years old staggered away with it on his back, we all taking the road towards the " Ten Mile Creek " on foot. It was a great providence we escaped with our lives; for I remember that the cannon-balls struck the stumps before and behind us (mother said), even when we were a mile out of town. We little witless things had no sense of danger, for we could scarcely be restrained from looking after the balls, thinking it a kind of ball-playing on a large scale! We trudged or toddled on a distance of four miles before we stopped. Fortunately, we got into good quarters considering the times. Our horses fell into the enemy's hands, and the house we left was burned and all our household efiects were consumed.

An old farmer by the name of George Lawrence, near the Four Mile Creek, took us in. He was a Methodist class-leader, the brother of John Lawrence, one of the first New York Methodists, and sometimes even then met his little class in the house. Mrs. Lawrence had a good voice, and used to sing the old-fashioned spiritual songs which suited the martial ideas of the time, representing the members of God's church as an army, ending with the lines—

> "We'll then march up the heavenly street,
> And ground our arms at Jesus' feet."

At first (till a part of the British forces, which had after their defeat retreated to Beaver Dam, returned and threw up defensive works on the north-west bank of the "Creek," about a quarter of a mile from Mr. Lawrence's house), we were at the mercy of the foraging parties from the American camp in the town. It is but just to say, however, they paid for whatever they got, which is more than the old people could say of the British soldiers when they came, who stole everything they could lay their hands upon. Even the dear old man went unpaid for the boarding of the officers' mess, which was entertained in the house; and was so abused at one time because the victuals were not better, that he sat down and wept to think his devoted loyalty should receive such a cruel recompense. Before the return of the British, our position was made a little lively by the appearance from time to time of American officers. One day, who should make his appearance but our old favourite, Pompey, bestrode by an American cavalry officer, well groomed and richly caparisoned; it was enough to make us sorrow deeply to see him wrested from us, and in the enemy's hands. We could hardly have felt worse if it had been one of our brothers we saw in captivity.

The summer passed very pleasantly at Mr. Lawrence's. It was a sort of house of refuge for a number of many different sorts of people. As there was a guard of thirty strong posted at the house, with sentries out upon all the roads or avenues, and as there was an officers' mess the members of which came there for their meals, it was no doubt thought to be a safe retreat for the otherwise defenceless refugees. There was old Mr. and Mrs. Stivers, Dutch people, whose two sons, Hans and Hinery, were doing duty in the " Provincial Dragoons," and riding express to various parts of the country, and a Mrs. Cassady, who came there to nurse a sick daughter, who performed, as we shall see, two very heroic acts, the last day of our stay in that place. I might tell of a good many queer things which happened while we were there; but I will only speak of the things which impressed my childish mind, and the relation of which would be likely to interest children.*

The garden had its plants and flowers, and contri-

---

* So I had concluded when this section appeared in the form of a "story" for PLEASANT HOURS; but I will, in this form, relate one incident on which I often heard my mother dwell with glee:— Some person in the house had lost ten dollars (in two five dollar bills, I think), and search was made for it in vain; and every person disclaimed all knowledge of the money. But a hired girl, out of a low family, one Maria Gesso, because of her antecedents, was suspected, but denied the perpetration of the theft. Mother devised a plan of detecting her, or frightening her to return the money. One day she she said, in the cook-house without, to young Mr. Peter Lawrence, purposely, when Maria was within hearing, "Peter, I have a plan for finding out the money-thief." "How is that, Mrs. Carroll?" "I will go to-night to the barn and fetch in one of the young roosters, and put it under a tub; and, every person in the house shall put his hand under the tub and stroke the chicken's back; and when the person who stole the money touches him, he will crow. Her intention was to daub the back of the fowl with something which would adhere to the hand. She knew that the guilty person would fear to touch him; and when palms were scrutinized, when the course of stroking was gone through with, the person with a clean hand would be charged with the theft, and if necessary searched. But the necessity for this "*hocus-pocus*" work was rendered unnecessary by the money being left on one of the beds in plain open sight, where the guilty person knew it would be found. It was found, and restored to its owner.

buted its share to our enjoyment. To watch the sheep was **very** pleasant, **and to see** them penned up every **night in a** high "bay" in the barn for safety, seemed **curious.** It afforded us pleasure to wander in the **fields to** play and look for flowers. One day, **however, we** twins got considerable of a fright. **We were al**ways taught to keep a safe distance from a **bull, and we** knew his bellow; while at **some distance** from the house we heard what we though**t that** animal's droning bellow—boo-o, boo-o—and **we broke** and ran for the house, upon returning **to which we found the** noise proceeded **from** one of the upper **rooms, where a hired girl was** driving *a large spinning-wheel,* only! **That was the bull.**

The soldiers of the guard seemed **to extract a** great deal of amusement out of us little ones, by doing **what** was not uninteresting to **us—snch as dressing us in** soldier's array, putting **a** "forage **cap" on our heads,** furnishing **us with a stick for a gun, and lading us with a** knapsack. Once **when thus** harnessed up, I fell over backwards with the weight, **and could not** extricate myself till some one came to my **relief. But all** this was trifling compared with what happened **on the last day of our** stay, and those that followed **thereupon.**

Children tired with play, usually fall asleep early **in the** evening; and "early to bed" **makes them** often "early to **rise."** On a certain beautiful summer or autumn morning, at an **early** hour, not too early for the sun to be up, I and my little mate were up and out; and though we had not yet breakfasted, each had provided him with a rod of elder, easily broken from the bushes, which we straddled, and our imaginations invested it with the attributes of a horse, and we were galloping up and down the road in front of the house, in imitation of Hans and Hinery Stivers, who had just cantered by, to execute some military command. The people of the house were rather about the door and yard than within doors. The table, with its white cloth, was laid for the officers' mess, but they came not; yes, Lieutenant McLeod, the captain of the guard, was there, and urged to take his breakfast, but he ate not; he looked very pale, and his hand trembled so badly that the cup of tea one of the women had handed him spilt its contents over his sword, which, in its sheath lay across his knees. He was a coward, and his fears were awakened by what was occurring without. What it was all about we little ones did not comprehend at that time, but we soon were brought to understand better—only I remarked that all the grown people looked anxious, and no one touched the breakfast. Our mother suddenly called us in from our sport; and not expecting that it was, as far as that place was concerned, destined to end forever, we carefully stabled our imaginary horses in a corner of the garden. The grown people heard, what we took no notice of, sharp but irregular shots of musketry here and there. Presently a little Irish soldier, who had been posted somewhere in the orchard, came running, scrambled up the steps, and attempted to enter the door, exclaiming, "Lord Jaysus! Where will a fellow hide?" To which Mrs. Cassady, the heroine of the hour, replied by pushing him heels over head down the steps, responding that he should "Go fight like a *man!*" Paddy turned on his heel, and scampered away to seek some other hiding-place. Poor old Mrs. Stivers the while walked the house and wrung her hands, uttering the piteous lament, "Och, mine poor Hans! och, mine poor Hinery!" In the meantime it was said that American Indians appeared in the road south of us, and the guard turned out and prepared for action. But the officer, not so minded, swore that he would "cut the first man's head off who fired a shot;" and then formed his guard and started in double-quick time for the cantonment on the banks of the Four Mile Creek. Thus this valorous lieutenant and his thirty armed soldiers left an old man and a house full of women and children to the tender mercies of what proved to be only ten Indians!

Presently the dreaded Indians appeared, not in a body, but Indian-like, in ones and twos and threes, stealthily surrounding the premises, some skulking behind this corner, and others behind that. Those that showed themselves seemed strapping, stalwart men, with painted faces, clad only in the indispensable waist-cloth and in gaudy-coloured printed calico shirts. Quarrels were frequent through the war between our own Indians and soldiers, and the gravest heads in our company for a time, such as my own mother, Mr. Lawrence, and Mr. Smith, a corporal of a Provincial corps, who had just come in from visiting the sentries concluded it was an *emeute* between British Indians and soldiers. The confab was in this state when some of the Indians appeared before the front gate, upon which the good man of the house went out, and offered one of them his hand, and it was accepted; but another savage came up with a scowl on his face, and seized Mr. Lawrence by his neck-cloth and made him his prisoner. Seeing this, Corporal Smith, whose gun did not chance to be loaded, put his hand behind him, and was in the act of taking out a cartridge from his cartouche-box, when an Indian, who was skulking among the weeds of the garden, levelled his fusee and shot our would-be defender through the hand and the cartouche-box into the small of his back, where the ball remained. He would have fallen, but he caught by the garden gate, and by the aid of his musket contrived to help himself up the steps, which were high, and into the house, whither the Indians rushed after him. To ease his pain, he lay down on his back in the middle of the floor.

With the curiosity of a child, I watched it all. Two Indians advanced towards him, and one stood over his head with an uplifted tomahawk, while another stood at his feet and presented his loaded fusee towards his breast, as though they would despatch him at once. At which the courageous Mrs. Cassady rushed forward and with her unlifted arm knocked the tomahawk one way and the fusee another, exclaiming, "Don't murder the man in the house." Her courageous bearing awed the Indians; and at her direction they assisted her in taking off his accoutrements, and after a little while he was led away a prisoner; and we afterwards learned that death put an end to his sufferings, three days after receiving the wound.

When the search began by the Indians through the house, mother thrust us four little ones into a pot-hole under the stairs, and stood with her back to the door and her face confronting the Indians, like a bear at bay against the hunters defending her cubs. Still cherishing the idea that they were British Indians after all, as one of them passed she patted him on the shoulder, and asked him if he were not "a friend to King George." She was the object of an ugly frown, but received no material injury. Our assailants passed through the house, upstairs and down, but, strange, to say, took no booty of any kind. The whole affair was so singular throughout as to lead to various conjectures as to who they were and what their particular object. Some doubted their being Indians at all, but thought them disaffected white men in the country around, only disguised as Indians, and that their object was to surprise and capture or kill the members of the officers' mess.

The surprise and sorrow of that day was increased by a son of the family, George Lawrence, jun., who had been out on duty with the militia company to which he belonged, being brought in with a buckshot wound in the thigh, which he had received in the skirmish which was general between the advanced pickets of both armies—the American, which lay in the town of Niagara, and the British, posted at the Cross Roads. I think there did not prove to be any reason for it, but the Lawrences resolved to retire further into the interior; and a waggon was got ready, furnished with a feather bed, upon which the wounded militiaman was placed, and they moved off, to be further away from the scene of conflict. And mother thought she must needs go also. She had no one to lean upon for guidance or support; father had been taken prisoner at the battle of Niagara. He had, it is true, been discharged on his parole of honour, and we had seen him once through the summer. But as he had taken service after his parole, it would have been death for him to fall into the enemy's hands; on which account he attended only to such duty in his department as lay farthest from the lines. The British army was preparing to vacate the camp at the Creek and to retreat. Mother with her children prepared to follow in its wake. We had eaten no breakfast, but each child had a large "sea biscuit" in his hands. When we arrived at the fort we met our brother Bill, just mounting his military horse to come and see what had become of his mother. He, too, had been on short allowance, and when we met him we were so glad to see him that, with the generosity and improvidence of childhood, we forced our biscuits upon him, and, as the result, never broke our own fast for twenty-four hours. What with our smallness, and feebleness, and the bundles we had to carry, it took us till the sun went down to toddle over the causeway and mud through the six miles of the dreary "Black Swamp Road," mostly skirted with woods. We found the road strewed with military articles shaken off the waggons in the flight from the approaching enemy. Some articles were picked up by the oldest boy, and preserved as souvenirs as long as the family held together, but alas! we found no food. Towards evening our frightened British Indians began to steal back to their camps, very anxiously inquiring of us if we had "seen any Yankees?" One of these poor fellows lay in the road, very sick with the "shaking ague." The violence of his headache led him to ask our mother for a "string," in default of a handkerchief, to tie around his head. Alas! she had none to give. The two older boys had a hard time of it, having had to carry us two little ones on their backs from time to time, my little twin brother pleading most piteously, the while, to be allowed to "lie down and die." But they tugged him through, and about sunset we arrived at Brown's Tavern, at the "Upper Teh Mile Creek," and got a supper of weak tea, bread, and skim-milk cheese, for which mother paid five dollars—a dollar for each one. Sleep that night was refreshing to us, weary and footsore as we were.

I had better not spin out my story in dwelling on any details excepting those which illustrate the topics on which the title of the present section pledge me to write. It is sufficient, then, to say that the mother and children found shelter in a small log-house, with a roof of bark, occupied by a woman who also had several children, to whom there was another added while we were there. During her sickness we had to make a fire out in the neighbouring grove, and stop there. I think, however, we did not fare very ill: there was a large orchard near, fruit was pretty well matured, and in war time all things were common, so that we treated ourselves to roast apples, not wholly without other accompaniments. Once we disturbed a nest of reptiles coiled together, preparing, perhaps, to hybernate for the winter, which gave us a great fright; but as snake stories are not very agreeable, I dwell upon it no further. When it began to be cooler, we removed two miles further westward, and stopped for a time at the "Twelve Mile Creek," near where St. Catharines now flourishes. But I do not remember much of our residence there. There could have been nothing very stirring, or I should have been likely to have remembered it.

In the fall it began to be unsafe, or at least it was thought so, to remain so near the frontier. It was after Proctor's defeat, and the British army was concentrated (intrenched) at Burlington Heights, at the head of the bay on the margin of which the City of

Hamilton now spreads itself abroad, and thither it was thought necessary for us to go. But how should we get there? All the horse teams were impressed to convey military or Government stores. Mother, however, now thoroughly cured of her religious despondency, was pretty energetic. She found a man who owned a yoke of oxen and cart, with whom she bargained to convey us the thirty miles, more or less, to the " Heights," for the sum of $20. We were piled in, and off we started. The jolting in that springless vehicle over the rough roads of that day did not, however, so shake up my ideas as to enable me to remember much about it.

We had an acquaintance at the Bay, who had often shared our hospitality, a Mr. Nathaniel Hughson, whose name is commemorated in that of one of the streets of the " Ambitious City." His place was sought for and found, and they did not repel us; but what could they do? His house was not very large, considering his family, at the best; and he had the meat contract for the army, which required a great many assistants and made a great deal of " clutter "—besides which, the house was crowded with soldiers and teamsters. Mother was fain to make a " shake down" on the floor, fencing its boundaries with such impediments as came to hand, into which we five turned for the night, and slept the sleep of the just.

Our next move was to the house, or place of a worthy German family, by the name of Smuck, or

"Smoke," as they were called, near the Binkleys, about half way between two distinguished places, which were then in the womb of the future—Hamilton and Dundas—we used to hear of a village of some celebrity then, some miles away, Ancaster by name, but I never saw it till forty years after. Our good entertainers were new settlers and had enough to do for themselves. There was a one-roomed old log-house, with an open fire-place, with loose boards for flooring. Then there was a newer part, an addition to the old house, also of logs, unfinished. Half of the place was floored, and half unfloored; but the chinking had not been put in between the logs, and there was no chimney, and there could be no fire, although the weather now began to be quite frosty. Although there was a sick officer in bed in the old part, we sometimes stole in to warm ourselves at the fire. This made the floor boards always to rattle, which greatly disturbed the weak nerves of the sick officer, made more irritable than his wont by the ague. One day he bid his "orderly" to bring his brace of horse-pistols (he belonged to our corps, the flying artillery) and threatened, with the emphasis of an oath, to "shoot a dozen of us." Happily he did not carry out his threat or I should not be writing these chronicles. Then he turned to my mother, and said, "Mrs. Carroll, I intend to have your husband tried by a court-martial and shot?" "Why, Colonel, what has he done?" "Why, for not sending you to Lower Canada? Do you not know that there was an order for all soldiers' wives to depart to Lower Canada?" "I hope you do not rank me with ordinary soldiers' wives, because my husband saw fit to turn out in troublous times to help defend his country—I shall not go." The mother defeated the Colonel, at least she silenced his battery; and next day he retreated himself.

But though the Colonel had left, there was not much room for us in the apartment warmed by the fire, and our part was too cold to be endured; so we were forced to lie in bed, by day as well as by night, to keep from becoming starved with the cold, a confinement rather irksome to restless childhood. At length our biggest brother, Jim, made his appearance: he had been in the militia, and took the measles, which affected his eyes, and, to a great degree, deprived him of his sight, on which account he was unfit for further service and was exempted. He had hovered about our path, and employed his time in working for the farmers, now in much need of assistance. He built a good fire for us in the shelter of the oak bushes: there we spent a good part of the day-time, alternately roasting and freezing, first one side and then the other.

Once a playful puppy took my mother's pocket to play with, containing all her money, to the amount of $100 perhaps, and she would likely never have seen it more, if he had succeeded in pulling it under the logs of the new house.

After a while, we got narrower, but warmer quarters.

In default of barracks, the sappers and miners and their assistants had made huts by digging places, perhaps, ten feet square, in the ground, to which there was an entrance made at one side, by means of a trench, like the descent to a root-house; the roof of slabs rested on the surface of the ground, and met in the centre; and the only light obtainable was what came down a low, but capacious chimney, and what entered by a hole in the door, about the size of an ordinary pane of glass, but innocent of the glass itself; so that if you received the light, you had to let in the wind; and if you closed the aperture to keep out the storm, you excluded the light. Once the hole was left open,—a snow-storm occurred through the night while we were all asleep, and the snow drifted in so badly, that we could not get the door open till the snow was removed by the slow process of shovelling it through that narrow hole. By barring the door, we were tolerably secure from intruders. Once there was a dreadful free-fight between our own Indians and soldiers, and some of the former were very badly beaten. One of them lay groaning all night by our chimney, but we were so alarmed with the fray without, that we dare not unbar the door to succour him. We hoped that the warmth of the chimney might keep him from totally perishing. Once our mother had to dress the back of a thieving soldier, who had been whipped till it was a complete jelly. Such is sin; and such the severities of martial law. Our water was obtained from the Bay by an almost interminable flight of steps cut in the very steep bank, while the slipperiness of the steps from the ice with which they were encased was such that we went down and up at the risk of breaking our necks.

When the winter was well on, a residence for the family and regimental harness-maker's shop for father, in one, was provided near what is now the centre of the City of Hamilton. It was more spacious than our last abode, but much colder. The far end of the chamber (reached by a flight of very steep stairs without a baluster) was unfinished, and a floor—nothing but lath and plaster between us and a shop below, kept by an old Scotchman. Once a dishonest artilleryman, billetted upon us, was prowling about in that dark, unfinished part of the loft, went through, and fell under the ire of the old shopman. There was no stove, you may be sure, and only a feeble fire on the hearth: to enable father to have his "waxed ends" soft enough to rive freely he had to keep a pot of coals by the side of his work-bench. The place was too open to expose us to any injury from the emission of the poisonous gas. While in this place we had to eat pork instead of butter; and eat it raw, for want of cooking. Sometimes the bread was without salt.

The spring came, and with it a genial sun, as also an order to advance to the Niagara River once more, the American army having evacuated the country. A well-known army teamster came and conveyed us along the road at the base of the Mountain, through the streams I have already mentioned, which interested me very much to pass. I learned the names of his fine span of mares, and have not forgotten them till this day; let "Jin" and "Doll" go down to posterity. In due time, we reached Queenston, where the regimental harness-maker's shop was located—over that of the blacksmith. There we were again a united family for a time—father, mother, Tom and Bill, and even poor camp-follower Jim was there from time to time. We also made the acquaintance of several non-commissioned officers, who were often in, each of whom had an individuality of his own, and felt his importance quite enough: there were Sergeant-Major Whittam, Bugler Eastham, old Mr. Thomas, the farrier (very pretentious), Petrie, the good-natured blacksmith; young Francois, the French-Canadian, who " blew and struck," the merriest fellow of the whole. The cold had passed away; we knew nothing of style, and did not hanker for it; and simple, but satisfying devices beguiled the time, such as the music of the Jew's harp. Petrie could manufacture them (the tongue cut out of a sword-blade), and play on them when made. I never heard that his range of tunes went beyond,—

> "Molly, put the kettle on,
> We'll all drink tea,
> Molly, take the kettle off,
> It will all boil away."

But he practically received many an *encore*, for we

never tired of the one, but called for it again and again. We had also an extemporized puppet-show of a character I never heard of since, except among those who learned it then and there, which was witnessed with unbounded delight. But it would take too much space to describe it so that one who never witnessed it would have a mental view of the play. I will not, therefore, go into details unless they are called for. Our social hilarities were brought to an end, by a journey required to be performed by father, who took mother and the four youngest with him, which will furnish incidents enough for a section by itself. Some will say, "Why have you not said more about religion?" Alas! there was no religion to tell about in those days.

No. VIII.

A THREE DAYS' COASTING VOYAGE.

IN my last section I described our family's residence in Queenston during the latter part of the winter and the spring of 1814. As soon as the spring was well open and navigation was considered safe, my father was ordered by the army authorities to go to York, now Toronto, and take charge of the military saddle and harness-making and mending department in that place. It was arranged for my mother and the four youngest boys to go with him. The eldest of these boys was about eleven, the second eldest nearly nine, and we two youngest five soon after we arrived in York.

The Government had provided for our transport in something like a schooner, called the *St. Vincent*, named after General Vincent. She was a poor old craft, rigged up hastily for the service. We embarked from the banks of the Niagara River, and dropped down the stream till we arrived at its mouth, the location and character of which my readers know from their school atlases, which are something we had not in my earliest school days. Arrived at Fort George, we did not dare to stand boldly across the lake, even supposing our frail craft could have endured the winds and waves, in which case, with a fair wind, we might have run across in half a day; but, alas! there was a cruel war between two English-speaking nations—a very wicked state of things, and just then the United States had the upper hand on Lake Ontario. Besides, our old schooner was very frail, and I guess was imperfectly armed. I remember there was at least one big gun on board, for I heard them fire it off, but I could not say if there were any more. So, also, there was a small company of marines (or sea soldiers) on board, for I saw them perform drill; and there were several military men on board, belonging to other branches of the service; but whatever they might have done on land, I think they would have been no great protection to our vessel. Besides, many of them were invalids, sick and wounded, who were being sent from the dangers on the "lines" to the hospitals at the capital.

From what I have said, it will be seen that we were not in a state to brave the enemy and the winds and waves, by seeking to scud straight across the lake, but we had to coast the great angle of the lake towards its "Head," as it used then to be called. Fortunately,

I think, our craft was so flat-bottomed that she could go quite near the shore, to which we could tie up at night, which was done. I am very sorry to say, that I have every reason to believe that the soldiers and sailors on board were arrant thieves, and instead of being the defenders of the peaceful farmers, they contrived to elude the watch, and to go on shore in small marauding parties under the cover of darkness, and bring away anything they could find. I know they brought calves, for one of them gave me a great fright by my encountering his bleat and his glassy eyeballs in the darkness of the "hold," to which I had gone, which sent me screaming for protection to my parents. It was said, though I am not sure that I saw it myself, they brought away a colt one night in mistake for a calf! Alas! all the tender things fell under the butcher's knife, but poor coltie was pitched overboard! Sin causes war, and war is always attended with cruelty and wrong. Let us pray that the "Gospel of peace" may so prevail, that the nations may "learn war no more." About the third night after leaving Niagara, we entered Toronto Bay, and moored the vessel under the guns of what is now known as the "Old Fort," though it was then called the "New Garrison." How this change of terms came about, perhaps I will tell at some future time.

No. IX.

OUR FIRST PLACES OF ABODE IN YORK, AND HOW WE CAME TO OCCUPY THEM.

I SUSPECT we spent the first night in what *you* now call the "Old Fort," if we did not remain in the vessel; a sleepy-headed child might be excused from not taking in the scene correctly at once. Soldiers' families were not allowed in the barracks, but a friendly artillery-man, a Mr. Elder, shared his hut with mother and the children. It was very small, and stood on the brow of an escarpment over the Bay, and the ground on which it stood, more than a generation ago, tumbled into the water. Mr. E. was well-conducted and kind, a well-informed Scotchman, but his wife had fallen into the too common fault of women connected with the army—*drink*. She may have mended when she got out of it. Years after, Mr. Elder became respectable in a civilian's position; and his son was often a good-natured playmate of mine. Poor Aleck Elder, once tried for his life! The ordnance land was then covered with swamps, which gave rise to little rills of water falling over the bank. In the mouth of one of these near the hut, George made a net of a basket, and caught as many little fish as both families could eat.

We were crowded and annoyed; we were neither in garrison nor town, and mother was exceedingly desirous to get out of the place; besides, father needed room for his mechanical department. There was an amiable and gentlemanly young officer, belonging to the 104th regiment, a native of New Brunswick, by the name of Haskings, who knew the respectability of mother's relations, the Ridouts; who, when he heard who she was, came to see us; and afterwards interested himself very much to get us a place. After we became acquainted with the people of the town, we learned how that Capt. Haskings, had ridden about the streets for days in search of a house. But every place was full, and no whole house could be secured all to ourselves. Our first abode was a tall, weather-beaten framed house, with a passage-way running through it, on the north-west corner of Duke and George Streets, the low two rooms on the east side of the hall of which we obtained as a matter of favour, and ate our first meal off a large chest. A little cross-legged pine table soon followed, and we began to exist. Still there was another family, besides ourselves below, and the upper part of the house was full of French-Canadians. A few mornings after our arrival, mother made an agreeable acquaintance. A comely young married woman, by the name of Barber, occupied a neat little house across the road from us. They met in the street, and found that both (at least Mrs B.'s parents) were from New Brunswick; and as they both knew, or at least knew of, many of the same persons, they began to question each other about this and that individual; and they soon found that they had a common knowledge and friendship of many people, which was, as we all know from experience, a source of pleasure. At length, said mother, as the plot thickened, "I wonder whatever became of Sally Rodney?" At this the young woman burst into tears [the first time I ever saw a person weep for joy,] and said, "Why she's my mother; and is alive, and living out on Yonge Street." Sally Rodney was a sinister daughter of Lord Rodney, a naval officer, who spent some time in New Brunswick, and lured one of the handsomest young women of the country from the paths of propriety; and Sally Rodney was the result. Sally had married fairly well, and we afterwards often met her. This her daughter married an agreeable man, an American, with some education, who was afterwards my first effectual school-teacher, and will come into view in the next section. Across the way from our place, mother renewed her acquaintance with the family of Stephen Jarvis, Esquire, respectable people, from Fredericton, grandfather of the present sheriff of the County of York. This was a solace to her. She and old Mrs. Jarvis were life-long friends and intimates.

No. X.

THE WAR-SPIRIT AMONG THE YORK BOYS.

CHILDREN will always take notice of *little things*, like themselves. A little boy or girl going along the road with a friend will draw the friend's attention to all the chickens, and birds, and kittens, and lambs, and rabbits, and squirrels in the journey. So, also, boys are more observant of other boys they meet with, or see, than their adult friends would be likely to be. On this principle, it is not strange, especially as I had two brothers a little older than myself, who were quite as observant as I, with better means of knowing; it is not strange, I say, that I should become acquainted with the sayings and doings of the York boys from about the year 1814, to, say 1818, if no further, when my years ranged from five to nine.

Boys, alas! are only too apt to be boisterous, rude, and quarrelsome in any place or time; but in York and its vicinity, during the war, and until Sunday-schools began to spring up in 1818 or '19, they were very much imbued with the war-spirit, and found great enjoyment in mimicking the military doings and manœuvres which they witnessed around them. True, there was no actual fighting to be seen after the battle of York, yet there were some " sham battles." One of these, especially, I witnessed, intended to represent a bush-fight, enacted on the outskirts of the town northward across the fields, perhaps into the woods, which then were quite near. The only victory accomplished was that of frightening all the hens and chickens and timid horses, and that of scaring the poor docile cows out of a day's milk, and far away into the woods.

This kind of work captivated the imagination of the youngsters, and they arrayed themselves, in twos and threes and larger numbers, against each other, pelting one another with stones and clods almost everywhere, insomuch that it was dangerous to walk the streets. As far as there were any schools, one school was arrayed against another, even on to a later day, as Dr. Scadding has shown in his "Toronto of Old," besides the one I have described.

The two great hostile sections arrayed against each other were those of the "Old Town boys" and the "New Town boys." What we now know as Jarvis street was the boundary between their respective dominions. All on the east side of that street belonged to the "Old Town," and were expected loyally to bear fealty to its military commanders; and all on the west side of the above-mentioned street were ruled as bearing allegiance to the "New Town" and its military authorities.

Henry Glennon, the son of a deceased physician, a neglected, unruly, bad youth, was accepted Captain-General of the Old Town boys; and Master Chewett, a youth more respectably connected, but quite as foolish, was the Commander-in-Chief of the New Town boys. I should think their forces pretty well balanced in point of numbers; for if the Old Town had the more compact, or dense population, the New one had a wider area to draw from.

They had had various encounters, "scrimmages," and parleys; but at length they met on a common near the dividing line between the towns, and adjacent to the residence of the deceased Dr. Glennon, a part of which house my father occupied as a residence and regimental harness-maker's shop; that is to say, at the corner of what is now known as George and Duchess streets. This I witnessed, though none of our family were allowed by our parents to take part in the misdoings. At first they were drawn up in two bodies, confronting each other; still they seemed to hesitate to encounter the danger and responsibility of actual conflict, and flags of truce passed between them, and a parley was being held. This, however, was interrupted, and an action was precipitated by some New Town boy shying a pebble which struck the Old

Town commander on the top of his head. His followers rushed upon the others to avenge the insult, and the battle became general, and missiles of all kinds flew about in a manner dangerous to all. Both sides had provided themselves with ammunition in the shape of small stones, which, however, being heavy to carry about, could not be largely accumulated, and was soon expended; and both armies were fain to supply themselves from the bed of McGill's Creek, which meandered in a valley where Queen street now extends. Parties were sent from both sides to the Creek to obtain the necessary supply of the munitions of war, and on meeting at this common arsenal, conflict ensued. One instance I mention. A large boy, Alexander Hamilton, of the Old Town, took up a large stone, and threatened to crush a smaller boy, fighting on the other side, unless he surrendered, and marched him in a prisoner, and he was bestowed in the garret of the Glennon house.

Nevertheless, the New Town boys had the best of it, and the Old Towners retreated and sheltered themselves in and around the common residence of the Glennons and my father. Matters now became too serious for any further toleration—every window was in danger of being broken. The old "Master Collar-Maker," a soldier of two wars, became aroused, went out, and soon quelled both armies—and there was a lull in hostilities. Whatever conflicts they may have had after that, they never came in near proximity to us. Thus we were saved from a spectacle we could well spare.

The case of poor Lloyd, the prisoner, was peculiar; he geographically belonged to the Old Town, for he had lived on the east side of Jarvis street. He was, therefore, regarded as a traitor. They detained him in durance vile, away from his widowed mother, till the next morning. A court-martial was assembled, which condemned and flogged him, and then released him, on condition of taking his oath that he would fight no more against them while he remained in the Old Town. In default of a Bible, he was sworn on a Roman Catholic Prayer-book! He escaped the consequences of his oath by the family moving, a few days after, into the New Town.

All I have narrated must justly seem to the well-taught boys of this day as very silly, as well as very wicked. It was the result of bad training. Gospel preaching and Sunday-schools came in a few years after, and rescued into the paths of 'virtue some of these boys; but my young friends must not be surprised to learn that many of them turned out ill—idle, drunken, and profane—coming to poverty and an early death. Learn to be thankful for your opportunities, and to improve them.

No. XI.

"NEDDIE," MY LITTLE PLAYMATE.

AFTER our parents came to live in the Town of York proper (for we stopped some time in an artilleryman's hut on the bank of the Bay, near the garrison, which many years ago fell into the water from the encroachments of the waves), we took up a house, or two rooms of one, on the corner of what are now called Duke and George streets. One of the first walks we children took was up George street, then overgrown with grass, till we crossed what is now known as Duchess street, into the farm property of Secretary Jarvis, which came down to the north side of said street, which, however, was innocent of a fence, for the soldiers had stolen it for fuel, such being the morals of war-time. Coinciding with what we now call George street, or in continuance of it, over the creek and ravine which I described in my last section, there was a bridge, which two park-lot holders had built on the line between their property as a means of reaching the back parts of their respective farms. It had once been a waggon-road, but the most of the planks had gone the same way as the fence rails (Oh! war, thou art indeed " a civilizer!"); but some of the planks, however, were left, and were laid lengthwise of the bridge, so as to furnish a means of egress and ingress to foot passengers—a pretty ticklish one too, for the bridge was high.

In crossing the narrow pathway for the first time, we met a little boy, who was returning from beyond the creek, whither he had been alone—for, as we afterwards found out, he was a fearless, self-reliant little fellow. He was dressed in a little black slip—mourning, perhaps, for a dead father; for he was the orphan son of a deceased physician, who had been in his lifetime capable, and in a good practice, but who, alas! had fallen by the hand of a destroyer whom doctors at least ought to know enough to avoid, but who, alas! has laid many of that profession low, as well as myriads of others—namely, DRINK. He was a plump, ruddy, pretty little boy; and, contrary to the custom among boys in York, we neither abused nor tried to frighten him, but asked him of his parents, his name, and age. He told us he was named Edward, that he was four years old, and that he was the son of Mrs. Glennon.

His father's late property was hard by, at the corner of George and Duchess streets, the then northern limits of the town, and his mother still maintained her possession of a third of it; and it turned out that the remaining two thirds of it soon after was hired by my father for his regimental shop and residence. Thus it happened that our two families became very well acquainted, and Neddie became the constant playmate of my twin brother and myself. And after that brother died, he became dear to me because he had known my dear playmate. He told us when we first met (I mind it well) that he was "four years old." He was therefore within a year of our own age, for we were five. Our tastes were consequently very much the same, and what was sport to one was sport to the other. Though, childlike, sometimes we had our disagreements and battles, upon the whole we agreed very well, and we longed for each other's society when apart.

After two or three years we both removed to other places; my family to a more convenient and permanent residence, and his mother and family to a little house on Yonge street, not far above Queen, given in lieu of her claim on what was afterwards called the "Lonsdale House," from that of the purchaser. Our respective houses were still comparatively near together, and continued so, although other moves afterwards took place. The "Old House," where we lived together under the same roof, was still to both of us a subject of fond and frequent reminiscence and a tie of affectionate regard.

Edward's parents had been born and brought up

Roman Catholics; but his father was no more; and, there being no stated services of the Roman Church in the town in that early day, and the Protestants having befriended the widow in her destitution, his mother had become more liberal than is usual with members of that Church. And well she might have been. Knowing that she had a great many mouths to feed— for there was Henry and John, Kitty and Theresa, Eliza and Edward—soon after her bereavement, that quaint but benevolent early citizen of York, Jesse Ketchum, drove a noble milch cow one day to the door of the widow, and never resumed the loan. The Church of England parson also called and gave her a present of money; but as he very judiciously counselled her to "take up some industry," his gift was not highly-prized; Mrs. G——, alas! like too many brought up in genteel idleness, regarded the advice to work for herself as an "insult," according to her own declaration. She sometimes, however, attended the ministrations of Dr. Strachan, and I should not wonder if Neddie, her youngest child, had been dedicated to God in baptism by the Doctor's hands. Sure I am, the boy learned the catechism of the Anglican Church in the public school, of which the Doctor was Rector, where the orphan received his tuition free. Once, on a vacant day, finding him playing at the door, Neddie took me through the school building, where, for the first time in my life, I saw an artificial globe. Showing how much my playmate was petted, I may tell that a well-dressed man on horseback meeting us that day, or near that place on another day (I won't be sure which), accosted my little companion kindly, and on opening his purse presented him with a large silver dollar! Upon the donor and his dollar hangs a tale, and as I do not pretend to be methodical, I may as well now tell it. It should teach my young readers the evils of dishonesty, untruthfulness, and boastfulness, and that unlawful gains are usually soon squandered. I do not call the well-dressed young man on horseback a gentleman, although at that time he had plenty of money to spend, and claimed to be a German Count, kept the most aristocratic company, and it is said that some of the most pretentious fair ones of the little capital were dying for love of him. He then had plenty of hard cash, but it was soon spent, and the last I heard of him was, that he was fain to support himself by attending a tavern bar. It was known afterwards that his only claim to German nobility was a German name; that his previous place of residence was the United States, where he had filled some clerkship, perhaps in a bank, or some Government office; but that being entrusted with a very large sum of money to convey from one place to another, he had decamped with it and fled to the British dominions, where at that time, I surmise, there were no arrangements for extraditing such felonious runaways. The rest of his history has been already told.

But to return to my playfellow. I have said enough

to indicate which way the religious proclivities (if they might be termed such) of the G—— family were tending. Ours, at our first acquaintance, were without any decided Church leanings—certainly not to either the Romish or Anglican Church. In 1818 the Methodist meeting-house was built, and my mother became a member of the Church, while I attended the Sunday-school; so that the religious affinities of my early friend and myself led to a divergence, and when, at the age of fifteen, I became converted, our intercourse was entirely broken off. For that I am sorry now, as I think I might have possibly done him good, if I had still conversed with him from time to time.

Yet I kept him in sight enough to know that his course was doubtful, if not downward, of which I am now to give an account for the purpose of admonition.

Sympathy for the mother would have opened prominent places for the children, if they had steadfastly remained in the places they had from time to time obtained. The mother had very little domestic authority, and the children did pretty much as they liked. The marked unsteadiness of the eldest son was enough to give all the others a wrong direction. He, often changed from place to place till he came to manhood, when he left the country. The two eldest girls did fairly well, considering their disadvantages. The youngest girl was subject to fits, lost her reason, and, at the age of fourteen or fifteen, fell into the fire, of which injury she died, thus releasing her friends from further solicitude. John, the second son, was the most stable and industrious of the lot; obtained a situation in Lower Canada; and in the long run rose to respectability and wealth, and did somewhat for his relations.

But now, to confine myself to Edward, my hero. Had he been wise and industrious, he might have done well. He was a comely boy, and naturally attracted people to him—he was popular among those of his own age. Then, he was favoured by the gentry, and might have obtained a good education free of charge; but he was averse to study, and only went to school by fits and starts. He did not like work any more than study, and when at home, did not render that aid to his lone mother he might have done. As a specimen of what a good son would never do, when his mother requested him to provide her some wood before he went away to play (wood was then to be had for picking up—it lay about the common), he flew into a passion, and exclaimed, "Mother, you are eternally wanting wood!" And I do not know that he would have procured her any, only I offered to bear him company and help him. A few armfuls of limbs, and roots, and big chips, procured me his companionship for the rest of the day. He who will not work for his widowed mother is not likely to work for others He went to be shop-boy; commenced learning the printer's trade, &c. In short, he was

"All things by turns, and nothing long."

After I went out into the ministry, at the age of nineteen, when he must have been about eighteen, I almost lost sight of my childhood's playmate for many years, although I often, as I do now, thought of him with tenderness and pity. I heard of him at long intervals, and I believe that this is about the substance of what happened to him during those years. He had picked up more education than had fallen to the lot of the most of his early associates; and he was handsome in young manhood; was naturally graceful; and, through his mother, had seen good society, which had exercised a measure of its refining influence on his external manners. Moreover, his brother had tried to introduce him to the means of self-support, and helped him in various ways. But I have reason to believe, that he had grown up an idle changeling, not wholly free from the vices of drink, licentiousness, gaming, and general wastefulness.

About middle life with me, I was appointed to a large western town, now for some years a city. There, by some means, I learned that a few years before a young man of the name of my early friend had come to the place, and, under the auspices of a wealthy brother in Montreal, opened up a large stock of goods, and commenced business as a merchant. He was prepossessing, and people thought well of him for a time. Genteel families opened their doors to him. In one of these there was an exceedingly fascinating young lady from New Brunswick, to whom E. G. paid his addresses for a time, not without encouragement, till she discovered certain flaws in his character, and saved herself in time. He idled away his time, neglected his business, wasted his substance, and fell into debt. His brother had to rescue him and close his business up; and was well content to be rid of the responsibility by giving him a small annual stipend, on condition that he would keep at a distance. He now sank to the position of a common loafer; and when I arrived at the place, he was the hanger-on of a tavern in a neighbouring country village, where he held some paltry position.

Before I left those parts, I took to preaching in that village, and I have reason to believe he once in a while came to hear me preach. Being one day in a shop in the place, a person came in with a dissipated look, but trying to maintain a shabby gentility in his appearance, in whose features I saw traces of my early playfellow. He affected not to see or know me, but I arose, went across the room, and, for the first time in twenty-five years, accosted him. Reaching out my hand, I said inquiringly, "Edward Glennon, I believe?" Affecting to suddenly recognize me, he said, "Mr. Carroll." But he was not inclined to be communicative, and soon withdrew. He never amended his course, but died soon after of the fruits of his irregular habits. Alas! alas! my young friend

No. XII.

RECOLLECTIONS OF THE LONG-LOG HOUSE.

IF I have ever spoken or written in glowing terms of the pleasures of the fireside, the images have been a reproduction of the remembrance of homely domestic enjoyment in the same long-log house.

The close of the war of 1812-15 found father, mother, the eldest son and brother, and the four youngest children, or brothers in York, and the second and third sons "on the lines," or in the neighbourhood of Niagara River. Although I think there was no need of it (they could have come by themselves), father went after those two, saw them get their discharge, and returned with them to our humble home in York. The weary journey was performed on foot. I remember the day of their arrival; and we were all glad of their return. We had not seen them for a year, and they were more manly-looking than when we had seen them last. They were yet in their regimentals. Tom was only eighteen; Bill was, perhaps, twenty-one; but both were large, powerful men. One of their pleasures when they arrived at home was to have little John, a child not quite six years old, climb on the knee of the eldest brother and read a part of the paraphrase beginning with—

> "Behold, the mountain of the Lord
> In latter days shall rise,"

to show his proficiency in that art—gained by spelling out the words by himself.

War times are wasteful times; and they had not saved much of their pay and prize money. They had been discouraged in trying to save by a disheartening incident. One of them had saved $100, which he inclosed in a letter, in ten golden "eagle pieces," and entrusted to a comrade, who was coming to York, to fetch it to his mother; but the messenger "got on a spree" by the way, and broke the letter open, and spent the contents in drink. True, after a time, he brought the letter, minus the money, with a drunkard's remorseful confession when his debauch was over, but never made good the money. Such is one of the painful fruits of drinking, then, alas! more common than now—too common although it still is.

The whole family had to turn to some industry. Two cows were purchased, and first an ox team, and then a span of horses, and the cultivation of neighbouring farms and fields, with teaming, wood-chopping, and wood-hauling, became their business; so that I will have no elegancies or luxuries to speak of.*

To have room for the whole family and labouring men whom they sometimes hired and boarded, and accommodation for their cattle and teams, they had to have larger premises. One of these was secured on the corner of what we now know as Bay and Richmond Streets, the only house then on those four corners, then the property of the late Andrew Mercer, from whom the Reformatory is named. The building was only of logs, but they were new, and they were dressed, or "hewed," as it was called. True, there was only five rooms in all, besides a capacious cellar, which served to store our potatoes and apples. There was also a barn and horse-stable, with sheds.

The reason why the remembrance of this homely

---

* Father and brothers cultivated what was called the "Jarvis Farm." It being the property of Secretary Jarvis and afterwards of his son, Saml. P. Jarvis, Esq., which intervened between Capt. McGill's farm (the centre of which was McGill Square, where the Metropolitan Methodist Church now stands), on the west side, and what then used to be called the "Selby Lot," then swampy and wild, (afterwards the property of Col. Allen, on the east side. The front of the Jarvis farm came down to Duchess Street. George Street's northern extremity ended at the Jarvis farm gateway, and Jarvis Street went through the centre of the Jarvis farm—through the very house itself. Quite a large stream ran across the front of the farm, now concealed by subsequent improvements. Beyond the creek was an orchard, which I used to be set to watch against the depredations of school-boys when the apples became sizable; but such tiny defenders as I and my twin-brother were treated with jeers by the lawless invaders.

place is so precious to me is this: all the brothers excepting William (lately married) were still at home, and he was often there. There was then a great deal more talking than reading. Most persons were dependent on conversations or oral communications for learning and mental entertainment; and our household contained several very great talkers. The oldest boys had all seen life, and had their war-stories to rehearse. Scores of old comrades or war acquaintances called and remained a longer or shorter space. Father was an old man of long observation in the world—in Ireland, the old Colonies, New Brunswick, and Canada. He had experiences as a mechanic, a soldier in two wars, farmer, lumberman, hunter, fisher, and I know not what else, with a great memory and great volubility. Mother, too, had her tales from her own side of the house, relating to two or three generations, which extended back to New Brunswick, and both New and Old England. Then, there were some half-dozen others, who in some way belonged to the household and joined the circle around the large open fire in the largest room, which was kitchen, parlour, dining, and sitting-room all in one. Among the work hands, or boarders, there was Nickerson, a journeyman wood-chopper, whose scheme it was to earn money enough to take him to Germany, where he expected to prove his heirship to an estate, and become a gentleman. There was "Old Boatswain" (or "Bosen"), a constant drinker, with a red face, an American, who had been in the American army, I think, whose dialect was New Englandish, with some frequently recurring expletives to help him in his lack of words. One of these phrases was, "Not that alone." Once, one of the company irreverently expressed a wish to go to heaven if he could have "a keg of rum along." Boatswain, equally profane, instantly assented, and true to his Yankee instincts, said, "Not that alone, but a kittle of biled corn." There was Sayers, an American, too, and unmistakeably such in dialect, who once undertook to sing what he called "an old seafarin' song," which wound up with an expectation, when his voyages were over, of—

> Sending for his friends and relations,
> And gittin' a bar'l of beer."

He, too, I think, had been in the American army. There also was Mitchel, who lived with his French wife in a room upstairs, who was an Irishman by birth, and a Protestant by education, who had learned the French language in the cities of Quebec and Montreal, but had turned Catholic to reconcile his father and mother-in-law to their giving him their "Sharlette," as he called her, whom, however, he had borne far from a well-to-do home in Montreal. Mitchel had been in the Voltigeurs during the late war. There was also an ignorant, uncouth fellow, a Canadian, whose name I have forgotten (I am sorry, too, it suited him so well). He had served in the navy on the back lakes during the war of '12, whose narrative of adventure ran upon "Lake Sincoe" and "Penatangashin." He was a widower, I believe, and was sometimes accompanied by a freckled, wrinkled, and wizened-faced little boy with a red head, who looked as though he had been *whipped up* rather than "brought up." It was said his father used to tie a rope around him and throw him overboard into the water to "make him tough," pulling him up again after he had a spell of struggling for his life. Old Cole, now partially blind, who had known brother James in the militia, sought refuge with us for a time, was an interesting song-singer.

Next to story-telling of all kinds, song-singing was one of the ingredients of our social enjoyment. None of these songs were very bad, but I fear they would all fall under the condemnatory prohibition of John Wesley, as those which "do not lead to the knowledge and love of God." Father was a melodious singer, with a memory well stored with songs of all kinds, embracing love, war, and Masonry. His "Jemmy Riley," the Irishman who stole the heiress, and thought to escape the penalty by putting her on the horse before him, to make it appear that *she* ran away with him, and not he with her; "Love in a Tub," which told that a lover obtained a rich wine merchant's daughter by getting her headed up in a particular cask, and purchasing it, closing the bargain by saying:

"I ve bought it, and paid for it,
And so it is mine,
Let what will be in it,
Beer, ale, or wine."

He had party songs, relating to his native isle; among the number were such as the "Green to the Cape," Croppy Lie Down," and others. Sometimes he gave us a refrain in the native Erse, or Irish. I remember some of the words, but fear to undertake putting them on paper. He usually sang "Burns' Farewell" with great pathos, and others equally pathetic. The time would fail to undertake to recount his *stories;* they were endless. Mitchel used to create unbounded hilarity by singing the Frenchman's aspirations of invading England " mit his flat-bottomed boat, to land zoost at Dover," which attempt John English, "mit his big ship;" "and ball big as a pumpkin," always frustrated. For of him the Frenchman sang :—

"He tump us, he 'trike us,
He make so much clattare;
He make tree, four, verra good ship
Fall down in the vatare."

This, of course, had reference to Bonaparte's threatened descent on England, which he could never carry out, the remembrance of which gave the listeners ecstatic pleasure; for all the Britishers were intensely loyal, so recently had they come out of the French and American wars. This feeling was also flattered by a song relating to a sea victory, which used to be sung by a young man, Barney Glennon, often in, who had served in the lake marine during the war. This related to the "boasting La Pique," which had "been taken by the brave British tars of the Blanche." Nickerson was a singer, and also gave us one song describing a nautical victory achieved by "Old Dreadnought,"—

"Whose sides were oak, her keel was box,
　Launched off the stocks,
　　Bound to the main."

One of Nickerson's Masonic songs, relating to Solomon's Temple, supplied us with some scriptural knowledge before there was a whole Bible in the house. About this time, however, the entire Bible came. Before that, there had been only a large Testament with a metrical version of the Psalms, the Paraphrases, and a few hymns, including some of Dr. Watts' and Bishop Ken's. Other books were rare, and of a very ill-assorted character for the most part. True, there were a few school books containing some good pieces in prose and verse, such as the "American Selections" and the "English Reader." The eulogies on Washington and Franklin, and other American notorieties, used to call out vehement denunciations from father's "Britisher" tongue. An allegory read in the family about this time, relating to John Bull and his son Jonathan, who had run away from home and cleared him up "thirteen farms" (corresponding to the then number of the United States), whom the old man would not suffer to enjoy the use of the mill-pond, used to tickle father's risibles, and produced bursts of laughter. A volume of songs about Robin Hood, Will Scarlet, Little John, and the rest of the outlaw's men and their joint exploits, gave us about all the knowledge we had of mediæval England. That work and the Newgate Calendar, with the doings of Jack Sheppard and others of that ilk, were not likely to give us youngsters very law-abiding notions. Nor had the autobiography of Philip Quarels, the bigamist, and Stephen Burrows, the jail-breaker, any better tendency.

How thankful my young readers and their parents and guardians should be, that the young are not now left to the companionship of such books! At present, I dismiss the long-log house and its memories.

No. XIII.

FOND MEMORIES OF CERTAIN DOMESTIC ANIMALS.

IT is good to have children brought up among the cats and dogs, horses and cows, and hens and chickens, to mention no more. The children learn something by watching the animals; the animals are company for the little ones; and the companionship nourishes domestic affections in a family. The brute animals owned by our family I know had the effects mentioned on me.

Our first span of horses, after the war, were old Jack and Bob. Jack was black, with a red nose, like a certain species of bear in our country. Bob was a bay, not so large as the other, but able to keep up his end of-the double-tree pretty well. He was the favourite, as he was good-tempered. Jack was peevish and cross; he would bite if he was not pleased, and we children kept a prudent distance from him. Bob would not bite, but if you gave him a smart slap on the side with your hand, he would give a piteous groan. If you were on his back and gave him a kick with your heel, as is often done, to urge him along, he would utter this groan. I never observed this peculiarity in any other horse. By this habit we once recovered him when he was lost. But more of this a little further on. We bought this span of horses after the war from an army teamster, who had allowed, if he did not encourage, the horses to go as fast down hill as they liked. Hence, when they came to the brow of a descent, they wanted to run, instead of "holding." This, of course, was very undesirable and dangerous; but father, being an old man, seemed unable to curb them, and the vice seemed rather to increase than otherwise. In one journey, father broke and lost a portion of his load, and was pretty badly injured himself. But Tom was a stout, resolute young man, and leaving another employment, he came home and took charge of the team, and soon reduced them to submission. His method was, to hold them with a strong hand, and to chastise them severely with the whip for any disposition to run; so that they became afraid to repeat it. This lesson may be of value to my young readers, if they ever should become teamsters, and have to deal with horses which have this trick.

Tom, like most young men, when he came of age fancied a horse of his own, and usually had one for his pleasure. His first purchase was of a first year's colt, which died before spring. His next purchase was a funny little pony, which rejoiced in the name of Button—which name I suppose he received because he was so small and so round. He was so round that it was almost impossible to keep a saddle upon him; and the boys, in striving to gain his bare back, often rolled off on the farther side. But then, that was no great disaster, as they had not very far to fall. How many hands high, or low, he was I do not now remember; or what breed of horses he was of. I should say he was a cross between a Shetland and a French-Canadian pony. He was, however, very beautiful, being very symmetrically formed, and as black as a coal. He might have drawn a carriage adapted to his size and strength, but he was not big enough to be matched against an ordinary-sized horse; yet we were once so forced to try and match him. Some dishonest person took old Bob out of his pasture and rode him far away, and we were ignorant of his whereabouts for several weeks. In the meantime the family ran out of wood, and some must be drawn from the cordwood piles in the "bush."* But as we had no single-horse waggon or cart, with harness to suit, there was no way for it but to try and extemporize a mate for old Jack, long enough to draw a few loads. Button was, therefore, caught, and harnessed up in Bob's harness, by making alterations, and giving him what the teamsters call "an advantage on the double-tree," so as to make

---

* Our folks bought large areas of standing timber and cut it up into cordwood, and drew it to town, and sold it for fuel.

his draft power correspond with his stronger mate. Yet, after all, poor Button seemed to cut a sorry figure. He seemed like a boy of ten years old put in a man's clothes, and made to keep up with a full-grown man in some piece of combined labour. Button's legs were too short to keep up with the other, and his strength too small to compete with the other member of the team. Besides, Jack seemed to feel contempt for his tiny mate, and to look down upon him with scorn; and when "Butty" failed to keep up, Jack's constitutional ill-nature broke out, and every now and then he turned and bit the poor little fellow severely, for which ill conduct Jack himself received chastisement with the driver's whip. But the mutual unpleasantness ended at last.

My father heard of a stray horse far back in the country, and went in search of him; but as he was a great pedestrian, and preferred walking, he went on foot. Besides, I do not know but that Jack was employed in ploughing, assisted or hindered by little Button. About the time he might have been expected home, and a few hours before he did arrive, one of the younger boys came in with breathless haste, saying he had seen a man ride old Bob down Yonge Street towards the centre of the town; saying that he knew it was our horse, for as the man started on, after stopping to inquire for "the nearest tavern," he urged the animal on with his heels, upon which Bob uttered his accustomed complaint. And by this utterance he was claimed, by an older brother, who chanced to be "down street" for an evening's walk. In those days, at the corner of what we now call King and George Streets, there was a well-known hostelry, or tavern, kept by a Mr. Hamilton, before which on that occasion, several persons were congregated, among whom was my brother Tom. A stranger rode up and dismounted, and my brother went forward and said, "You have got my horse." The man said he did not know whose he was; but an old man, tired of riding, had offered him the horse to ride into town, with instructions to stop (as he understood it) at the first tavern. "Well," said Tom, "to prove that he is my horse, when I slap him on the side he will groan;" and suiting the action to the word, he did slap him, and the horse complained as usual, and the stranger resigned the possession of him. The man had been guilty of no dishonest intention as circumstances after proved. My brother brought the horse home to the "Long-log House," and Bob was put into his old stall, and received the welcoming whinny of his old mate, that had gone with him through the war, laying by for the nonce his constitutional crabbedness. Not long after the horse's arrival, father came in, and expressed great disgust that the man should have disobeyed his directions. But the truth was, the man did not understand the old Irishman's terminology. In those days, on the east side of Yonge Street, a few yards north of where Queen Street now crosses it, the Widow Glennon had a little house, and kept "cakes and beer" for sale. Father had said to the stranger: "I am tired of riding; take this horse, and ride on till just as you enter the town, you will see a *shebeen shop;* leave the horse tied there for me, and I will find him." "Shebeen" was the word he misunderstood for tavern, and hence the mistake. That was a pleasant evening around the wood fire in the "Long-log House." Bob, that had been lost, was found; and father had returned. That old team served the family several years, and when they were sold, in their old age, to strangers, I was very sad and sorry. It went to my young heart to see them led away.

But my strongest attachment was to the "old brown cow." The family had several cows, first and last—sometimes three or four at a time—but Old Brown was a fixture and an institution in the family. My dear mother preferred her to all others, and that was enough. She had been the favourite cow of an artilleryman, about to be removed from York, and he reluctantly offered her for sale, and my parents bought her. She was of the very best type of Canadian cows, than which there are no better for milk, no matter what breed they are; she was large and long, with smooth horns, brown in colour, plentiful in very rich milk, and easy to be milked, for being gentle in temper, she readily "gave it down," as it was termed, and often yielded milk till the day of calving.

Other cows were bought and sold, but **Old Brown was**

kept; and when we had but one cow, she was that one. Often was it my task to feed her in the winter, and often to seek her on the extensive commons and free pastures that stretched away north and west (especially) from the town, until I began to feel all the regard for her which I felt for other members of the family—and more, for others at times offended me, but she never. Alas! at about the age of twelve there was a dispersion in the family, and most of our effects were sold, and among the rest the old cow. This affected me much, and I could not bear to see her removed. Upon this change, I went to live with an older brother settled on a new farm, fourteen or fifteen miles from the town, for the space of over a year, of which sojourn I may have something to say before my stories are ended. Often I had to walk, on one errand or another, to and from the town. In one of my journeys, I discovered that a farmer on the roadside had purchased and possessed "Old Brown." The thought that any one else than ourselves should possess our old friend filled my heart with grief and eyes with tears. As my eyes affected my heart, so I used to turn away from what seemed "Old Brown's" captivity. This grief was increased when I discovered that she had met with an accident, and had been cut or maimed by a falling tree, or limb, and had to wear habitually a large swathing of canvas around her body. I could not bear to look at her—her eyes seemed to reproach the family for allowing her to go among strangers, in her old age. The sorrow produced by the sight of her was of a mingled kind: it recalled the happy early associations of a family then dispersed, though destined to be afterwards gathered for a time, yet never under very happy auspices.

The great Linnæus, the naturalist, believed that instinct would survive death; and John Wesley, on Scriptural grounds, believed in the resurrection of the brute creation. If there is any such resurrection, I shall be glad to see "Old Brown" again—and many a faithful horse which I have since ridden.

No. XIV.

THE GHOST LORE CURRENT DURING MY CHILDHOOD.

AFTER looking over the foregoing section, giving an account of the various entertainments around the large open fire of the Long-Log House, I am reminded that one of the most exciting subjects of conversation was omitted, namely, that of "Spooks," or apparitions. These were a subject of confabulation in our family before going there; nor were they entirely extinguished by our removal from that place.

Our previous residence, at the corner of George and Duke Streets, was near an old dilapidated, unfenced, neglected burial ground; that in the midst of which now stands the old Central Presbyterian Church. There were a few graves in this resting-place of the dead upon which considerable care and expense had at one time been bestowed. Some of the palings were yet standing, but they were grown full of wild shrubs. One grave was covered with a large, table-like tombstone, resting on four pedestals, covered with an elaborate inscription, the purport of which I once knew well, but of which I can now remember nothing precisely. The tradition which figures faintly in my memory relative to that grave was something like this: a young gentleman of respectable, well-to-do, if not wealthy connections, coming from Kingston on horse-back post haste to York, undertaking to cross the Don before there was a bridge, or at a time of its temporary removal, was unfortunately drowned. His body was afterwards recovered and buried in the grave described. The spot was afterwards reported to be haunted. A luminous vapor was said to have been seen to exude from graves in that burial spot, which might have arisen from the emission of some kind of gas generated perhaps by the decomposition of animal remains. Yet like a true orthodox ghost, it was only to be seen at night. The result was, although myself and other children often amused ourselves in that graveyard in day-time, and conducted various kinds of plays on the tombstone, no possible persuasion could have induced us to go anywhere near it after night-fall.

Apropos of the sprites which lingered around that locality, after we had removed to the Mercer House, at one time the following tale received a "nine days" currency: One Barney Maguire, an ex-soldier of the Glengarry Highlanders, who had escaped with his life from the decimation inflicted on that corps in the charge made by that regiment into the ranks of the invaders at the battle of Niagara, had married the daughter of a worthy citizen, who lived on what we now call Ontario Street, had been with his wife on a visit to his father-in-law on the night in question, and remained till a late hour, and then started for his residence to the west of us on Newgate Street (now Adelaide); but, for some reason, on his return walk, he had kept one street nearer the graveyard than his most direct route, so the story ran. Opposite the "city of the dead" a human form came out and followed the party, apparently desirous to speak to Maguire; but for fear of alarming the ladies (his wife and some female friend) he abstained from accosting the apparition. When, however, he reached home, he went in and confided the child he was carrying to the hands of its mother, and went out again, and opened a colloquy with the mysterious visitor. It was the spirit of the drowned man, who confided some important message, or agency, to Barney, the purport of which was then given with minuteness and particularity, (for such tales have usually all necessary details supplied as they pass around to make them consistent); but I confess they have all passed from my recollection, especially as interviews with Maguire exploded the whole as a *canard*. Nevertheless, the rumour in the meantime, led each person in our fireside circle to refurbish the ghost lore he had in his possession, handed down to him from several foregoing generations of his ancestors, and to relate it for the delectation of the company.

Some of these were pokerish enough. One of them, from my mother, related to New Brunswick, and was to this effect: A solitary resident in a little house on the banks of the St. John River was cruelly murdered, after that the place was undeniably haunted, so much so, that no boatman, fisherman, lumberman, or indeed any traveller, would peril his night's rest by lodging under that roof. However, a party of wild young blades in going up or down the river, were driven by stress of weather to seek the shelter of that deserted house for one night. On entering, one presumptuous fellow, as it was very dark, cried out, "Come, old Blank, strike up a light!" When suddenly to their great dismay, the place became as luminous as day, and old Blank sat crouching in a corner. Deponent said they left more hastily than they came. Mother also told how she had seen a man's double in day time, before his death, at a moment when he was proved to be miles away, near a spot where he was soon after buried. This was related to show that there were more things in heaven and earth than were dreamed of in the prevailing philosophy. There were many of our Highland Scotch and Roman Catholic Irish acquaintances who related tales by the hour, not only of fairies (the good people)—*uttered softly*—but of the "Banshee," and the "Brownie," which we liked the excitement of listening to. I cannot say that any of our people believed in them; but in the possibility of apparitions and in the authenticity of their occurrence in many cases, we had the heartiest belief. The belief grew in me, and as Dr. Stephens said the apparition of old Jeffry in the Wesley family, "opened the right of way for the supernatural" in my soul.

But the belief occasioned me a great deal of superstitious terror. And while the spook stories went around (a baneful thing to allow among children), I always stole from the outer edge of the fireside circle to the inside of the circle, despite the burning heat of the fire, and the danger of being roasted alive. For hours the sweat would pour off me, but I dared not stir. The hold which these stories had taken of those who listened to them, especially the younger ones, could be seen in their staring looks, or the dilation of the pupils of their eyes and their glistening eye-balls.

Scarcely less exciting were the recitation of the barbarous incidents of the Indian wars, which had passed out of New England into New Brunswick. Those were mostly authentic, and so the more terrible. One of my mother's stories was of a woman, who heard her little child at play in the door-yard to shriek out. She knew that the savages were upon them, and it would not do to go out, even to look after her child, but to stick to her only means of defence:—She was making soft soap, and a large pot of it, scalding hot, was simmering over the fire, over which she stood ladle in hand, and as the Indians opened the door, the front rank met a hot reception. They yelled and broke, but she stood to her guns, and as each successive rank came forward to the assault, they were welcomed in a similar way. Till at length they all scampered off, writhing and screaming with agony. When she ventured out her child was dead, but she herself was undisputed master (or mistress) of the fort and field.

Many, many years after, when there were but few remnants of the aborigines left, and no danger was experienced from them, a scarred old Indian called and asked for something to eat. She gave him a comfortable meal and otherwise treated him kindly. So communicative did he feel that he said to her in a way of inquiry, "You no remember makum soap of Indians?" "Yes! was you one of that band?" "Well, what became of the scalded Indians?" "Some berry sick, good many die." "They deserved it, the rascals!" was her reply.

These reminiscenses might be multiplied indefinitely but the reader has had enough for illustration; and perhaps he will say, "*more than enough.*"

But, perhaps, before I dismiss things terrible and improbable, I shall tell that about 1816. A report was raised that a wild man, or *yahoo* ("yo-ho," it was pronounced) had been seen on Yonge Street, near the Gallows Hill, by one Whitesides, if not others, which obtained currency for a short time. No one seemed to think the thing unlikely. My own father spoke, as a parallel case, of having seen a wild man, naked but hairy, by the roadside, in one of the Southern States or Provinces, by whom, or which, his horse was very much frightened. I mention these particulars to indicate the beliefs or credulity of the people, and the kind of conversation which obtained among those by whom my childhood was surrounded, and the consequent influences under which my own mind had to be developed

No. XV.

HOW I EARNED MY FIRST FELT HAT.

I WAS then about eight years of age, ever since which I have done something towards my own support. Do not suppose that I had gone bareheaded till then. I had worn a cap, and that cap of home manufacture, sometimes of one material and then of another —of yellow nankeen, or green baize, ornamented sometimes with a tassel at top, and when that could not be obtained, by a large covered button and an appropriate forepiece. But then, that was only a *cap*, and not " a store cap either." I can remember how consequential I felt, years after, while wearing at my work, a peaked cap of red-worsted, known as a *bonnet rouge*, bought with my own earnings " out of a store."

Yet up to the age of eight years, as I have said, I had never owned a veritable hat; and I sighed to have one—it would be so much more manly. Every boy of any manlike pretensions wore a hat; and if I only had a hat, it would be a long stride towards manhood.

And was it not a happy day when mother went to the hatter's and brought home a hat for each of the three youngest boys! But how great was my boast, compared with the others, as I could say, "I earned mine!" It had been paid for by my own hoarded earnings, a lot of little pieces of silver, amounting to one dollar.

The way in which I earned the money was this: we still lived in the "Long Log-house," on the corner of what we now know as Bay and Richmond Streets. The square directly opposite eastward all belonged to one man, who owned a great part of York besides (indeed he owned the land on the three opposite corners to us) enclosed with a high picket fence. The fence, or stockade, protected a meadow and an orchard. The gentleman's residence was on the south-east corner of the block, that is to say, on the north-west corner of what we now know as Yonge and Adelaide Streets. That gentleman was the son of a shiftless, if not drunken father, who ill provided for his family, and bound out his son where he suffered great hardship and cruelty, from which he had relieved himself by running away and coming to this Province, where he had an older brother then living. Industry and good habits marked him ever after; especially he foreswore all intoxicating liquors, in a day when the evils of drinking were not generally seen. He fell into good business habits, married prudently, came to York and bought out the business for a song of an American leaving the Province on the eve of the war; prospered and made wealth with uncommon rapidity. But, in his prosperity, he did not forget his early hardships; but the remembrance of them made him thoughtful of his poor relations and sympathizing to all in destitution, especially to poor boys, particularly if they were industrious and trying to rise.

This person was homely in his ways and quaint, or odd, in his expressions. This, joined to his known benevolence and kindness of heart, caused him to be familiarly known by his neighbors as "Uncle Jesse."

Uncle Jesse had, among several other dependent persons, living with him, a nephew—a sister's son—by the name of John Jones. John was four years older than I, but being small of his age, and very fond of play, he seemed to be a mere boy for many more years. Among other boyish characteristics, John did not like to work alone. Unless he had company, he was not very persevering, if not looked after.

In the early spring of 1818, Mr. Ketchum had caused a two-acre field, bounded by Queen, Yonge, Richmond, and Bay Streets, then without a building of any kind upon it, to be ploughed, manured, and every way prepared for a crop of potatoes. The seed was brought on to the ground, and John Jones was set to work to plant them. He was wholly alone, and it seemed a formidable undertaking for him. He naturally hailed any boy that passed to get company out of him, if he could not induce him to help. During the first day of his operations, I and my little twin brother were passing, and he called us in, and asked us to drop the potatoes in the drills for him while he hoed the earth upon them. My mate refused and went home; but, being naturally obliging, I complied, and John started to work with renewed vigour. In a few hours the uncle came to see how his nephew was getting on, and was not a little pleased to see him so reinforced and prosecuting his work so well; and being desirous to reward and encourage me, he opened his buckskin purse, filled with small pieces of silver, and offered me a piece of what was called "cut money" (money used to be cut up in lesser pieces in those days to make change), one half a quarter doller cut in two; but showing my preference for a piece of "round money," he gave me a regular "York shilling." There was no stipulation between us, but, at John's earnest solicitation, I went every day; and every day the good man visited us and gave me a York shilling. Eight days had elapsed before we had completed our task. Every day I took my piece of money to my mother, and at the end of the eight days I was the *owner of a dollar*. With that dollar, as I have already said, my mother bought me a hat.

Like all children, we wanted to put our hats on at once; and needing hats very much we were allowed to wear them. But going to work with them on in a very warm day, and being employed in burning the brush that had been cut down on a field, then farmed by the family (a field which now constitutes the

Queen's Park), the coloured glaze which stiffened the crimson lining of our hats, and which we had greatly admired, melted and lost its colour and its gloss, and caused us sorrow and disappointment : so unstable are our earthly delights!

But I was consoled by the good opinion which I had earned of Mr. K., which led him to propose to my parents to have me come and live with him; and although I did not immediately comply, I went into his employment in after years, and enjoyed his friendship until the good old gentleman's death at a very advanced age. My little story carries its own moral on its face.

No. XVI.

THE "ELMSLEY FIELD," AND ITS ONE TRAGIC MEMORY.

THIS field was a block of land facing Yonge Street from its west side, containing about forty acres, perhaps at the time when it first came under my observation, mostly cleared, well fenced, and with a large barn in the centre of the clearing. It was the northern half of the block, formerly possessed by Chief-Justice Elmsley before his death. If any person is curious to know the history of that particular portion of his property he has only to turn to Dr. Scadding's "Toronto of Old," page 392. At the time to which I refer, Chief-Justice Elmsley was deceased, and the heir-at-law of the northern section of his property in that locality (he who was afterwards known as the Hon. John Elmsley), was a minor, and living in Europe, probably for the purpose of completing his education; and the property was managed by Alexander Wood, Esquire, who kept a shop on the north-west corner of King and Frederick Streets.

I have already said or intimated that my father and brothers purchased wood lots, and cut and sold the cordwood from off them, and farmed various pieces of land. About the time the Jarvis farm was to pass out of their hands, they engaged with Mr. Wood to till and crop a large part of the Elmsley Field, he himself cultivating, in the most approved Scotch method, the other part. My brother James was the principal manager of this particular enterprise, but all the younger ones were more or less employed from time to time about the place. The time it was in our possession must have included the years 1817 and 1818, the former certainly.

I have several minor memories of the field, mostly of a pleasant kind; such as its broad expanse, and the fragrant "smell of a field which the Lord had blessed;" the pasturing of our two cows there, with the pail of milk "Old Brown" gave one morning before she went, and the beautiful calf that followed her from the field at night (of Pink, the calf herself, I had my special memories); the pleasant memory of burning brush and rubbish. And where is the boy that does not like to kindle a fire and see a blaze? And the not so pleasant memory of riding, along with my little twin brother, our span of horses, round and round, on the barn floor, to thresh the grain, in the absence of modern appliances for that purpose. I say "not so pleasant memories," for ever and anon my bare feet got a scraping between the horse's side and the boarding of the barn, which tore off the skin and made them bleed.

But I am to relate a tragic memory of that place. I will be likely to tell elsewhere how that we two youngest boys attended school the whole of the summer of 1817, at what was the extreme east end of the town, that is to say, on King Street, east of Ontario. On arriving at the school-house for the afternoon, after partaking of our dinner, on the 11th of July of that summer, the children who had remained at the place told us that there had been a squabble on the street, and that one gentleman had given another gentleman a caning; and while they were talking, the person who had used the cane made his appearance with two or three others, to whom he seemed to be describing what had happened. He was a very young man, but tall and large. He was dressed in a frock-coat and white pantaloons.

We neither heard nor knew anything further for that night; but, on the morning of the 12th, at a very early hour, my brother William, who was married and living in a small house which he had erected on Yonge Street, near the corner of what is now Yonge and Albert Streets (the first erected in McCauley Town), was getting his team ready to start with a load of Government stores to the Holland Landing, a method of forwarding which then furnished employment to those who, like my brother, kept teams for hire. The sun was scarcely risen, the dew was on leaf and spray and all nature seemed in repose, save that a close carriage (almost the only one kept for hire in the town), belonging to William Darius Forrest) generally called "D'Forrest," who kept the most flashy hotel in the town), was proceeding very slowly, almost lingering, and stopping—till there was the report of a pistol heard, and a few seconds after another. Upon which my brother observed that the driver on the box of the carriage whipped up his horses, and put them at the top of their speed. After another short interval, the carriage was seen returning not very fast, but with no person visible but the driver. My brother said to him, "What have you there?" He answered, "The body of John Ridout: he has been killed in a duel by Samuel Jarvis."

These names reveal the two principals in the broil and in the death-dealing duel. It is, perhaps, too early for the history of the inside details of the quarrel which led to this sad catastrophe. Suffice it to say, that there had been a family feud of some standing between the Ridouts and the family of Secretary Jarvis; and George Ridout and young Samuel Jarvis had been prevented some time before, from satisfying their injured honour by the arbitration of pistols, through the vessel in which they had set sail for Niagara, where the duel was to have been fought, being so long becalmed outside the Point, that she was overtaken by the officers of justice in a row-boat, brought back to town, and bound over to keep the peace. But unhappily the quarrel was resumed between Samuel Jarvis, a young man from 20 to 30 perhaps, and a younger son and brother of the Ridout family. On that fatal 11th of July, Samuel Jarvis had called John Ridout into his office, and after some altercation told him to leave, or he would kick him out. The same day they met in the street, and the younger man (being the larger and stronger) inflicted chastisement on the other. For the further and fatal issue of the quarrel they were both answerable. Each challenged the other, and the whole was evidently arranged that night, while their mothers, sisters, and other friends were sunk in peaceful repose. Jarvis obtained Henry John Boulton as his second, and Ridout secured James E. Small as his second. And, oh! sad mockery of law and justice, both were legal men! Boulton was Solicitor-General, and Small was an able pleader at the bar; and both of them afterwards wore a judge's ermine.

The story told of the duel was, that Ridout being young and nervous (it was his twentieth birthday), had fired by mistake at the word "two," instead of waiting for the true count; his ball cut the necktie of the other. Seeing his mistake, he rushed forward to his antagonist, and exclaimed, "I hope I have not hurt you?" What a pity that at this stage of the deplorable business, there could not have been some means employed to prevent the matter from going further, and the loss of a promising young life prevented! But, alas, no! they were all cowards, afraid to infringe the injunctions of a barbarous code of law, the poor victim was put back at his eight paces, and deliberately shot at, the ball passing through his chest, the seat of vitality. He fell, and was carried into the barn and laid on a board with his head a little elevated. The carriage presently arrived. Those accessory to the homicide placed him in the coach, and then each one consulted his own safety by flight, leaving the dying man to pour out his blood and give up his life without friend or foe to witness his death. He died before the carriage reached town. Those of our family who went early, as usual, to their work in the field found the blood-stained board in the barn, and the spot where he fell still wet. Some time after, I can remember seeing the grass stiffened with the clotted gore now dried by the sun.

A reward of ten pounds was offered for the recovery of the ball, and two of my young brothers, respectively of the ages of *twelve* and *fourteen*, searched a wide area around for the bullet a number of times without success. To say nothing of the passionate or stunning grief of his relatives, there was no right-hearted person but felt sorrow at seeing a promising young gentleman thus led as an ox to the slaughter. His violent death made a strange, vivid impression on my own childish heart and mind at the time.

The particulars of the principal's trial and acquittal; as also the failure of an attempt to criminate the seconds, after the lapse of ten or twelve years, are given by Dr. Scadding in the work above quoted. But there is reason to believe that Mr. Jarvis was never able to acquit himself at the bar of his own conscience from the "cry of his brother's blood," and that he lived and died an unhappy man.

Some months after the occurrence, when public excitement had somewhat abated, the feeling in our family was awakened anew by an occurrence in the Elmsley Field, which our brother James related at the fireside the evening after. A genteel stranger, a young man, came to him in the field and asked him if he could point him to the spot where John Ridout fell in a duel. Brother said, "I can put your hand on the spot that was wet with his blood," and led him to the place. The person seemed very much struck and moved indeed.

> "This stranger's eye wept,
> That in life's brightest bloom,
> One gifted so rarely,
> Should sink to the tomb."

Seeing him put his pocket handkerchief to his eyes, James presumed to remark, "You knew him, sir?" "Oh! yes, he was a very, very dear friend of mine indeed." Brother did not recognize his appearance as of one he had seen before, yet did not presume to ask what had been the relation between him and "the loved and lost." Whether they had been fellow students or companions-in-arms (for though young, they were old and large enough to have shared with almost all the other young gentlemen of the country in its defence during the recent war), or what other tie had bound their friendship, we never knew.

NO. XVII.

THE RISE OF AN INSTITUTION WHICH INFLUENCED MY DESTINIES FOR GOOD.

THIS was the building of a Methodist meeting-house, and the establishment of regular preaching and other services in the Town of York. There was an English Church in the town at the time of our arrival, and for long before. But it was then in a very dilapidated state. It had never been much of a structure, not large, a framed, clapboarded building, which had never had a steeple, or a coat of paint. Some low wag scrawled upon its walls—

" Doctor Strachn,
" If you'd have the good-will of the people,
" You must paint your church and build a steeple."

Report said that the building had been used as a military hospital at a time of pressure during the war. The church lot had been fenced with rails, but the soldiers and the rabble had burnt them up. As it was, it was the only place where the decencies of public worship had been statedly conducted until the event to which I am about to refer. Transient preachers, among the rest the Methodists, had given occasional sermons,—in the Parliament buildings, in hotel ballrooms, and in private houses, but no other denomination had a church of any kind, and, therefore, could not collect, much less preserve a congregation. The Episcopalians were the most regular church-goers of that day; and they were principally, though not wholly, of the aristocratic class, such as our aristocracy then were. Thus, the best bred and most pretentious people had most of the form of religion, so far as it related to public forms. You could see on a Sunday forenoon our would-be aristocrats in their gigs and elegant coaches, with liveried footmen up behind, driving to that old church, the servants, dogs, and horses awaiting in the street their more devotional masters, or owners to issue from the sacred enclosure. Some indeed walked: among these was a remarkable pair, who passed our door on almost every Sunday while we lived at the corner of George and Duchess Streets, coming down the oblique waggon track from Don Flats, looking, as a woman of my acquaintance used to say, "like a couple of old-fashioned picturs," the old gentleman with dangling cue, I think, three-corned cocked hat, sloping, single-breasted coat, long buff waistcoat, with large pockets, breeches, stockings, and shoe buckles; and the old lady dressed equally primitively, with scoop-bonnet, kerchief on her shoulders, &c., but all of the best material. This was old Colonel Playter and his wife, in the costume of the early reign of George III.

The religious notions of our family, as far as we had any at that time, strange as it may seem of a family which had been identified with the army, were of a Quaker cast. Consequently, the ritualism of the Church of England was scarcely adapted to attract us to her altars. True, the Presbyterian family into which William had married were temporarily going, off and on, to the Church; and William and Annie's first baby must needs be carried to the Church and christened; but then the parson would not perform the rite upon the child until the father was baptized, which was conformed to by him,—the first one of our household who received water baptism. But this conformity, as yet, was not attended with any vital religion.

In the summer of 1818, just before we removed from the Mercer house to a home of our own, provided for the family by Brother Tom, I came one day from the nearest store (and the only one for a long ways) and told my mother, that I had met the man who had come in from the country to put up the meeting-house, speak of raising the frame that day, and that, contrary to the usual practice of the times, there would be only cakes and beer, (instead of raw whisky) given at the raising. My father loaned them the log chains which drew up the timbers. Soon it was enclosed, and service commenced before it was finished. Next, one Sunday, after we were settled in our new home, father and mother went to the preaching, and father returned alone, for mother had "stayed to class." In that meeting she joined the Church on trial; and not long after, while a hymn was being sung, she found the peace of God for which she had sighed nine or ten weary years. After that she went every Tuesday night to class at the leader's, Mr. Patrick, and I usually accompanied her with the tin-lantern of the day, over holes and hillocks across the commons for company. As in duty bound, she received baptism; and I being the only one of the family she could control, she led me forward one night when baptism was being attended to, and asked the rite for me. As I was a sizable boy, I had to promise for myself, as well as my mother for me. The notable James Jackson performed the baptism. The Sunday-school, which I have elsewhere described, was commenced about a year before that. In the meantime, my twin-brother had died—I think without being baptized. During a severe fit of sickness, from which he was expected to die, Thomas was baptized. George and Nathaniel not for another five or six years, at the time they made a profession of religion; and poor sightless James, not till some years later still. Thus, one by one, here and there, all the members of our Quakerized, nondescript family were formally initiated into the visible Church of Christ. But the frame meeting-house became our religious home as far as we availed ourselves of it, and countless blessings, even of a material kind, resulted therefrom. In that spiritual birth-place of my mother, and as I shall have to describe in due time, I myself most assuredly passed from death unto life. In this short sketch, I have supplied a link, necessary to make the chain of events in my lowly boy-life continuous.

NO. XVIII.

HOW I CHANCED TO GET THE FIRST PRIZE.

SIXTY-THREE years ago this September (1881) there was no Sunday-school in "Muddy Little York," now the fair City of Toronto, nor had there ever been one. But there was one organized soon after—that is to say, about November, 1818. Sunday-schools were then new and rare anywhere in Canada; one had been set on foot in Brockville by the Rev. Wm. Smart, in 1811; one was organized and taught by the Rev. Thomas Burch, Methodist minister, in Montreal, during the war of 1812, and when the Wesleyan missionaries came to that city in 1815 they likewise established one. But though the Rev. Thaddeus Osgood, General Missionary, supported by some New England society, spoke of such an institution in a humble school that I attended after the war was over, it came to nothing till three years after.

In the autumn of 1818 my dear mother returned one day from a visit to Mr. Ketchum's, and told us at home that Mr. Osgood had been in town, and that Messrs. Ketchum, Patrick, Carfra, and Morrison were going to teach a school every Sunday afternoon in the new Methodist meeting-house on King street, and it was decided that we, the three youngest boys, should attend. We were hardly in presentable trim to make our appearance there, in point of clothes and shoes especially; but an extra effort was made by father and mother (the particulars of which would make a strange story by itself), and on the bleak November afternoon appointed we were there, and so early that we had the honour of kindling the fire in the sheet-iron stove out of the chips and hewings from the timber of which the frame of the newly-built house was made. At length the patrons and the intended teachers of the school arrived, and we were called to order, and the lessons began. There were few books of any kind in that early day, and not enough Bibles and Testaments. My first lesson was the fragment of a Bible, a psalm, pasted on a shingle, which I read and committed to memory.

This school was under the patronage of the "American Sunday-school Union," which had provided spelling and lesson books, bearing the device on the title-page of clasped hands in token of union. Beyond this, I do not remember that there were any appropriate books such as Sunday-schools now have; no hymn-books, for we sang out of the books for the congregation; no library books, certainly; and no reward books or prizes of any kind for a year or two.

The first attempt of this kind was the offer of one single book as a reward for the scholar who should answer a certain question, which had been asked and was under consideration for weeks. The question had been addressed to the first class of boys—or young men, almost, as some of them were—but soon the whole school had come to be interested in the matter. It was Christ's question to the learned among the Jews (to be found in Matt. xxii. 42-44; Mark xii. 35-37, and Luke xx. 22-44), *How it was that Christ, who was David's Lord, could be also his son?* The question was not answered the day it was proposed, and they were directed to take it home, and it made a great stir in many of the homes of the children; but it was not answered the next Sunday. But the managers of the school resolved that it should go to them again; and a book was to be bought for the one who answered the question. This was bought, and exhibited to whet the eagerness of the contenders; and, as it happened, the first book purchased did not satisfy the teachers, and another was bought. In the meantime, the question was agitated in the several families represented in the school for a period, at least, of two or three weeks. At length the day was set when the inquiry was to be determined, and all was eagerness and expectation, both in and out of the school.

I was not even a candidate, for I was not in the first class, but in the second, a little boy between ten and eleven, while some of the first class were nearly or quite twice my age and size; nevertheless, I had thought about the question, and with the aid of my mother had made up my mind what was the true answer.

The day and hour came, and the question went up and down the class, and no one of them could answer it. My class sat close behind, and I watched the state of matters with interest. I was always eager, but, in those days, very bashful. Fortunately, there was a little boy sitting beside me, not quite so old, but larger, who was not bashful. His father was the teacher of the big class: said I to him, "Alfred, I could tell!" He immediately spoke out, "Father, John Carroll says he can tell!" As the class was now fairly nonplussed, Mr. P—— condescendingly turned to me and said, "Well, John, how could Christ be David's Lord and God, and yet be his son?" "Because, sir, Christ was both God and man; and as a man, He was of the house and lineage of David.'" "Well done! well answered!" That was all the reward I obtained then.

The questioning went on; and those big boys were asked, "Why did the Jews refuse to believe Jesus to be the Messiah?" It went up and down the class, but none could tell. Alfred Patrick turned to me, and said in a low voice, "John, can you tell?" "I think so," said I. "Father, John Carroll says he can tell!" The teacher once more addressed me, "Well, John, why was Christ rejected by the Jews?" "Because, sir, He did not come with the pomp and splendour which they expected the Messiah to come with!" "Good again!" Now, by a sort of general consent of the authorities of the school, I was transferred to the first class, but put at its foot. In those days the practice of going up and down, according as a pupil succeeded or failed, obtained in Sunday-schools just as they do now in secular schools—so I began at the bottom. But the questioning still went on, and before the school was over I was at the head of the class. That was supposed to be reward enough for such a little fellow for one day, without the book; I had been admitted to the first class, and I was not inclined to complain.

But what was to be done with the book? A singular conclusion was come to for a Sunday-school—the institution of a lottery! It was thought and said, "They have all done their best; and though John answered the question, yet as he was not a proper candidate, he has been amply rewarded already; therefore each one shall have a new chance—they shall ballot for it. As many slips of paper were cut as there were scholars in the class—they were all left blank but one, on which the prize was marked; they were then worked between a gentleman's thumb and finger, each into a little roll, put into a hat, and shaken up together. The hat was passed along the class from the foot to the head; and each boy as it passed him was to put in his hand and take out one of the little billets The hat came to me last, and there was but one left to take—it was really no choice; but, oh, joyful day to me! when they were unrolled all the rest were blank but mine, and I had drawn the prize! The first Sunday-school prize that I ever heard of being given in the town! Was I not glad? My brothers, of course, congratulated me; but no sooner was school over, than I started for home to tell the good news to my mother, and outstripped the rest. In crossing the green in front of our house, and coming in sight of those looking from the door, I lifted up my prize and brandished it before their eyes, exclaiming, "I have got the book! I have got the book!" I need not say that my success occasioned great delight to all my friends, but especially to my tender mother, whose "baby" I now was, that my little mate had died. I was sorry he was not there to share my pride and joy.

My young readers will be inclined to say, "One book was not a great deal to make a fuss over; I have fifty books." Yes, but I had never had one of my own before, unless it were a school book. Others will say, "What sort of a book was it?" Well, it was not a book about religion, strange to say, though obtained from a Sunday-school, and it exerted a beneficial influence on me, of a certain kind, all my life. It was a pretty 18mo., printed on nice clear paper, with a pasteboard cover of a wavy-like design. The title was, "Picture of the Seasons," and the matter a description of spring, summer, autumn, and winter as seen in Old England, adorned with pictures, and illustrated with poetry mostly from Thomson's *Seasons*. I read the book over and over again to myself and to my friends, particularly to my eldest brother, James, whose sight was so impaired that he could not see to read for himself. The book, besides affording a vast amount of enjoyment, exerted a training influence upon me, which followed me through life: it made me observant of scenery and of the material works of God; it gave me a taste for descriptive poetry and the graphic in style, and probably had some influence on my own style after I began to write. A noticeable effect was to beget a desire in my breast to see the British Isles. —a desire which, after the lapse of forty years, was destined to be gratified.

The only conclusion I shall draw from the facts here recorded is, that while it is a privation not to have enough books, it is possible to have too many —so many that the attention is distracted among them. Certain it is, that a few good books, well studied, are better than a great many superficially looked over. Young people, make a thorough use of your books that are worth reading; and if you have more than you can master, give them, or give the use of them, to those who have none.

No. XIX.

HOW I INVESTED MY FOUND MONEY.

A LITTLE more than a year after acquiring the Sunday-school prize, our family was in a transition state, and we were all in some measure upon our oars. For several years we younger ones, with our dear mother, were principally dependent for support upon our dear brother Tom, yet unmarried and still uninjured by some ill connections and mistaken moves which afterwards made some impressions on him for the worse. He had made some property in the town, which he had lately exchanged for a farm in Whitchurch; and we were all delighted with the prospect of living in the country, and were packed up to move to it. I had even bought the fish-hooks by which I hoped to catch the trout in the purling stream which ran through the farm which we hoped to make our future home, when suddenly our fine team of horses was missing. They had strayed, or had been stolen. All were in search of them for weeks, during which time it was impossible to move. It turned out, in the issue, that we went not to the farm. Boy though I was, I was very sorry; for I was always very fond of a country life, and I had sense enough to see that the several dead-heads in the family would there be of more assistance to the bread-winners of the household than anywhere else. To all human appearance, in the the long run, it appeared we were great losers by remaining in the town; my brother changed all his property for a stock of goods in the saddle and harness line of business, and after a time lost it all, and had to start again in a humbler sphere, and the rest of us were scattered abroad. The only compensation was (and it was a great gain, if the same event would have failed to happen to us in the country), that, after some years, the religious opportunities we enjoyed in the town issued in the conversion of the three youngest of us boys. But that is not the matter I set out to tell about, but how I found a piece of money, and the use I made of it.

It was during our time of suspense. I had been called away from a situation where I was earning a few shillings every week, to get ready for our moving; and after our loss I went wandering about the commons in a vacant sort of way, in hopes of finding our stray horses. I was a little lame in one of my feet from some cause or other, and thought myself lamer than I really was, and was helping myself along with a long stick, and nearing home, when suddenly I saw in the road where Adelaide Street now runs, between Bay and York, something shining in the dust, and sprang forward and grasped it—it was a well-worn quarter-dollar. It was long since I had had any money I could really call my own, and it cured my lameness at once, and I threw away my stick, walking (if I did not run) with alacrity. I always reported my gains to my mother, and usually gave them up to her as a matter of course. She was the treasurer for all the boys, as she had to cater for the whole. By her wise management the "many littles" made a sum to keep the family afloat after some fashion.

But just at that time I very much desired a little money to spend as I liked. And how was it, my young readers will feel curious to know, I did want to spend it? I will tell you: As I had passed up through our straggling little town, which had but one business street, and not much of a one at that, I discovered that a new book and stationery, toy and variety store was opened on King Street, among some new houses, opposite the English Church, or where St. James' Cathedral now stands—that is, on the south side of King Street, a few doors east of Church Street; and my eyes had gloated over the books and pictures in the window so long as greatly to inflame my desire for a new book.

"But chill penury repressed the noble rage
And froze the genial current of my soul ;"

and I was going home depressed, when I saw the glittering prize in the road. I had always two reasons for wishing books to read : one was, because my eldest surviving brother, James, was then almost totally blind, and unable to read himself, albeit the contents of a book was a great solace to him in his loneliness. He was very hard of hearing as well, and one had to sit very near him to make him hear what was read; but I was so small, and he was so big, that I could sit on his knee opposite his best ear, and make him hear very well. I must just say, that the unnatural pitch I had to assume very much injured the intonation of my voice, which was one source of unpopularity after I became a public speaker. In the meantime, what gave my dear brother pleasure afforded me delight; I, therefore, always associated the pleasurable prospect of getting a new book with him.

I entered the house and said, "Mammy, if you will not take it from me, and let me spend it as I like, I will tell you of something I have found." She assured me that unless it were wrong for me to keep it, she would not take it from me. I then showed her the quarter-dollar, and as there were no houses near, as the the road was little travelled, and the money was nearly buried in the dust, it was impossible to imagine who had lost it; and that, therefore, it was the property of the finder—it was mine!

Receiving permission, I turned on my heel at once, hurried back to Mr. Leslie's, entered the shop, which I had not dared to do before, and turned over the smaller books which lay upon the counter. At length I selected a stitched book with a cover somewhat stiff, and containing, perhaps, fifty pages. There were no pictures to tempt me, but the book was fresh-looking, and contained a great deal of matter in verse, which always attracted me, and it chanced that its price was just one quarter-dollar, and I bought it and carried it away.

My new purchase contained two principal poems, accompanied with notes in prose, with two or three lesser pieces also in rhyme. The two longer ones were, first, " The Borders,"—the complaints of English people in the north of England of the " bordering Scots," who " despoiled their fields and ravaged all their farms." I know not the authorship; it might have been Sir Walter Scott. I knew nothing of him then, and for long after; but it was accompanied with notes, which gave the reader an insight into monastic and civil life in the middle ages. The whole thing was weird and interesting to me and my auditors when I read it. My mother appreciated and explained it the best of any. She had heard the " Chevy Chase " sung by an intelligent Scotchman, and tales of those olden times told around her father's kitchen fire on the banks of the St. John, New Brunswick, in the last century, by that strange medley of persons from all parts of the world, whom the glow of old Quaker Ridout's genial fire attracted to share his gratuitous but ample hostelry

After some years I lost my book; but in the course of still further years I read the "Tales of my Grandfather," "Rob Roy," and the "Chevy Chase," as well as the more general histories of those times, by which the allusions of my "Borders" became more intelligible to me.

The other longer poem was the now well-known production of the Moravian poet, Montgomery, entitled the "Wanderer of Switzerland," one of his many pieces written in the interests of freedom and fair dealing. The story was very touching, and we all mingled our tears with the old wanderer. I read this and the other tale over and over; and the perusal, besides affording me a great deal of pleasure, begat within me a sentiment, which has been deepening ever since, of hatred to all oppression and unfairness, whether civil or ecclesiastical—whether from crowned heads, aristocratic oligarchies, or democratic majorities and mobs. May they all perish forever?

No. XX.

A TRAMP TO THE BUSH IN SUGAR TIME, WITH YOUNG LADIES.

WHEN we came to York there were two families, pretty much on a par with ourselves, intimate with each other, with both of which we became connected—the one directly, the other only remotely—two members from each of which come into my unpretending story. The one of these families was of Highland Scotch origin, the other I do not know from where—perhaps England. The first were the McIntoshes, the second the Hamiltons. There were four daughters in the first family and one in the other, and several sons in both. My second brother, William, had married the eldest daughter, Annie, in the McIntosh family, and my brother Thomas was destined to marry the second daughter, Jane. There were two other daughters, twins, Isabella and Eliza, at the time of my story seventeen or eighteen years of age, very comely in appearance. Bella was tall, straight, and graceful, if not majestic in figure, with a full face and rosy complexion. Eliza was darker in complexion but smaller in person, and lithe and graceful in her movements, with small and lady-like hands and features, vivacious in manner and conversation, frank and very amiable. Caroline Hamilton, who was destined to marry their handsome brother Charlie, was the almost inseparable companion of the twins, Bell, and Eliza. Miss H. was tall and graceful, but not so beautiful in face and features as her more favoured companions. Her brother Wilson, or "Wilse," a tall, handsome, vivacious fellow, was Bell's acknowledged admirer at that time. Eliza's intimacy with the handsome young American, Charles Thompson, destined to be her future husband, was not as yet, I think, very pronounced—it was two years afterwards, I know.

About the year 1819, my brother William, the husband of Annie McIntosh, had settled with his wife and two children on the lot drawn for his military services, consisting of two hundred acres in the edge of the "New Survey" of the Township of Toronto—say, as the road went, fifteen or sixteen miles from the town. The time to which I refer was the early spring, or breaking up of winter, 1821, when I was between eleven and twelve years of age.

It seems the younger girls in the two families had projected a visit to William and Annie during the sugar-making time that spring; and, from what afterwards happened, I suspect they had engaged, or expected, Wilson Hamilton to be their escort. But when the time came he was too busy in the shop to leave, or at least to spend all the time they expected to be away. But ladies, especially young ladies, do not easily relinquish any project they get in their heads. Defeated in one resource, they resorted to another: they tramped on (for they were on foot) up to the west end of the town, where my mother resided, in hopes of getting one of our boys to accompany them. But Thomas had started business, George was in his situation, and 'Thaniel was away on a journey in almost the direction they were going, but further. They must have some masculine escort, and young and small as I was, they asked for me and I was away on an errand; but just as they come to the door, hesitating whether to go on or turn back, I made my appearance, and mother joined her request with theirs, that I should go with them.

I liked sugar—and where is the boy that does not? —and once I had, when thirsty, taken a good drink of sap, and the remembrance of the sylvan nectar had lingered in my memory, and almost the taste of it in my mouth, during the three or four intervening years. Besides, I longed to see my brother's residence in the bush; but there was a drawback—I had never felt the refining influence of a sister's presence and love, and I hardly knew how to behave in the company of girls; besides, my brothers had a silly trick of teasing me about little girls, until I was afraid to be seen speaking to one. I was almost afraid and ashamed to consent to go; but being urged, did consent, got ready in a trice, and went; and the young ladies expressed their delight again and again. It was pretty late in the day when we started to tramp the intervening fifteen or sixteen miles along the rough and still largely unsettled road.

We passed up the Dundas road (Queen Street), turning south at where the Lunatic Asylum now is, till we came near where the Dundas Street Methodist Church stands; then west, including one jog on the road, till we reached the Humber, where Lambton now flourishes; on up the hill and across the Mimico, where Islington now displays its beauties; and on up Dundas Street till we reached the place of turning back into the new settlements, of which more after a little.

Shall I tell you what the road, or country, was like those fifty-nine years ago? On the north side of Queen Street there were nothing but farms and farmhouses until the turn west, north of the Asylum, was reached. After that it was all dark pine woods for three or four miles, excepting some squatter or woodchopper's shanty, till you came out where an industrious German, by the name of Friday, had taken up a location, and joined a little farming with charcoal-burning and tar-making. Then, there were no houses along the plains among the scrub oaks until we reached the Humber, with its saw-mills (the first or second I had seen) and tavern there. Then no more houses till we reached the Mimico. After that, a very few rough log houses, with a great deal of woods between, till we came to where we must needs turn north. There, fortunately, the school was just breaking up for the day, and, upon inquiry, we found there was a young man, who lived only a mile and a half from my brother's, just returning after his day's studies. Ebenezer Austin was fairly educated, intelligent, and rather polite; besides, the sight of the young ladies put him on his best behaviour at once. We had something like a road until we reached his father's, at which time it became quite dark, and we had to go the rest of the way across fields and through the woods; but young Austin was only too glad, with lighted hickory bark torch, to be the guide and cicerone (explaining the history and mystery of all we saw) to the fair town girls. At length the light from the roaring log fire on William's hearth, well on in the evening, was a welcome sight to us all; for we were very tired and very hungry. We would not accept the proffered hospitality of the Austin family, noted for their kindness; and I, with my boyish bashfulness, even refused to go into the house. But I made myself welcome where I was known. We did ample justice to the abundant farmer's fare served up by the acknowledged taste of my sister-in-law, of well-known housekeeping capabilities. I soon became sleepy, and mounted by a ladder to my bed in the loft, made on the floor near the chimney, where the constant fire below heated the boards. I stretched my weary legs, feeling the cat-tail couch a luxury, and soon fell asleep, and, boy-like, slept till late the following morning.

Looking around in the morning sunshine, I observed that four adjacent clearings (two on each side of the well-cleared road) made a fair opening in what was forest all beyond, for the wilderness bounded our horizon—everywhere a wilderness of large trees, crowded with "underbrush" beneath. All within the encircling forest was rudely made, but new—fences, barns, and houses. One of the condiments that made our breakfast still more appetizing was furnished from the sugar-bush; namely, pure, new maple molasses, than which nothing can be more delectable.

The breakfast, moreover, was swallowed with eagerness, for we were "all agog" to be off to the sugar-bush. It was simply the nearest forest land to the north end of the clearing, for the sugar maple was a prevailing kind of tree in that hardwood forest, and large ones they were. The trees were tapped for a large area around—that is, a notch was cut with a sharp axe on the south side of each tree, at an angle from the perpendicular of about forty-five degrees, and at the lower end of the notch a "spile" or spout of basswood was introduced into an incision made with an iron instrument. The sap was caught in basswood or ash troughs, made on the ground—it was before the day of cooper-made pails. Once a day, at least, the troughs had to be emptied, for when the sap ran freely the troughs were filled within twenty-four hours.

Sometimes we emptied the sap-troughs both morning and evening, just as you would milk a cow; and when there had been rain, or a fall of snow and a thaw, why then the water thus caught had to be thrown out, that it might not dilute the sap.

The boiling place was in the centre of the sugar-bush. Everything was rude and extempore in those early days; no arches or fixtures for the boilers, and no store puncheons. There was a capacious "store-trough" made out of a large tree. The great pots or "sugar-kettles" were strung on a strong pole resting on crotches at either end of the fire; then two large logs of suitable length were rolled up from either side under the pots, which, with kindlings, chips, and smaller wood, both round and split, of which there was plenty close at hand, set on fire, soon put the whole in a roaring blaze. The largest pots were filled with the new sap, which was emptied into lesser ones as it was boiled down to greater strength, called "syrup," the strongest pot of which was kept simmering away more gradually until it became molasses; and the molasses was boiled over a still slower fire; for the nearer to sugar it became, the more likely it was to boil over, or to burn. The pots, during the whole process, had to be skimmed often to get rid of the impurities which came to the surface in the form of scum. An egg, or a little piece of fat pork, served as a clarifier, by making the sediment more observable in the scum. I was never lazy, but rather officious in assisting at whatever was going on. I tendered my services to aid in the business, and soon learned to "gather sap," to "tend the pots," to feed the fires, and even to cut down and split up a sizable tree for fuel. Of course we all drank a great deal of sap, syrup, and molasses, and ate a great deal of hot sugar, which is very fine. "Sugaring off" was a very nice process, as it required an experienced manager and a very slow fire; and for that purpose it was generally done in the house. Some of the richest molasses was taken in pails, put over some coals in a pot, and slowly simmered away till it became gritty when cool; it was then nearly ready to pour out into the moulds, which were usually such pots and pans as came to hand. William made a square box, which could be taken apart when the sugar became hard, which made a very pretty mould. The final test that the hot sugar was ready to pour out was to take out a little to cool on a lump of snow, which, when it became cool, if it cracked like a piece of glass when struck with the finger nail, it was ready to pour out. If the desire was to make flour sugar, instead of cake sugar, they kept stirring the pot till it was thoroughly cool, or poured it out into a receptacle, and stirred it, and it became loose and nearly like brown sugar bought in the stores; and I believe, if left a little more moist, and poured out into a keg or some other vessel whose bottom was open enough to allow all molasses or soft sugar to run away, it would crystalize and become a sort of granulated sugar, hard and clear—very nice, indeed.

One day William made his visitors some taffy, which they ate with great delight. He boiled a small pot of syrup or molasses down till it was in a state of consistence to "sugar off," when he poured it out upon a wider surface of clean snow; and then, so soon as it was cool enough to be handled, oiling his hands with some clean fat, he manipulating it very much as a shoe or harness-maker manipulates his wax, pulling it out, folding it together, and pulling it out again. By this means the gritty feeling passed away, and it became stringy, and possessed the taste and all the attributes of taffy. The young ladies were hugely delighted with it.

And the young ladies themselves became a delight as soon as it was bruited abroad in the settlement (and it is astonishing how such matters travel where there is little else to talk about); sundry bachelors (one particularly), dressed in their holiday clothes, contrived certain errands to William's log-house. Alas, poor fellows, I think they wore out shoe leather in vain! In a day or two after our arrival, who should burst in upon us at the "sugar camp" but Wilson Hamilton! After that my functions as an escort passed into his hands, and I did not remain even "second in command."

After the best part of a week spent in the woods, we bent our steps homeward, five in number instead of four, as we came. While walking onward by myself in a piece of woods, I was accosted by a grave but kindly interlocutor, or questioner. He was a sizable gentleman, well-mounted on a good horse, with the usual paraphernalia of equestrians in those days, clad in a broad-leaved grey hat, and drab overcoat, and of measured speech, but not Quaker dialect; whence I judged he was not a " Friend," but one of the Methodist preachers who were our almost only evangelists and civilizers in those times. Seeing me, a small boy, all alone in the woods, he seemed solicitous for my safety, and wished to know whence I came, and whither I was going. My very ready and frank answers appeared to assure him that I might be entrusted to work out my own objects; he bade me good-bye in kindly tones and a very pleasant voice, and spurred on his steed at a faster pace than I could keep up with. Mrs. Charles Wesley said that " the piety of the early Methodist preachers was an excellent substitute for a polite education." The stranger gentleman's inquiries left a tranquilizing influence on my boyish heart. Inquiries into the whereabouts of the few itinerants in the Province, made since then, have rendered it probable to me that I must have been accosted by Isaac Bateman Smith, as by "an angel unawares." Peace to the memory of those men of God! I reached home in safety, and my sugar-making adventure furnished food for conversation for many days after—as the cake of sugar in my pocket-handkerchief sweetened my porridge.

No. XXI.

"OLD GRAY," THE MILL HORSE.

IF I have not already told my readers, I tell them now, that I spent *three* or *four* years (perhaps I ought to say *five*, in all, including two or three several intervals) in a tannery, from the age of twelve to seventeen, and that for two of those years I was considered as a regular apprentice to the tanner's and currier's trade. Some will think I ought to be ashamed to make the confession. I would be ashamed if I thought there was anything sinful or mean in a business which is so important to civilized countries. My "Boss," or master, raised himself by following this business from the low estate of a poor boy to be one of the very richest, most respected, and most useful men of the town during the course of a long life.

In every trade, "the youngest apprentice" has usually, for some time, to do many things not properly of the trade, but preparatory to it. In our establishment this bottom rung of the ladder was grinding the bark. In many large establishments at the present day, along with other advanced conveniences, the bark is ground by water or steam-power; in our earlier and ruder times it was ground in an iron mill, by horse-power. John Jones, already mentioned, when I first knew the establishment, was the bark-grinder, but when John was promoted to the "beam-shed," the "flesher," and the currying knife, others were employed to do this work. Two other boys intervened between him and me. At length I was called to mount the mill "brow," for the bark was pounded and put in the hopper above stairs, and fell into a place for its reception below, whence it was carried away out as wanted to the tan-vats. I ground the bark both before and after I became a regular "hand" in the tannery.

I might here say I have pleasant recollections of that dusty loft, both before I was converted and afterwards; for, by pounding up bark for the hopper in advance, I found a good deal of time for reading. Before conversion, Richardson's Pamela and Clarissa, with similiar works, were read there; and after my conversion the precious Bible, the Methodist Hymn-book, Bunyan's Pilgrim's Progress, Doddridge's Rise and Progress, the Lives of the Early Methodist Preachers, with many, many other good books, were read and pondered in that loft.

But at the beginning of this section I had no idea of writing anything very grave or serious, but to give some pleasant reminiscences of an old horse, which served his generation better than some boys and girls, for the innocent entertainment of my young friends. The sort of horse required for the mill must be a quiet and steady one, and regular in his gait. Now, these qualities are seldom found in a young horse; for young horses, like young people, are apt to be flighty and frisky. Hence the bark-grinding generally fell to the lot of an old horse. The horse that did this work was required to be kept without shoes, else the iron would cut up the floor of the mill-loft too much. If horses had pride and ambition like sinful men, old and young, the mill-horse would have felt very much like an old mechanic when his deficient sight and unsteady hand seem to rule him out as unfit for the nicer work (or a full day's work at least), and he is set to mending and patching, or to do odd jobs of this or that; or rather felt like an old preacher when, perhaps, only because he is old (that is to say, has spent so very many years in study, and has such a long and ripe experience), is ruled out of the popular pulpits he used once to fill, if not out of the pulpit altogether; or off the platform where once he used to be welcomed with applause, and assigned humbler work to do.

Now, to my certain knowledge, Old Gray had had his day of flash and popularity with young folks, for he once belonged to my own brother. He was not a very large, but a very well-formed horse, of an iron-grey colour. Moreover, he had been very free and spirited, and very showy in harness. I can remember when he and his mate were considered a dashing team. He then rejoiced in the buxom name of "Larry;" but, alas! years had passed over him, and he had become white; his ribs, once covered with flesh, began to show like an old man's wrinkles; instead of being round as in his prime, he had become " slabsided;" besides being old, he had been too willing, and the " free horse" had been overtaxed, just as it often is with a willing labourer in the Church, or in the ministry. He had descended in the estimation of his owners and the character of his work, till at last my kind-hearted old master bought him to grind his bark, and knocked off his shoes. He had plenty of grass in summer and hay in winter, but very few oats. The plea was that his teeth were not good enough to chew them; just as some very pleasant things are denied to old people on the supposition that they "no longer care about such matters." But I must in justice say, that though Old Gray did not get many oats, he got many a feed of bran or potatoes.

Upon the mention of potatoes hangs a tale. He generally had his noon baiting in a vacant, or pasture lot (would you believe that it was ever vacant?) at the north-east corner of Yonge and Adelaide streets, not far from the bark-mill. There was not always a halter lavished on Old Gray, but I pulled him along by his very long mane, or "foretop." His great age had given him experience. He knew what my movements meant as well as I did myself. When the twelve o'clock cannon fired, he knew it was time to be unharnessed, and whinnied vociferously. The boys used to say that he called out "Jo-oh-hon!" Yet he did not often show the same alacrity when I went after him to fetch him to his day's or half-day's toil. I think he showed the most reluctance at noon-time, when he had not had long enough time to fill his stomach. In the larger field, when I had caught him, I generally utilized his back to save the labour of walking, albeit the height of his backbone made it a little like riding on a rail; but sometimes, after, by dint of kicking my heels into his sides and slapping him first on one side of the head and then on the other, to guide him in the absence of bridle or halter, I had got him to the gate, and was occupied in trying to unlatch it with my toe, he would suddenly start off, and gallop to the far end of the field, when, putting his nose to the ground, which I had no power of holding up, he would kick up his heels and slide me down his neck, upon which I had to recommence my task of bringing him to the gate. But at the time I was going to speak of, he was in the nearer and smaller pasture-field already described, but at the farther side; and as I approached to catch him, having nowhere else to run, he galloped to the gate. My good-natured, kind-hearted old "boss" witnessed the performance, and interpreted it very differently from what I did, and broke out in his usual quaint words and nasal drone to commend and order the reward of the old horse: he exclaimed, "Gray, you fine old fellow. Run to your work, eh? John, go and get a basket of potatoes and give him a good feed!" So my return to work was delayed until Old Gray had munched about a peck of potatoes.

I do not remember the facts of his death. I think it occurred during a year's absence of mine from the establishment. Unlike the fate of some human beings, I never heard a word spoken against Old Gray (but, on the contrary, a great deal of kindness expressed), after his death. Peace to his memory! I, at least, have done what I could to give him posthumous fame.

No. XXII.

GOING ON A BUSH FARM.

IN several of my sketches I have made references to a crisis in our humble family history by which our joint residence was broken up for a number of years, and the several members of the household were scattered in various directions. Thomas, the patron of the rest, was married and had gone to live by himself, taking his mother along. A temporary residence was found for poor James, though finally he followed me to the country. 'Thaniel was at a trade. An opening in a business he understood offered itself to brother George, lying partly in the township of Toronto, and partly in Trafalgar. And, as I had always showed a preference for country life, it was decided that I should join my brother William on the bush farm whither I have already conducted my young readers on a sugar expedition. This breaking-up occurred in the month of March, or April, 1822, when I was between twelve and thirteen years of age.

George's route and mine lay pretty much in the same direction, and it was decided we should travel together to the end of my journey at our brother William's. We were very disproportionate in size; he being a stout fellow of nineteen or twenty, and I being of the tender age already given, and small even at that; but each had his wardrobe packed in a bundle upon his back. We started, after an early lunch, on a raw short day, to trudge fourteen miles, less or more, on foot. At Wilcox's tavern, on the farther side of the Mimico, we took a short rest; and my brother regaled himself and me (such, alas! was the custom of the times, no one seeing the danger), each with a glass of whisky. It was a mercy that converting grace, a little more than two years after, abruptly and completely put a stop to an indulgence which would have been very likely to have proved my total ruin.

From the Mimico (for the first time to me) we took the "Back Road," which was some miles shorter than the one by the Dundas Street and the turn at Custed's. About night-fall we reached our brother's log-house and enjoyed his blazing fire of burning logs. His wife, for that season, was boiling all the sugar they made over the domestic fire, and the new sugar and molasses added to the social pleasures around that homely hearth. The next day my fellow-traveller started for the embryo village now called Streetsville; and after a few days returned with the news that arrangements were made for his steady employment in that region for several months to follow.

It will devolve on me now to tell how I was employed, and some of the things which befell me during the year and a quarter, or so, of my residence there. The sugar-bush; learning to chop, reap, rake, bind, and pitch grain; going to mill on horseback, hunting the cattle, getting lost, &c., &c., will probably be some of the subjects on which I will dwell for the entertainment of my readers.

First, the sugar seasons. I passed through two of those during the time I remained. At the period of my arrival it was pretty well over for that year; and I have said the boiling was attended to in the house. The sugar-bush was some distance, and the sap had to be gathered and poured into barrels on an ox-sled, which was then slowly drawn to the house. The work of gathering the sap henceforth was mine; and, the next year, boiling it down over the camp-fire in the woods, to which was added the work of chopping and fetching the fuel to keep up the fire under the sugar-kettles. The early spring is subject to storms, and often our sap-troughs were filled with rain or soft snow, which, so soon as the downfall was ended, had to be thrown out, that the sweet discharge from the trees might be obtained undiluted. Once, about nightfall, after a heavy shower of wet snow, I was sent to empty the sap-troughs at the roots of the trees which had been "tapped." I might here say, that heavy frost would arrest the discharge, and if that continued so long as to dry up the incisions or cuts in the trees, they had to be "tapped" over again. Warmth and sunshine were always favourable to the sap's "running." But to return to my errand. I had heard of owls, and their hideous noises, but learned that they were harmless; nevertheless, when I had got well into the bush, I heard all around me such doleful noises as *ooh-ooh*, *hoo-hoo*, and *coo-o-o*. I could not persuade myself but I was threatened by a pack of wolves, and I broke and ran for dear life to the house, for which I was chidden and ridiculed by my brother. My cowardice occasioned them inconvenience.

After one of those heavy falls of wet snow the first spring, just as we had finished our breakfast, an old Highland Scotch settler, living three or four miles from us, burst into our house with his two stout lads, John and "Jamis," as they called him, each with his axe in hand, and began to lay before my brother the danger of his forfeiting his lot and "betterments," if the "settlement duties" on the rear end, the fifth concession, were not completed within a fortnight. Besides the clearing and fencing of five acres, the road upon both ends of a two hundred acre lot had to be cleared out to the depth of two rods. Mr. Wallace was a distant relative of the Highland Scotch family into which two of my brothers had married; and when the decision of the Government relative to the completion of the settlement duties was bruited about, Mr. Wallace's ties of clanship would not suffer him to rest till "Wulliam" was extricated from his peril. Two other kind-hearted neighbours came to our assistance; and by the end of the second day the work was so far done (save two ungainly trees, which stood on the precipitous bank of the "Tobico," which crossed the road, and which they agreed to "report impossible") that two neighbours could testify to it on oath. This was the first time I crossed our forest farm to the "other line;" and when accomplished, I thought myself quite a travelled person.

The two Wallace boys and Mr. Rutledge's son Thomas were my first acquaintances, among whom the town boy was quite a lion. I am led to fear that my conversation did them no good. Alas! alas! for the days spent in sin and folly. All praise to the grace of God—within a few years my friend Thomas and myself were, I believe, truly converted, and entered on a religious life.

No. XXIII.

DRIVING AN OX TEAM.

I WAS in the midst of an account of a year spent on a bush farm, and I had only given the first section of that story. Sugar-making was the first thing that I learned; the next thing I shall mention is driving oxen.

I knew that my brother William had gone on his farm with a noble pair, or "yoke," as they were called, of tall fine oxen. But I also knew, that a year or two after one of them met with an accident, and that the other was sold. Just before that time I knew that Thomas, in the way of trade, had become possessed of a team of younger and smaller ones; and Bill coming to town, somewhat down in the mouth about the breaking up of his team, Tom, with his usual impulsive generosity, gave him his steers—or rather one of them only was a steer—the other was what farmers know as a "stag." It was these, about a year after, that had the fate of receiving a boy teamster, in my own person.

As I became greatly attached to them, I will describe their looks and other things about them. They were about four years old, more or less, when I began to drive them. Like many domestic animals, they had received the names of distinguished personages. Not wholly forgetful of the old war memories, one was called "THE DUKE OF WELLINGTON," and the other "PRINCE BLUCHER;" but for short, they were usually known and distinguished as "Duke," and "Prince." "Duke" was of a lively red colour, but his face was as white as the drifted snow and I think also his feet, and the "native white and red" contrasted beautifully with each other. He had a large, kindly eye, and a good temper; and, therefore, I confess, he was the favourite. When he put out his nose for a "nubbin" of corn, if I had it to give, you may be sure he never went without it. "Prince" was not bad tempered, but he was less demonstrative than "Duke," and looked somewhat sullen. His colour was a dusky brown, or dun. His horns were the thick, straight ones of a bullock, and would have been sharp-pointed, had not their tips been taken off by a saw. Only for their being blunted, no doubt one of them, on one occasion, would have put out my right eye. I was sent to the barn one day in great haste for a couple of sheaves of oats, I think to feed some visitors' team; and just as I was clambering over the logs which fenced off the "bay," where the fodder was kept, with the oats under my arm, "Prince" thought it would be a fine chance to get a mouthful of provender, and seized hold of the heads with his mouth; I held on, and he gave a pull, when down I came, oats and all; and the blunt end of one horn struck the bone which defends the right eye; and if the horn had been sharp-pointed, it would not only have pierced the skin, but would, most likely, have slipped into the eye itself. But a kind Providence spared it to me. I was bruised, but not cut; I scrambled up, fought off the cattle, and ran for the house. "Prince" looked to be the stronger ox of the two, but "Duke" was the quicker, and on the whole they were very well matched, and performed a great deal of work in "snaking" logs, drawing loads on the sled, in summer as well as winter—waggon, as yet, we had none—and harrowing the land; for as yet we had no regular plough, and the land because of the yet undecayed roots, was unploughable.

I thought I had performed a great exploit when first I found I could yoke them up. As there are many town boys, and even boys on old farms where all the work is done with horses, who may not know how it is done, I will tell them. Well, then, I used to take the yoke under my left arm, which was about as much as I could do; first pull out the bow-pin, carrying it my teeth, and then work out the right end bow, and, carrying it in·my right hand, walk up to the "off" ox, which was "Prince," and lay that end of the yoke on his submissive neck. The bow was then thrust up through the holes prepared to receive its ends, which was a pretty tough job, for I had to keep the other end of the yoke, bow and all, up to a horizontal level with the end of the yoke on the ox's neck. But when the bow-pin was inserted in the end of the bow where there was a mortice to receive it, it held its place as a sort of key. It was then only the work of a minute to pull out what was called the "near bow," and beckon to the other ox, bow in hand, to come near accompanied with the words, "Come under, Duke!" The docile creature would lower his head, and come forward at once, and put his obedient neck under the yoke, and was then fastened in with the bow and bow-pin, as the other. Next, with a wave of the hand to direct them, they would obey the word of command to "go," "haw," "gee," or "whoa," as I wished. All may not know that "haw," in ox language, is to come near—come this way; "gee," is to go to the right, or go from you; and "whoa," is to stop.

The most of growing boys like any kind of teaming, and I was fond of driving the oxen; they were company for me, on which account I got attached to them, and it was not very hard work. The hardest work I had to do was harrowing, because the fields were full of stumps, around which I had to turn up the harrow. This implement was made of strong, heavy wood, in the form of the letter A; this was well framed together, penetrated with heavy iron spikes, each weighing a pound at least, if not two. The clevis by which the harrow was drawn was fastened to the apex, or small end, of the triangle; to this a chain was attached, and the oxen drew it over the ground, by which the soil was torn to pieces; but as it met with many obstructions, mostly undecayed roots in the ground, it twitched and jumped about, which tried my quick temper, I am ashamed to say, very much. But my principal difficulty was in going around the stumps of trees. The stump often stood right in the line of my straight course across the field. It was very desirable to get as near the stump as possible, because the grass and weeds were likely to fasten themselves among the roots, therefore, I was forced to "haw," or "gee" the team around it. When once around it I must bring them into their former course as quickly as I could. To keep as near the stump as possible, and to have the harrow directly behind them when they got around, I had to lift the harrow on its edge, so that the "teeth" would not fasten among the roots, and to hold it there till it had passed the stump, when, as quickly as possible, I had to throw it "teeth" downwards again, so as to get hold of the first soil beyond it. This required all my strength—for the harrow was very heavy—and all my patience too; because often the poor, unknowing brutes would jerk it rudely out of my hands, defeating my purpose, and giving my slender arms and back a great shock besides. I was then without grace, and often lost my temper and beat the poor oxen, much as I thought I liked them, unmercifully using words the while that I have long since deeply repented of. I have heard of a wicked man who "did not believe that any but a real Christian could plough among stumps without swearing;" there was a neighbour who made pretty bold professions of religion, whom he regarded as "a hypocrite," because he thought he "did not feel all he professed to;" one day he saw that neighbour in the back part of a very stumpy field ploughing; he also heard his voice, as he thought, in anger and swearing, and he waited to have the pleasure of hearing the shouting class-leader swear; but as the ploughman drew near, and the plough was flying from side to side, he heard the good man sing the chorus:

"Oh! the way is so delightful in the service of the Lord;
"The way is so delightful, Hallelujah!"

Said the eavesdropper, "Limburner is a Christian for no man could plough in that stumpy field without swearing, unless he was a Christian." If he had listened to me in those days, I am afraid he could not have made any such report.

Driving the oxen before a sled I liked well enough, though once I fell into some trouble which put me about a little. My brother sent me about six or seven miles on a dark, short autumn day, to get a load of live hogs, which he had purchased from a man who was selling off his stock, as he wanted to fatten them for his winter's use and to sell. He had a good crop of corn to feed them with. With the carelessness of a boy, I went off without my jacket, that is, just with my shirt and trousers on. We had no sled with a box, and I was expected to borrow one by the way, which, the sequel will show, made my trouble worse. The neighbour, dear Summerfeldt, let his name go down to posterity, was obliging and the sled was borrowed, the outward-bound journey accomplished; the pigs caught, and their feet tied together, and loaded on the sled, and our faces (mine and the oxen) turned towards home. About the middle of the afternoon it began to rain, and about a mile and a half from home it became dark, and that was not the worst of it; more than half the way there was bush, and the sled road was full of mud-holes, which the oxen would always shun if they could; in trying to do this with one of the worst, the team shied off to one side and the "nose" of one runner passed to the wrong side of a sapling, while the oxen dashed on, pulling the sled apart and letting the pigs on to the ground. There was no way of fixing up, and nothing for it but to unhitch the team, leaving my load just there, and drive them home, to which, as being hungry and missing the lumber of the load, they had been trailing over bare ground, they dashed off in double-quick time. It was humiliating to report a disaster in connection with my first piece of distant teaming, of which I was ambitious and very proud. My brother chided me for what he called my "carelessness," especially as we had to exclaim, "Alas! it was borrowed!" A night journey to untie the pigs and drive them home was no light matter, for pigs are notoriously hard to drive. The next day my brother went that far with me and mended the sleigh, and I drove it back to its owner. The sorrows and toils of that first day increased my relish for the big wood fire, quickened my appetite for supper, (when has not a growing boy an appetite?) and gave a relish to weary bones for my humble bed. And "kind nature's sweet restorer, balmy sleep," did that night, in contradiction to Dr. Young, "light on lids" which had been "sullied with the tears" of a hard-working boy, with no mother near to sympathize.

No. XXIV

MORE BOY'S WORK ON A BUSH FARM

I HAVE told how I went to live with my elder brother, married and settled in the "Bush,"—how I learned to drive oxen—my having to go to mill on horseback, &c. I must particularize two or three other kinds of boy's work on a bush farm.

1st. *There was my learning to chop, and my efforts therein.* I admired chopping very much, and aspired earnestly to possess the skill and do the work of an axe-man. Chopping is indeed delightful work; it is clean; the smell of the newly-cut timber is most agreeable; you are constantly seeing the result of your operations, and the progress you are making, and there is a feeling of triumph when you have "knocked down" a tree two or three times the thickness of yourself and fifty or a hundred feet high. It is good work also, if not over-done, to develop the chest and the muscles of the arms—there is a great sleight in the right swing of the axe, and the exercise is very pleasurable. But then an axe is seldom found light enough for a growing boy, and too heavy an implement is very wearying, and very often the handle is too long, with the danger of giving yourself a poke in the stomach.

However, I was pretty well provided for. William was a very adroit and skillful axe-man, wielding a seven-pound axe. One originally smaller, and that had the "bit," as they called it, pretty much worn and ground off, had been "jumped," that is, furnished anew with a steel edge, and provided with a handle half a foot shorter than one for a man (William made his own axe-handles, and the shaping and smoothing of them was a nice little job for a long winter evening before the big open fire, which often furnished the only light for the operation) and I was very proud of it myself. It was with somthing of the pride of manhood that, after my breakfast of a morning, I whetted my axe, tied my trowsers with a tow-string around my legs to keep out the snow, and tramped through the deep drifts to the "chopping" on the margin of the cleared land. The "underbrushing," (cutting down the underwood and throwing it into piles, as also cutting the fallen timber into lengths for drawing) was usually done before the snow was so deep; being light and easier done by one of inferior strength, it usually fell to me. When a forest is underbrushed it looks open and park-like, and the large trees are easily attacked. There is great skill required to fell a tree safely. First, you must see that there is no tree in the way to obstruct the one you wish to cut down in its fall. If there is, that one must be chopped down first. As to felling a tree, the skilled chopper first looks at the "lean of it," and unless he has some special reason for throwing it another way, that is the way he will cause it to fall.

The most usual lean is to the south, or south-west, the result of the prevailing north-east winds; and the north side may be known generally, even in the absence of the sun being visible, by the moss which the dampness causes to grow on that side. The first notch is made on the leaning side, on the side towards which it is desired the tree should fall. It is cut three or four feet from the ground, according to the height of the chopper. It is cut usually half way through the tree, the upper part of the notch slopes the most, the lower side, or bottom, is straighter across, or horizontal. Then the woodsman passes to the other side, and cuts a similar notch, only it is made a couple of inches higher up, which greatly contributes to throw the tree the opposite way; and it might be very disastrous if he did not. If the tree is very straight the notch will have to be deeper, for in that case, it will balance on a very narrow pedestal, but if there is the smallest lean in the world, you will not have to cut the second notch much more than half as deep as the first, before the tree will begin to nod and quiver at the top, which is the first indication of its coming down, when the chopper begins to think of consulting his safety, by getting out of the way. The final warning is a crack, after the last few sharp, quick blows of the axe.

The true way to escape the falling tree is to run to the right or left of them, not certainly opposite either notch, not even to the last made one ; for if the tree should "lodge" against other trees, it will be liable to slide back over the stump, and crush the chopper, as I have heard it to have sometimes happened. The only danger is, (if you go far enough to the right or left) when the tree falls " across the butt," as it is called, which it might do if the notch was clumsily made, that is, cut in more on the one side than the other. But the most of bushmen know how to plan the whole operation and to calculate their chances so well, they are in no fear, and it usually turns out as they calculated. There was a tall Scotchman, named Tom Bell, in those new settlements, who had so good an eye and was so experienced and so cool, that, on a bet of a quart of whisky, which, alas, was then too much drank, would walk (not run) out under the falling tree, and so calculate it, that he would allow the branches of the tree top just to switch him on the heels as it reached the ground.

The fall of one of these monarchs of the forest makes sublime resounding, which is pleasant to hear at a distance. This operation of felling trees I learned to achieve (although not the biggest ones) while on that bush farm, and the operation greatly delighted me.

Planting potatoes was another part of my work; and, if I remember rightly, that was all we had to do with them, in the new black vegetable mould in which they grew, until they were dug—the hills being built as large when they were planted as they ever were, and in the new soil, there were no weeds. But then the labour of planting was very hard, the ground being full of the yet undecayed roots of trees and bushes which, after a slight harrowing, if it got that, had to be cut up and drawn to the potatoes with a hoe, purposely heavy and made of a material that would hold a sharp edge. I remember a very hard day's work in planting a patch for myself in an old stack-yard which my brother had given me to cultivate, at the foot of two large maple trees, necessarily full of roots, on a very hot day. It was a holiday, and my brother and his wife were absent; but cheered by the hope of raising a little crop, the sale of which was to procure me some pocket money, I worked away till I had completed the job, which left my hands, hardened as they were, blistered, and my slender arms so sore that they ached for days; but, alas! I never sold my crop, and, therefore, never realized the money.

I learned to reap in harvest-time,—there were no horse-reapers in those days, or smooth fields in which to use them, and nearly all the harvesting was done with a sickle. I became possessed of one, the sole inheritance from my father, and I learned to use it, of which I was very proud.

Pulling and "topping" turnips was another of my attainments and occupations in the autumn. The turnips were a sweet, luscious kind, and I regaled myself while I worked. We had no apples and these were a fair substitute for them.

The turnip harvest and potatoe-digging extended into the beginning of the cold weather, with rain and frost, and was sufficiently dreary, groping with the hands, as we did, in the cold, wet earth.

The threshing was done with a flail, and took up a good part of the winter, as it was all done by my blind brother, who taught me the art, and myself. Standing on the barn floor was very cold for the feet, and the log barn was very open besides. All my toes were more or less frozen that winter of 1822-23.

I will leave the failure of some boyish hopes for another section—such as the fowling-piece I failed in getting—my calf that died—my pet squirrel that was killed—and the pig I left and never claimed.

No. XXV.

"OLD KATE," THE MARE, AND I.

I USED to hear a Scotch song sung when I was a boy, a period when there were more songs sung than hymns, entitled "Courting the Old Gray Mare." My brother William married a bonnie Scotch wife, and in the long run got a mare as part of her dowry, but I don't think there was any courting done for the mare, and she was not a "gray," either, but a chestnut. My first ride was on her bare back on a distant errand of some miles. The next morning I was very stiff and sore, and could hardly walk, of which I complained, and was told to "supple myself by working," a prescription which answered the end in a few hours. Such was the *regime* that boys were under in my day.

One of my most painful experiences in connection with Old Kate was this: My dear mother had made us a visit, and there was no way of sending her home to town but on horseback, and there was no saddle but a man's saddle, borrowed of a neighbour a mile off, to whom it must be returned at a certain time positively. I was to accompany mother, who dared not ride faster than a walk, in the capacity of a runner, like the servant of the Shunammitess (read the 4th chapter of 2nd Kings). This was for mother's protection and safety, and to bring back the mare, and if I mistake not, a bag of salt. We had a slow and toilsome but safe journey to town. The mare was put in a paddock, but when I went for her in the morning to prepare for my return journey, she was gone: she had jumped the fence and returned to her old haunts, and boundless bushy pastures, then widely stretching on three sides of the town, east, north, and west. I was in great distress, for the saddle should be returned, and the salt was needed, as sister-in-law wanted to prepare her pickles. It was in vain that I started, bridle in hand, taking some tempting thing to catch her, scouring the commons far and wide—there was no sight of Kate. How many days I sought I don't now recollect. At length I resolved the saddle should go back to its owner, if I carried it the whole fourteen or fifteen miles. I packed it up as compactly as I could and swung it on my back, taking also salt enough in a handkerchief for sister to start her pickles with, and turned my face westward. I had one sympathizing friend, my dear old mother; she did not desert me, but walked slowly along by my side encouraging me, a mile and more out of town, up Dundas (now Queen)

Street, hoping that I might get a lift. A short distance from where the Lunatic Asylum now stands a farmer's waggon overtook us. It was pretty well loaded with something in barrels, and there were four if not five men on top of the load: the grave, and I believe good owner, a tall young man, I think his son-in-law, who drove, a younger man his son, and an old gentleman whom they were giving a lift on his way. Mother accosted them, and interceded for me, and they kindly took up not only my saddle, but myself. I received my mother's parting kiss and blessing, and we started. Once in a while some of us walked to lighten the load and ease our jolted bones. In these intervals I heard the older men talking about serious matters. I am sure my good Samaritan was pious.

But, oh! troubles never end! About a quarter of a mile east of the " 'Tobico " it was found that the endboard of the waggon had come out, and the irons were all lost. They must needs, therefore, stop, and go back to seek the missing things, and, if not found, repair the damage some other way. I was fain, therefore, to transfer the saddle from the waggon to "my mother's colt," and spur him on his way alone. I toiled on the three or four miles to Mr. Austin's, who owned the saddle, where, of course, I left it. I then cut across the fields and woods for home. The load was off my back, but there was a load on my heart—I was in dread of a severe scolding. When I stood in the doorway, crestfallen enough, brother, sister, and the children were at their supper. I was called pretty sternly to account for what they thought my truant conduct. I explained in lugubrious tones how the mare had escaped from the field—how I had sought her, like Saul his asses, in vain—and how I had been forced to walk home. "But what will Mr. Austin do for his saddle ? We would not have had him treated so for anything ?" " Yes, well, but I fetched it home to him on my back." " Oh, that is well ! We're glad he has not been put about for want of it. You had better come and get some supper." I had a relish for it, for I had eaten nothing all day but the piece my careful mother had put in my pocket.

But my principal horseback experiences were in going to and returning from mill. This convenience for the settlers belonged to a Mr. Silverthorn, and was situated on the 'Tobico, midway between two thoroughfares, about four miles from our place, if I went around by the road; but I could make it in three if I cut across a wide expanse of woods where there was no road. We had no cart, or waggon, or sleigh, for a horse, so that the grist had to be taken to the mill on the horse's back. The way was to take two bags, neither quite full of grain. The grain was fairly divided in each bag from the centre, so that one end might balance the other. They were then thrown across each other on the horse's back, something in the form of an X. In returning from mill, pretty much the same was done, only the flour was put in one bag and the bran in the other. These did not usually balance so well. Sometime in her life Kate must have had a very sore back; for she was exceedingly sensitive behind the withers, and very hard to saddle and to mount. It was, therefore, a ticklish job to get the bags placed properly on her back; but especially it was difficult to get on top of them oneself. William generally started me off all right; and, in returning from the mill, the miller did the same; or if I had to do it alone, I brought the fidgetty beast to the high platform at the mill door, and threw on the bags and then jumped down on them myself, in doing which it was a chance if I did not knock them off again. But if, by any accident, which sometimes happened, the bags came off on the road, far from human help, then a rusty with the old mare, and much lugging and toiling were the result. One of these troubles I will relate. It may seem a trifling thing to tell, but it caused me as much anxiety till it was tided over, and as much joy after I was extricated, as the Right Hon. William Gladstone felt before and after the last election in Midlothian. I have hinted that I sometimes crossed the woods for a short cut. I think I seldom went that way loaded from home, but I sometimes returned that way. The first time that I did so I was not loaded; for some reason the grist could not be ground that day, and I returned empty, and I thought I would try the short cut; but in doing so, I lost my way, and tried in vain for some time to find it, and became distressed and alarmed. My mother taught me to pray when a child, but I am ashamed to say, I had given it up. Trouble, however, made me pray that day; I was off the horse trying to grope my way, and I fell on my knees in a thicket, and prayed earnestly to God to deliver me. Prayer soothed my mind. I rose from my knees, and had only gone a few steps when I came out on the "Back Road." Most, gladly, therefore, I led the mare up to the nearest fence, jumped on her back, and rode home with joy; alas! I forgot to pray till the next trouble came, which was the serious one I started to tell about.

This time I started from the mill loaded, and determined to take the shorter way again through the woods; as it was late in the autumn, and the leaves being pretty well off, the forest seemed more open. It was pretty much an oak forest, and the woods were full of hogs feeding on the acorns. It would be a serious thing to have the bags come off and left there —the hogs would tear the bags and devour the bran and flour; and, alas! they did come off. There were miry places in the cow-path that I was striving to keep, which the mare always tried to shun. In doing this, at one time she hugged a tree so closely in striving to keep the firm footing made by its roots, that, despite all my pulling at the bridle and kicking in her sides, she rubbed against the tree and pulled both me and the bags from her back. I had just strength enough to pull the bags out of the mud, but to put them on the restive beast was a task I could no more perform than make a world. What was to be done, If I did not stop and watch the bags, the pigs would eat up their contents; and if I did stop no one was likely to come to my help, for I was in the heart of the forest where there was no thoroughfare, but I must remain to be chilled to death and perish. I determined to act. Fortunately the pigs had neither sighted nor scented my bags; I clubbed and frightened the herd from a wide area around the bags, mounted and made for home. When I came out on the road, I saw, to me, the most pleasant sight in the world—a young farmer, by the name of Wilcox, going towards his home on "The Street," to whom I told my trouble. I had never known him personally before, but he expressed great sympathy, said he had experienced milling troubles himself when a boy, and turned off his way to where the bags lay, fortunately yet untouched by the hogs. He reloaded and remounted me, and started me on my way rejoicing. I never saw him to thank him since, but trust he will receive his reward in heaven. Peace to his memory!

I suffered the most from the cold from those milling journeys in the winter time. I was innocent of flannel underclothes on back or legs; and I have no recollection of a top-coat. Boys in those days sported no long boots—the first pair I ever owned I earned about two years after—much less overshoes; the coverings for my feet were one pair of socks, and a pair of low shoes, open enough to let in the snow. True, in snowy weather, I think, I sometimes wore a pair of long oversocks, which, drawn over my pants, kept the snow out of my shoes, but I seldom resorted to them. On the mare's back (and I dare not get off to take a run for fear I would pull off the bags, and neither I nor the load could be reinstated), both body, hands, and feet were often agonizingly cold.'

As a counterfoil to these sad tales, I may say, I remember one very pleasant ride on Old Kate. It was harvest time, and the weather was fine. It was thought the reapers must have something better than hot spearmint tea, which they usually drank, to keep up their strength (one was a tall, lusty Highland woman, the best reaper in the field), and I was packed off, three or four miles, with a small bag of wheat and a keg to the distillery to exchange for some whisky. I did not mean to call the journey pleasant because of the object of my errand, although, with the light we all then had, it was considered a matter of course; but my journey was pleasant, because the weather was fine, and I met no accident by the way; albeit, I liked the excitement produced by a glass as well as older people. I may yet tell how religion saved me.

Since the above was first in print, I have been reminded of a journey and an experience in which Old Kate was a partner, which reveals some of the peculiarities of "roughing it in the bush." "The McIntosh

Boys," the young men of that family, owned a large, good lot of land on the Centre Road of Toronto, near where Carter's Church was afterwards built. Its only "improvement" was a large clearing, well-fenced, laid down in grass. It was mid-summer, and young Robert McIntosh had been out, with one or two hired boys, securing the hay. Their supply of meat had run out, and the night before the journey he had spent at my brother William's place. Meat had been secured, and I was to accompany Robert in the morning with the mare, to carry the bag of meat, on the top of which I was seated. We rose very early and started, expecting to breakfast at the shanty. Robert was a large good-humoured young man (and large people are more apt to be good-natured than little ones), and I liked him —indeed, better than any of the brothers. He walked by my side and beguiled six or seven miles with chat And when we arrived at our journey's end, while Kate was munching the cut grass, Robert must needs prepare and serve the breakfast for our two selves. And here was the unkindest cut of all. The meat, gentle reader, was not fresh meat, for there was none to be had; but salt, just out of the brine. There was no time to parboil it, but it was cut in pieces and fried in a pan, which process brought out a film of salt all over it. To eat it was terrible, very provocative of thirst, and our tea was made by putting the leaves in a tin cup, and pouring hot water unto the tea. There was no milk, I am sure; that there was sugar I am not sure. If there was, it was not sufficient to overcome the strength of the tea, which was astringent enough. This liquid, in default of any means of keeping back the leaves, we strained through our teeth. I had a thirsty journey in returning with the horse. But a cup of spearmint-tea (a most delightful and healthy beverage) at night, made all right again. I would not be without the experiences of that day for a good deal.

No. XXVI.

MY PETS AND PROPERTY IN THE BUSH, AND WHAT BECAME OF THEM.

MY pet squirrel.—A neighbour, Mr. Jacob Markle, called at the door one day and said that he had rescued a family of young creatures from being burned up alive. The case was this: it appeared that a black squirrel had made her nest and brought forth her young (four in number), in a log-heap in Mr. Markle's chopping. Unaware of their presence, he set fire to that heap with the other piles. The cries and flurry of the little creatures, when the flames began to reach them, revealed their presence; and the kind-hearted man ran to their relief, not, however, till one of them had been somewhat scorched on one of his hind-legs. I was told, that if I would come up and get him, I might have that one. The rest were soon appropriated by his young relatives; and by the time I found leisure to go for him, which was not till the next Sunday, (in those days, it was well if my

Sundays were no worse spent than in such acts of mercy), by which time, he was nearly healed and quite tame and domesticated. I put him in my bosom and brought him home. He proved to be very tame, and attached himself to me at once. We provided a nest for him among some tow in a little basket, but he would sleep nowhere else at night but in bed with me, not without being followed by some company that I could have done without. When I had got into bed of a night and lights were out, I could hear Jackey's purring sound (which he always made when he was satisfied) clambering up the bed-post, when he would dive under the clothes and into my bosom. His purr was a sort of goo-oo, whence my ordinary pet name for him was "Goo," which he always answered to when called.

His ordinary food was bread and milk, which he shared with the cat and kitten, getting usually the lion's share, by dashing into the middle of the dish and crowding the others away. In that respect his habits were something like those of a pig. His manner of feeding upon any soft substance was like that of a racoon and bear, and so far as I had the chance of observing, was that of gathering up and crowding the food into his mouth with the paw. The dog had no particular liking for him, but Goo was enabled to elude all pursuit at all times by running up the corner of the house, and on the roof if necessary. I need not say, that I was greatly attached to him, and loved him very much. But, alas! I was doomed to be early bereaved. He was so tame and fearless, that he was often exposed to danger; and one day, seeking to get into the cradle along with the baby, my little nephew, seated in its foot, and not seeing Jackey, rocked the rocker on to his head and crushed it so badly, that I was fain to destroy him to put him out of his misery. Many a sigh I heaved for poor " Goo!"

A more valuable piece of property came from the same source as the squirrel,—property of which I never realized the final benefit. Perhaps it was because this, like the other, was a piece of Sunday work. Our neighbour told me, that he and his wife were to be away the following Sunday, but the bees were threatening to swarm; and that if I would come up and keep a certain young person, who was left in charge, company and aid her in the event of the bees swarming out, he would give me one of a litter of small pigs too numerous all to be brought up at home. I agreed and went, found the young woman very talkative and pleasant,—got a good dinner,—and stayed till the sun became so low that the bees were not likely to swarm for that day. The pig was then caught, and I carried it the mile or more back to my home. It was a little sow, not of a large kind, but pretty, and of an unusual colour—mostly red. She got such things as were to spare about the house, among others, milk being tolerably plentiful. In imagination, I anticipated the product of my potato patch to be large—they were to be dug, and cooked, **and fed to** the pig—and she was to grow large, get fat, **and to** bring me a good sum of money. She did grow nicely, but it was thought best not to kill, or sell her the first year; and before the second autumn came around, I saw fit to leave the farm suddenly, in a fit of discontent, and to throw up my interest in the pig and another piece of property from which I had expected much, but realized nothing in the end.

But I must tell my young readers of my bull-calf and what became of him :—Where my brother Nat was learning his trade in town, the cow had a fine calf, which it was thought a pity to consign to the butcher's knife, he being larger and prettier than usual. 'Thaniel bought him for me as I was to be the farmer; and after being left a reasonable time with his dam, and being taught to drink milk and flour and water **as a** substitute for his natural aliment, it was thought he might now live upon grass, and I went for him. I shall never forget that journey. I walked the fourteen, or fifteen miles to town, stayed with my friends over night, and started tolerably timely the next day, Bossey's strap in hand and a switch to make him step along, for my bush home. The poor little animal soon learned to trot along in front of me and to keep in the road, being recalled from any wayward tendency by a timely twitch of the strap. But it was not very long till he became tired of such continuous travel. The journey was wearisome to me, but I was cheered with the thought of my journey's end: the admiration that would be given to my calf, and the stately ox Bossey was to become, the suitable mate I was to get for him, the fine team I was to have, and the display I was to make some day at the log rollings! But it was a cause of sadness to me, that I could say nothing to impart comfort or hope to my meek, obedient little slave. This was one of the first times I felt a sorrow which has followed me all my life while urging on a jaded animal without being able to inform him of the rest and food that were to come. I could not afford him more than a few minutes' rest at a time to nibble the grass by the side of the road till noontime, which found me at the stream called the Mimico, where a kind family, by the name of Smith, gave me a lock of new hay to feed my calf, and I lay down beside him on the grass to enjoy the pleasure of seeing him eat and rest; but the lengthening of the shadows admonished me that we must be pushing on, and I urged him forward, taking the shorter branch of the road, which here diverged. On and on we went My legs became weary and my heart was sore and sad to have to whip up my mute companion—nay, if I remember right, he often " bawled " with hunger and weariness. But perseverance will bring the most tedious things to an end, and, about sunset of a long summer's day, I let down the bars and turned him into the meadow, where the aftermath was rich and tender. But the foot-sore little animal was too weary to eat, and he lay down on the soft grass. When we had partaken of our *supawn* and milk, I was cheered by my brother's coming in from outdoors with the news, that "the Bashan bull had gone to feeding." I must wind this story up with a not very pleasant finale.

The calf had very good pasture till the frost came, but at his tender age he should have had more; and the lack of milk in his early life and his long journey told against him, and he entered on the cold weather not in very good condition to encounter and pass the winter. He was turned into a stackyard where he had hay enough, but he should have had warm mashes, and cut potatoes and turnips. The last two I might have fed him, but, boy like, I had lost my interest in him—the novelty was gone. I failed also to provide him as good a shelter as I might; for want of a roof of bark, or something of that kind, the snow fell and rested on his frowsy little back. He became dull and inactive, and one cold morning I went out and *found him dead!* And I am afraid that his unworthy owner was largely accessory to his death. The thought of it has often caused me sorrow and anguish. Let no little boy follow my example. Compassion, as well as self-interest, should have led me to a more kind and careful course of conduct. I deserved the loss which followed: we took off his skin and gave it to the tanner, as the custom then was, "to tan on shares," that is, to give me a "side" of calf, or rather "kip" leather, as it would be called, for the whole skin; but before the process of tanning was complete, I left the bush and heard no more of it.

Thus, you see, I did not make my fortune by going to the "bush." And my pleasures were no better than my profits. The woods were full of game. Often as I made a short cut through the forest (something I was too ready to venture on, and by which I was once lost for a long time), or wandered far into the woods in search of the cattle, I was often startled by a flight of pigeons, or the whirr of the partridge. One of these with her brood of young ones, once led me a long but bootless chase. No wonder I longed for a sportsman's gun, something which I never possessed. On this subject, my kind-hearted brother Thomas raised my hopes; he had seen a fowling-piece which he expected to get for me, and the prospect greatly elated me; but, alas! there is "many a slip twixt cup and lip;" something came between, and I was destined to be disappointed. My boyhood was largely one of hardship and disappointment; but they were no doubt intended and wrought for my spiritual good, as a culminating disappointment, a year after I left the woods, led me to repentance, prayer, and conversion. But particulars about that by-and-by.

I had almost forgotten to tell one successful hunting exploit in which I was a sharer. While on the subject of game, I should have said, that though I never acquired the fowling-piece for which I was sighing, my brother had a gun, an army musket, a genuine Brown Bess, which was too heavy for me to handle, and, as will be seen before I have done, almost any one else. We had a neighbour, Archy Armstrong, a good-natured ne'er-do-well. All he was possessed of was a dog (which would have starved only that he fed himself on green corn on which he kept fat,) and a wife and four or five little girls almost totally destitute of clothing He occupied a house and small clearing on a fifty acre lot belonging to a brother of his, a bachelor, who resided in another part of the country, and who allowed him to occupy the place free of rent. Archy was almost as much away as John, for he had to work abroad for the farmers to procure a livelihood for his family. On one of his visits home, he had reported to us that havoc had been made in his corn patch, next the woods, and that the black, coarse hair left on the log fence showed that the depredations had been done by a bear, which had left part of his coat behind him in scrambling over the log fence. That night the men and boys, with the dogs, organized an expedition, armed with guns and axes, and scoured the adjacent woods in search of Bruin, but in vain. On Monday Archy went away to his work (for, alas! I must confess to another instance of Sabbath-breaking,) and the neighbourhood relapsed into quietness; but this was not to last always. A few days after I was aroused from my slumbers by my sister-in-law punching the underside of the chamber floor where I slept with a broomhandle, and after sundry yawns, I stretched myself, got up, and put on my clothes and went down, when I learned that Mrs. Armstrong had tree'd a bear by the help of their dog and ours, and that I was to go south to Mr. Rutledge's in search of more men and dogs, and if they were to be got, more guns. I dashed off through the pasture field, giving old Kate a great start, which produced such a snort as made me think for an instant that I had encountered another bear. Mr. R. was from home, but Thomas turned out with me, accompanied by Prince, their dog. We had now a formidable pack.

When Thomas and I arrived on the scene of action, the three dogs were barking fiercely at the root of a branchless "stub" about twenty or thirty feet high, up which Bruin had hugged his way and was holding them at defiance. The night was damp and very dark but Mrs. Armstrong, a genuine pioneer, had kindled a fire, which not only cheered us with its genial warmth, but shed some light on the field of action. The great want was to get a good shot at the bear, sufficient to settle him, rather than to provoke him to turn on his pursuers. William put a heavy load of balls and slugs in "Old Bess, a hand and a half"—load enough, if it did not kill the bear, to burst both stock and barrel of the rusty gun and destroy the gunner. The next thing was to get a "rest" for the heavy musket, which few could hold steadily at arms' length, the fence being too far away for that purpose, to say nothing of getting a clear sight of the game. William said, "Thomas," (the bigger boy), "will you let me rest the gun on your shoulder?" Tom thought it the better part of valour to decline the honour of this advanced post. I volunteered, in a fit of bravado, or foolhardiness, not but I suspected it might be perilous—in two ways: the gun might burst, and where I had to stand was in close proximity to the bear, if he should be only wounded and show fight. But placing ourselves near enough to get a good range, while his wife held up a burning rail to give him light on the subject, William banged away; and down came Bruin like a bag of sand, having, as we found after, received a bullet through his jaw and another through one of his paws. Then came the tug of war; he fell among weeds and long grass—the dogs pitched in and occupied his attention pretty well, and William rushed in with the axe; while each furnished himself with anything that came to hand, that would deal a blow. But the difficulty was to hit the bear without hurting the dogs, yet ever and anon, the head of the axe came down upon him. At length the beast succumbed to the injuries he had received, though he showed great tenacity of life, moving himself by involuntary muscular action after we had the skin half off his carcase. He was young, but large and fat, his meat weighing about 200 pounds—the most delectable flesh I ever tasted—like delicate young beef. A hind and fore-quarter fell to each of the two families, and the offal went to regale the dogs. His flesh, and the particulars of the bear hunt, were to regale our visitors, at least as long as the proverbial "nine days' wonder" lasted.

Coon-hunting, was a usual nocturnal amusement, and furnished an available meat-market, to Archy Armstrong. Occasionally we shared the product of his chase, (for which he was always amply made good); and we found racoon to make a delectable pot-pie or stew. Thus it is, that tyrant man revels in the slaughter of the inferior animals.

In the meantime, facilities for mental and religious information were not much, while I remained on the bush farm. I always liked a book, and would read if I had one of tolerable interest; but we had none of any account but the precious Bible. The historical parts of that I would read by myself; and the more devotional and doctrinal parts I read at the request of my blind brother, who came to live with us after a time, for his edification. One borrowed book I remember and read: it was Lieut. Byron's Narrative of the Loss of the Ship *Wager*, lost off the coast of South America, a thrilling and sorrowful tale, the main facts of which remain with me till this day. Yes, and we had Blanco White's Master Key to Popery.

The Methodist preachers, I afterwards learned, traversed those new settlements, but they never chanced to come very near us; and neither I, nor one of our household, ever once heard a sermon during the fifteen months I lived in the woods. Once I went three miles to a so-called Sunday-school, but there was no religious man to conduct it; no prayer was offered, and it consisted of an hour's reading of the Bible, "turn about," which constituted the whole of the exercises. But that, and a singing school which followed on its heels, taught by the mail carrier between York and Ancaster, furnished an opportunity for the young people to see each other, which comprised the principal part of what devotion there was in the whole matter. No wonder, that for want of better occupation, we fell into something like Sabbath desecration. But a change came at length; in five years from that time, there was in the heart of the neighbourhood, a school-house in which meetings were held; there was a society; and I myself, for four months, was, strange to say, one of the preachers! I must not, however, anticipate

No. XXVII.

A CHRISTMAS WEEK THAT ENDED WRONG.

FEW holidays had I in the bush; but it was determined that the Christmas week of 1822 should be mine to go to town, and spend with my mother and the few friends I had left in York, old and young. What strengthened the project was, that my nearest boy companion, Thomas Rutledge, was to have a vacation at the same time, to be spent in the same place. From the close of the war of 1812-15 till, say, 1825, a great many Irish Protestant families, who had come to this country through New York City had been detained there during the conflict between Great Britain and the United States; but when the war was over, some earlier, some later, they began to stream away across the intervening wilderness, many of them in conveyances of their own, towards King George's dominions, some of them stopping in the Town of York, and some penetrating the newly-opened wilderness in the region round about. Many of those who went to the country left relatives in the little capital. Mr. Rutledge's family was one of these; and it was among some of his relatives that Thomas was to spend his Christmas week, and we were to go out and come back together. The prospect of company made the project of my trip the more exhilarating. My most presentable suit of clothes was a summer suit of jean, and I had no top coat that was presentable; the weather, also, was cold. What was to be done? Young people will half freeze themselves for the sake of appearances, and I determined to wear my summer suit. So far as I can recollect I put some warmer garments under, and I don't remember that I felt the cold very much. The activity and restlessness of my boyhood was a counteraction to the cold.

Here I must make a general confession that will explain some things at the close. In those days, among all my acquaintances, lax ideas of what might be done, or not be done, on the Sabbath, prevailed. No one would think of performing downright labour on that day; but then, no one scrupled to perform a journey to see friends, or otherwise, on that day, and thereby save a week-day for work. In accordance with this idea, the two boys were to leave the bush early on the Sunday morning preceding Christmas, spend the week in town, and return on the succeeding Sunday. We left early, therefore, without the scruples and fears with which I, at least, came back. With the alacrity and hopefullness of boyhood we started off, taking hold of each other's hands, in places where the road was smooth, and trotting along together like a span of colts.

At length I greeted what had been the scene of my boyish haunts for seven years, and saw my mother and friends. The week was spent pleasantly enough, according to my boyish notions, a good part of it at old Mr. McIntosh's, sliding on a pond with William, Janet, and David, the first two of whom have been long since in their graves.

But my return journey was not to be so pleasurable as my journey out. Calling through the week at Mr. Graham's to see Thomas, and make arrangements for our return, I found out he was to get a ride home with friends who were to drive a team out, but whether before or after Sabbath I forget; but I was not to have his company, but to return alone. I still thought it necessary to return on Sunday, to be back at my Monday's work. It was rather low water-mark with my poor mother's piety just then, and she did not interpose strongly against my Sunday return journey. In the meantime she had prepared a number of additional articles for my wardrobe, and these I was to carry in a little pack on my back. Mother "rose up betimes and sent me away." It was an early hour of a cold morning that I walked up King Street, and saw not a human being until I came opposite the old wooden Methodist Meeting-house, midway between Yonge and Bay Streets, when Mr. Patrick, the class-leader, who had been my Sabbath-school teacher, had been kindling the fire in the stove to have the chapel warm for early service, came out on the road and turned towards his residence in Bay Street I had been a favourite scholar with him and as love is the effectual loan for love, I liked him very much, and was glad to see him. I, therefore, hurried up and accosted him (he was short-sighted and did not readily pick me up through his spectacles). I was thinking how glad he would be to see me, and how manly I would look, stick in hand, with my pack on my back, totally forgetting, for the moment, all he had taught me about the sanctity of the Sabbath. He turned and looked at me with surprise and displeasure.

"What, John, is that you? Where are you going?"

"Why, sir, I live in the country now, have been in the town for a week, and am now going back again."

"But why must you go back to-day, this is the Sabbath of the Lord, you must remain till to-morrow."

"But I can't, sir, I am expected back."

"Any expectation of your friends cannot excuse you for breaking the Sabbath."

"I think I shall have to go on, sir."

"But if a tree falls upon you by the way, and kill you, what excuse can you give at the bar of God for breaking his Sabbath?"

This terrified me very much, for it was quite windy enough to blow down trees, but I would have been ashamed to go back to my friends, and I slowly and silently moved forward, and I may say sorrowfully, too, for I was sorry to have forfeited the good opinion and incurred the rebuke of a man I revered and loved so much.

On I went trembling. But so long as there were no trees along the road near enough to reach me, I felt pretty safe. This was the case along Dundas Street (now Queen) till I got into the tall pine woods which stretched from Col. Givens' to the plains. Through those dreary three miles my eye scanned and measured each tree in the vicinity of my path, to determine whether it were tall enough to reach me in the road, the centre of which I kept as nearly as I could to escape the judicial infliction from either side. I prayed in my heart, but it was that I might not be killed; and when a roadside tree seemed dangerously near, I kept to the other side, and went past in double-quick time. In the "Oak Plains," I went on with confidence, as there were no tall trees. Thus I pushed on till I reached the Mimico. There, as I had some coppers in my pocket, I went into Wilcox's tavern and bought and drank a glass of whisky, no one in those days doubting its propriety, even for a growing boy, especially on a cold day. Alas! people thought a person might stop drinking just before the point of drunkenness was reached, although he had placed himself on a slippery inclined plane, the natural tendency of which was to shunt him off into perdition. The whisky raised my confidence a little, not enough, however, to make me take the "back road," there being too many instruments of God's displeasure against Sabbath-breakers on that road. However, the way seemed long and I wanted to abridge it by a short cut; but in doing so I had to pass by the door of a Mr. Cook, who kept two ferocious dogs, and I was always very much afraid of dogs. These I had defied when on horseback. But now I was on foot and alone, and they came out at me, open-mouthed. I did not know but the dreaded judgment was to come in being torn to pieces by two ferocious dogs instead of being crushed to pieces by a tree. But I bethought me of an expedient: I had part of my luncheon on my person in the shape of some Boston crackers. I, therefore, employing all the soothing words I could think of, doled out the crackers to the dogs, till this form of *backsheesh* had carried me beyond the frontier the dogs felt bound to protect. I then cut across the woods, the nearest way to the open glade, where there was no fear of falling trees; thence I pushed on home. Still, through the swamp the trees were too near for perfect composure, till at length the long-desired opening furnished by "our settlement" burst upon my gratified sight, and, before the sun was quite down I found myself, uncrushed by a tree, within the protecting strong walls of our log-house. Thank God, that he spared me to repent; and in the long run repent I did! I have just bethought me, that the notion I was out of danger as soon as I was out of the vicinity of the trees, was like the mistake of poor Plunket, a big, eccentric and wicked Irishman, who lived some years after in the lower part of the Province. He and some others were out in a boat on the Lord's day on one of the expansions of the Mississippi called lakes, when it blew very hard and the waves ran so high as to endanger the boat of upsetting. The wicked man was very much alarmed, and prayed and promised if God would but spare his life to reform. When they got to land, he was overjoyed, and exclaimed to his companions, "I tell you what, boys, that was well done! It was a good thing God Almighty did not kill me when he had a chance." He, too, was spared to repent, and professed conversion afterwards at a Methodist camp-meeting; a certain sermon being the instrument of his awakening, which led him to say in the experience meeting, that, "Mr. Pollard was the boy that did it."

No. XXVIII.

AN IMPULSIVE ACT—A SUDDEN DEPARTURE FROM THE BUSH.

TWO several formations in my boyish mind, one of longer and the other of more recent standing, led to this. The crisis was painful, and I hope no other poor boy may pass through a similar one. I would pass it over entirely, only that it forms a transition from one state of boy life to another. My boyhood was a pretty hard one all through; and having an active mind and a taste for reading, which furnished me with food for thought, which many other boys had not, I was often led to cast about in my mind for some other condition in life.

My first tendency to a roving disposition arose from books of adventure, such as Robinson Crusoe, the Buccaneers of America—a kind of sea pirates—and such others as I could lay my hands on. I was not averse to effort, and was confident of my ability to tke care of myself; and, like many another foolish boy, I should very likely have left home and "gone to seek my fortune," as we boys used to term it, only for my attachment to my mother and unwillingness to give her pain. I felt she was too good a friend to wound in the smallest degree.

Some weeks before the start that I made, which I am about to relate, a new source of discontent, real or imaginary, tended to revive these revolvings in mind of the fortune-seeking project. It was hard for a slender, growing boy in the bush, at best—frugal fare, and work, work, work. But the winter had gone, and the spring broken. That season brought great activity to prepare the fields and get in the crops; the fall supplies began to diminish, so as to require economy, especially in the matter of meat; and lighter diet must be substituted, not over satisfying to a hungry boy. These, with the relaxing effect of warmer weather, made me feel weak and discontented. I was several days in a sullen state of mind, and my feelings were no doubt expressed in my countenance. On the day referred to, I was discontented with my dinner, and went back to my work in the field feeling angry and gloomy. Both brother and his wife were away somewhere. I thought it a good time to leave, and went to the house to tell my poor blind brother James, to whom I had a strong attachment; but for some reason my heart failed me, and I made no sign to him. I then started down through the meadow, to the house of Mr. Rutledge, thinking I would call out Tom, my young companion, and tell him to make my flight known, after I had got well away, for I did not wish to give any one needless alarm, as though some evil had befallen me. But Thomas was away from home, and I went on, skulking in the woods on the sides of the road, lest I should be identified by neighbours and turned back. When I got out to the corners, where I must needs turn westward, away from all that knew me, or eastward, to York, where I was known, I stood and hestated for sometime. Had I possessed a reasonable amount of my clothes to make me in any measure comfortable and presentable, and had been able to leave word with any one who would not impede my flight, but after a time carry back word that no bodily harm had come to me, which within a reasonable time, would reach my poor mother, who otherwise would be distressed beyond measure, the probabilities were that I would have turned westward and gone to where I was not known; seek temporary means of support, by such work as I could do; and then when I got money, have gone farther. In that case, the Omniscient could only tell what would have been the result to me. But I had seen no one with whom I could leave my message; and my clothes were scanty, and they were torn. They were my ordinary working clothes, of course—coat, vest, pants, shirt, shoes, and stockings. I was innocent of anything more, and had no top-coat. Remember, too, it was a dark chilly day in the month of April (1823). Besides, my pants had met with an accident and were torn badly on one side in front; so that, to be at all presentable, I was fain to put my hand through the place for a pocket, and hold them together from the inside.

Being in such a plight, my instinct led me toward the town where my mother lived. Even that was a sad resort. Thomas was just then out of business, and it was low water mark with us all, George having gone to the States. On my way town-ward, greatly to my embarrassment, I met a neighbour (in some sense a relative), the old Highland Scotchman, Wallace, whom I have already mentioned. I could not pass him without his seeing me, but when I met him said as little as I could. I could not, however, escape his keen eye and ready questions. I told him I was going to town. But why was I going in such a plight? Then I told him the real state of the case. He chided me for leaving my brother; and I defended myself on the ground of hard usage, of which I had brought myself to believe I was the subject. He tried to get me to return with him, by the promise that he would "talk Scotch to them." But I felt it impossible to face them after what occurred; and when he almost attempted to turn me back by force, I wept bitter tears, and screamed with terror. Whereupon he allowed me to pass on, with the pledge that I would go to my mother's and nowhere else. He was to have taken my brother's in his way at any rate; and I have reason to believe that he lodged there that night. His statement of my charges exasperated them very much. I was glad, however, that they were saved from suspense, though they might have cause for anger. I did not take a good way of severing my connection with the place. Withdrawing my services was the termination of my quota of contribution for keeping James, and, just at that time of year, put William to great inconvenience. Upon second thoughts, I would have reversed what I had done, if I could. Not without solicitude, I thought, " Who will rake and burn the leaves and stubble? Who will drive the oxen to harrow the fields? Who will ride the mare to mill? And who will do their errands? Who will hunt the cattle?"

There was, no doubt, a providence in the issue of the movement in the long run. I would not have had much chance for education if I had stayed in the back country; and, going on as I had been, I might not have become converted, and then my whole life would have been worse than blank.

It was dusk before I reached my mother's, and I met her at first in a dark pasaage way; and, though surprised at my sudden appearance, it was not till I had gone into the light that she saw the dejected, weary, dirty, and ragged plight I was in. But, oh! the never failing attachment and ready resources of that mother! She provided me supper and a bed, and soundly I slept from weariness and sorrow; and she mended and made for me while I slept, so that by the morning I looked passable for week-day appearance. After fixing me up in the morning, she said, "Now, John, you had better go and see your early friend, Mr. Ketchum. You know he always took very much to you; perhaps he may find a place for you." I went "with my heart in my mouth," as the old saying is; received a kindly greeting, and patient listening to my story. After a little chaffing—he always liked to tease boys—he said, "Why, yes, John, you were always a pretty good boy to work; we must find something for you to do. What must I give you a month?" "Will four dollars be too much, Sir?" "I don't know, that's a good deal of money. Do you think you could melt the ore, and hammer out the metal, and make four dollars in a month?" It was hard to answer anything so quaint. But he soon relieved me from embarrassment, by saying, 'There, go along and help Luke, the Frenchman, at that 'ere job he is at!"

This was a great boon for me. No one was required to kill himself with hard work in that establishment; the food was good, abundant, and well cooked; and I had a good feather bed to sleep on at night, with plenty of clothes. And, although as yet none were truly religious, it was of good augury that every one of the boys in the common sleeping-room bent his knees in prayer before retiring to rest. For very shame sake, I was forced to bend mine also, and to say the Lord's prayer, which my mother had taught me when a child. Alas! another whole year passed before I began to pray in earnest. I fear I shall have to tell some stories of the following twelve months which will show that I was not religious. My work was in and around a tannery, but I did not commence to learn the trade for two years from that time.

₊ After seeing the above in print, and pondering it at leisure, I am led to believe that some of the prudent, worldly-wise class will think that I should not have made such a disclosure relative to myself and friends; but if an autobiography may be written at all, it ought to be literally accurate relative to all matters great and small, however delicate, that were significant in shaping the character and complexion of one's after life, else such a personal history is of no value to the reader. And it must be confessed that the tendency in most persons is, to such concealments and colouring of facts, that their statements are of no validity whatever. And what wonder if a person who afterwards made a fair record should have once in the course of his boyhood have had such an escapade as the one I have recorded. It would scarcely have seemed boy-like if he had not; and I am writing of a boy and not of a man.

As to my brother, I should, perhaps, further say, that we did not meet again for fully a year after my leaving and then in friendship without any allusions to what had past; and a year after that again, when my renewed conscience was tender and sensitive about my past sinful life, I made a very humble confession of my unfriendly remarks respecting him with many tears. Indeed, one who heard it, thought that I humbled myself too much. He spoke very kindly, but made no concessions on his own part. Henceforth, however, till his death we were on terms of the most brotherly friendship; and always took sweet counsel on religious matters, regarding which, in all fundamental particulars, we were in perfect harmony. He attained a position of wealth and respectability which none of my other brothers were fortunate enough to achieve.

N.B.—As to those who wish to establish their respectability by leaving the impression that neither they nor their relatives ever had a strait, or a want, or a struggle, I think they are simply detestable for their pride and affectation.

No. XXIX.

SOME ACCOUNT OF MY DEAR OLD "BOSS."

BEFORE I go any further, I had better give some account of the gentleman I had worked for, off and on, about two years, and under whose roof I was to reside at least another two years and a-half—first as a hired boy, and then as an apprentice. I give this account because he was a very remarkable man, and just now for certain reasons, he is very much talked about. Indeed, his career furnishes a good example, and many valuable lessons for boys. If I call him "Boss," instead of MASTER, it is from no want of respect, but because that was the term most generally used in this country at that time to express an employer, or one who gave the word of command.

About one hundred years ago there lived a numerous young family in Spencertown, in the State of New York, United States. They were poor, mostly, I suspect, because the father was a poor manager; and, from some hints I received from time to time in the early day, he drank as well. **Alas!** it was a common fault in those days, and by no means as discreditable in public estimation as now; thanks to the improved public opinion brought about by the efforts of the Temperance Reform. But I am bound to say, that the shiftless father, became thoroughly reformed, so far as drink was concerned, late in life—thanks to the influence exerted over him by his virtuous son. But when I came to know the old gentleman he was in his dotage, and was very childish in his talk, (if, indeed, he had ever possessed any manly sense) repeating the same little stories and rhymes many times over. In this Ketchum family, for that is the name of the person I am writing about, when it was completed, there were at least six children—three boys and three girls: of the former, Seneca, Jesse, and Zebedee, or Zebulon, I suppose, for Jesse's children used to call him "Uncle Zeb."

I should have said, perhaps earlier, that the mother of these children, (from certain tender hints and reverent allusions to her by her son Jesse) was as wise, and true, and prudent, as her husband and their father was lacking in those qualities. I suspect our hero, Jesse, the mainstay of the family, received an impulse in the right direction from his mother, of whom he always spoke with great respect, not without a tinge of the regretful and mysterious. She died comparatively early, long before her husband, and in their native home in the United States. What were the circumstances of her death I knew not, but her life and character had been good. Jesse Ketchum, among the many wise saws and maxims he was wont to utter in after years, used to say, "I have hope of a child, though he may have had a bad father ; but if has had a bad mother, I can't expect any good of him."

I may as well here say, that there was an incubus adapted to crush the energies of this family (a matter too well known to be ignored ;) there was an hereditary taint of insanity in their blood, but upon which side of the house I know not. I rather supect that it was the active intellect of the mother that gave way under the pressure of domestic cares. I hardly think the husband's mind was ever stiff enough to snap. This legacy in the family was an evil against which Mr. Jesse Ketchum had to fight all his days, and greatly added to his cares and burdens, while it gave occasion for his exemplifying his unfailing brotherly kindness for many long years.

Seneca Ketchum, the eldest son and brother, aside from occasional aberrations of mind in later life, was a man of energy and ability. He early left home, came to Canada, and became possessed of some property, about seven or eight miles out of York, (now Toronto) on Yonge Street.

Jesse, our hero, the next eldest, was born on the 30th of March, 1782. The way I came to know his birthday, was this : Mr. Ketchum was one day among some friends in company, when the conversation turned on their several birthdays; he was led to say that he was born on the last day of the month of March, when his own little boy spoke up and said, "Daddy came very near being an April fool, didn't he?" This made a laugh in which the father joined along with the rest.

He was early bound out to a master, most likely till twenty-one. What the business was I do not know, I suspect not the one he afterwards adopted; but from some incidental allusions, I surmise it was farming. He never spoke amiss of his master, but his mistress was a cruel, capricious woman, and when a woman gives away to ill-nature, she can be very ugly and tyrannical indeed. Whether she had any children of her own or not, I do not know, but it was evident she did not feel a mother's affection for poor young Jesse Ketchum. I myself heard him tell a tale of her cruel caprice: he had by some means obtained a new coat, and wore it to his work in the field. It being easier to work in his shirt' sleeves, he took it off and hung it on a bush; and with the heedlessnes of a boy, came away and forgot it. His mistress coming along some time after, found the coat, and in order to make out a case against the 'prentice, tore the coat to ribbons, and held it up as the work of the hogs, in whose power she alleged Jesse's carelessness had left his garment. Whether she got him punished as the cause of the accident is more than I clearly understood.

As any boy naturally would, the lad revolved in

mind an escape from such tyranny. The last straw which broke down his endurance was her punishing him for having as she said, ill-treated one of the geese by pulling out its feathers; which charge she made up out of the fact, that in pulling a goose out of a fence she was vainly trying to pass through, she dropped a quill, which he appropriated to make a pen to write his school copy with, green quills being his only material for pens.

Young Jesse Ketchum availed himself of the first chance of making his escape from the bondage of his stern mistress, and made for Canada, whither his elder brother had gone before him, pursuing his journey on foot, without money and very destitute of clothes. If we had the particulars, no doubt the details of the fugitive's hardships would be thrilling. But the God and Father of the friendless preserved him and provided for him, and brought him to his brother's place in peace and safety. After events proved, as an observing old lady used to say, that "Jesse Ketchum was sent before, like another Joseph, to provide for his kindred." He soon became his brother's partner in the business of the farm and tannery; and his brother sometimes suffering from aberration of mind, the principal management fell to the younger brother, who soon began to display that wonderful capacity for business which distinguished him through life, by which, without any apparent bustle or effort, wealth flowed in upon him from all sides.

A young, energetic widow, a Mrs. Love, with one little daughter (who had lost the husband of her youth in a tragic manner, he having been shot in a night-hunting expedition by mistake for a bear), kept the house of the brothers. Jesse became attached to Mrs. Love, and married her at the early age of eighteen. She was his senior by a few years, and, therefore, she was prepared to be his counsellor. She was shrewd, capable, managing, and very industrious; and aided him in both gaining and saving. She "looked well to the ways of her household. The heart of her husband safely trusted in her. She did him good and not evil all the days of his life. She sought wool and flax, and her hands held the spindle and distaff." All her household for years, were clothed by her home manufactures. Her husband, therefore, was known in the gate, sitting among the elders. Nor did she forget to "stretch forth her hands to the poor, or to reach them out to the needy." She was a cordial co-operator in all her husband's charities. Especially they were the life-long benefactors of all his relatives and their descendants, the family, all but his mother, having been early transferred to Canada.

At the opening of the war of 1812-15, he was led to buy a tannery and several surrounding blocks of land in the Town of York, at a sacrifice to the sellers, from aliens retiring to the United States. This applies especially to the property of a Mr. Van Zant. There was a great demand for home manufactured leather for none was admitted from the States. Prices during the war were high and money was plenty. Cash flowed in upon our hero, and he had a chance of buying town-lots and farms for a mere song, which after a few years had increased in value—four, five, ten, and at last *a hundred times.* A similar purchase was made in Buffalo, N. Y., with the same results.

I don't think that Mr. K. ever professed any very marked Christian experience; but from our earliest knowledge of him as a householder, his character was that of a Christian man. He was never known otherwise than strictly moral and temperate. Indeed, he was far in advance of the very best part of the community in the avoidance of the drinking customs of the day; he "took no snuff, tobacco, or drams." "No manner of work did he, his son, or his daughter, his man-servant, his maid-servant, his ox, his horses, and mules, or the stranger that was within his gates, perform on the Sabbath." Furthermore, he joined hands with the parson of the town in striving to break up Sunday skating upon the Bay, by taking the names of the skaters, and threatening them with the law.

I surmise his early religious proclivities were Presbyterian; and I am sure those of his wife were emphatically such. But before there was a Methodist or Presbyterian Church in the town, he kept a pew in the Episcopalian Church, which he and his family strictly attended, and where he also, I believe, used to commune. When the Methodists built a church in

1818, he was a frequent attendant and a teacher, as we have seen, in the Sunday-school, which was the first to be organized; and one who knew his views well, believed that if his wife had been as much inclined to that people as he was, he would have cast in his lot with the newly-organized Methodist cause. His house was always open to all the travelling ministers who came and went in those days, the Methodist itinerants among the rest. From an early day family worship was conducted twice in each twenty-four hours. Every one of his large household was required to be present; every one who could read, was provided with a copy of the Bible, and the lesson was read in the "verse-about" manner.

All the candidates for settlement as Presbyterian ministers found a comfortable, loving home with him; and the first one settled in the town, the Rev. James Harris, never had any other home from the first till he married Mr. Ketchum's second daughter, Fidelia, and went to live in a residence erected for him by his generous father-in-law. The land on which the church stood was his gift; and the building itself was almost wholly built at his expense, as it was planned by him and the grounds were beautified by his hand. Don't I remember how the ministers who came, (some of them, all the way from Brockville) to install the young dominie, were lodged at his house; and how their jaded horses were taken out by some of us boys to one of Mr. K.'s adjacent farms to revel in the best of pasture during their needed rest of several days. That farm was just beyond where the Mount Pleasant Cemetery now displays its undulating surface and its white cenotaphs.

Mr. Ketchum often boarded the school-master, and took private lessons from him to remedy the defects of his early education. I remember that grammar was one of these; and I suspect, that those lessons were all the board money the pedagogue paid.

My old Boss's practical wisdom crystallized into cautions to young beginners not to "eat up their seed potatoes," and not to spend all their time over "the wind work" of a subject—mere talk. A refractory boy, or horse, had "too much democracy in his constitution." The large assembly room in a new mansion he erected, about 1820, was not the ball room, for he disapproved of dancing, but it was "the fourth of June room"—the place for celebrating the King's birthday!

He often talked lovingly to his horses and cattle. "Mink," a favourite black horse he had raised, was often caressed by the arms of his master around his neck, while he was pronounced 'a fine old fellow." A neighbour, one fine May morning found him driving his well-fed cows out of the yard, talking to them the while, and saying to them, "I have fed you all winter, now go away on the commons, and go and hunt! Go up there by Mr. C.'s and go and hunt." Though thus thrust out they did not fail to receive something tasty when they came back to be milked.

But I must check my pen, for it would take volumes to tell of all the poor boys and destitute families he befriended, helping them in the very best of all ways, by giving them employment, and by putting them in a way to create for themselves a home. Some other of his quaintly amiable ways may come to view in the further narrations I have to make.

Not to leave this section incomplete, I must not forget to say, that he was born in Spencertown, N.Y., in 1782; came to Canada in 1799; removed from Yonge Street to York probably about 1811 or '12; went away to Buffalo, N. Y., the place of another large property, in 1845; and passed away to the place where he had laid up imperishable treasure, September 7th, 1867.

No. XXX.

BUTTERNUTTING ON SUNDAY, AND ITS PUNISHMENT.

THE last year of my unregenerated life, the one immediately before my conversion, was a perilous one for my morals and my soul. There were a great many men and boys employed in the establishment in which I was employed, with a good many comers and goers besides, none of whom were truly religious at that time, although a revival came the following year which made some change in some of them. In the meantime, none of them were a safe copy to follow; and those whose age and size gave them a claim to matured manhood, and whose company, as an aspiring boy, I affected, were more likely to lure me to wider fields of indulgence than I had yet explored. Alas! these explorations were mostly made on Sunday, including sometimes the garrison, among the soldiers, not excluding the military canteen, where the older ones treated the younger to drink.

It is true, our good old Boss enjoined upon us to attend some church, which we usually did at least once a day; and the churches we attended were either the Methodist or Presbyterian. My spending part of the Sabbath with my mother, and her proclivities for Methodism, led me to attend the Methodist meeting-house the oftener; albeit my place of residence led me often to my master's church.

But, the morning service over, the scattering away after dinner was seldom in the direction of any church. Our devotions were oftener paid to the blackberries, choke-cherries, hazelnuts, and butternuts, in the fields and woods of unlimited extent surrounding the town on three sides.

One Sunday afternoon, John Jones, of potato-planting memories, asked me to accompany him up the Flats of the Don, where butternuts were said to be plentiful. We strolled along down Newgate Street as far as what we now call Jarvis Street, then across the ravine which then intersected what used to be called Lot (now Queen) Street, just where the creek which coincided with it a long way, broadened out to a tangled, marshy expanse, which has since received the euphonious name of Moss Park. Then we zig-zagged along till we got into the road which led between the cleared lots on the west and the pine woods which stretched everywhere away to the Don River, which had always been known as "The Park," which road now constitutes Parliament Street. On we went along the sandy, dusty, stumpy waggon way, through the woods which have since given place for the Church of England Cemetery and the Necropolis, within which were the remains of old Castle Frank. Then across sundry gullies and undulations of the ground went we, until old Col. Playter's meadows, dotted here and there with lofty butternut trees, opened to our view.

John was a good singer; had both voice and science for sacred music, in which he had been trained. Some little time before he had been at a Methodist meeting and had heard them sing the chorus to the hymn, commencing—" Come, ye sinners, poor and needy,"— with which he was much taken, and which ran thus:

> Turn to the Lord and seek salvation,
> Sound the praise of His dear name,
> lory, honour, and salvation,
> Christ, the Lord, has come to reign !

This he sung a great many times over to beguile our tramp, which began to be irksome, when, as I said, the wide, green meadows, bespangled more or less with flowers, the shrubs and trees, and here and there a glint of the silver stream, burst upon our sight.

A word or two about my fellow-transgressor will be necessary, to account for some things which are to follow. He was now nearly twenty-one, and very anxious to take rank in all respects as a man. He had lately taken to chewing tobacco, and sported a quid in the hollow of his cheek big enough to show itself on the outside, which he thought added to the manliness of his looks; and provided himself with an enormous tobacco-box, which came together with an emphatic snap; albeit, he had to keep these things on the sly from the Boss, who was down on such indulgences. But if his tobacco-box was large, he was small himself, which was a great grief to him. True, he was strong and wiry, and few could out-work or out-wrestle him. He was plucky, too. But then he wanted to look muscular, as well as display muscle. For that purpose he, when dressed up, wore a good many clothes, such as vests and drawers, to swell himself out, and at that moment he had on two pairs of trousers—a linen pair, which he wore in the tannery, under his Sunday pants, to fill up the latter to the right proportion of plumpness.

The trees were tall, but the branches when reached were loaded with the largest and finest nuts. John divested himself of his coat and mounted into the tree tops, and shook down the fruit to me, who gathered them together; and a great heap was the result. But what were we to do with them now we had gathered them? Our handkerchiefs did not suffice to hold them all. John bethought him of a plan to carry the surplus; he took off his under trousers, tied up the legs and filled them with nuts, buttoning them at top, in which way they made a sort of duplicate bag. Shouldering them up, we came on until we got so near the town we saw that for the present we must conceal them ; for we would not have liked to go through the streets in such a plight in daylight on any day, still less on the Lord's day. That would have been utterly impracticable considering the character of our employer. It was, therefore, agreed to cover them up in a way they would not be found by others, and come with a bag and get them under the cover of the darkness of the following Monday night. We, therefore, turned into the woods, somewhere near where the Primitive Methodist Church now stands on Parliament street. We soon found a large log from under which we scraped the leaves and earth, and stowed away our nuts, then scraping back the leaves and rubbish to cover them, leaving the place as natural looking as possible, and making a mark on the roadside to show us where to turn in, the little man resumed his under clothes, and we made our way back by supper-time, looking as demure as if we had been to an afternoon service.

We had many an anxious thought and colloquy about our hidden treasure during the course of the following day ; and when our work and supper were ended, rolling up a bag, we stole out of town, and by the time it was nearly dark we arrived at the spot we were in search of. The log was there, all right ; but, oh! to our woful disappointment, not a single nut! Some wanton boys, like ourselves (the squirrels could hardly have taken them all away in twenty-four hours), had found them and borne them off. We had been justly punished for our Sabbath-breaking. We turned towards the town chop-fallen enough. For the sake of better light, and other reasons, we came up King street. Opposite the market stood the " English Chop House," kept by a man who was afterwards converted and became a zealous Methodist class-leader— I speak of Mr. Bloor—and my senior treated me to some refreshment of a kind to enliven our spirits for the time and counterpoise our depression. By the following autumn I had found an enduring source of satisfaction.

No XXXI

A MISSPENT SUNDAY THAT ENDED WELL.

MY last story, of a misspent Sunday afternoon, had at least a ridiculous finale; the misspent whole Sunday, of which I am now about to give an account, had one element of the ludicrous along with the sinful, but, thank God, ended well, and put an end to all Sabbath-breaking by me forever. I must tell it all, with its preliminaries, adjuncts, and succeeding events.

I have told my readers, young and old, before this, that my father lost his hundred acres of wheat at the Grand River, by the war; as also his beautiful span of horses and waggon, by their capture by the Americans, at the Battle of Niagara, May, 1813; besides the loss of all our household effects, the burning of the house in which we had been living, for which he had put in a claim of something like a thousand dollars, more or less, at the close of the war. After waiting a great many long weary years, perhaps one-half of that sum was granted him out of the insufficient war-loss fund; but after the grant was issued, it was many weary weeks, or months, before the money was paid. For some time after the issue was made, the position of the family, which was now worse off than it had been for some years previously, began to look up in hopes of getting what would at least give us a start in some newly-projected efforts to improve our fortunes.

On the Sunday morning, in 1824, to which I now refer, I rose from my bed with a hopeful heart, took my breakfast, and joined some irreligious companions, for a day's forbidden pleasure. Although it was the holy Sabbath, as far as I can remember we projected a walk over the Garrison Common, including a call at the canteen; but the day was doomed to be overcast by two circumstances, the one trivial, the other serious. Along with putting on otherwise my best, I put on a beautiful pair of new shoes, the most elegant I had ever ventured to buy. I knew they were painfully short for me, but their finish was captivating, and I could not think of relinquishing them, hoping "they would stretch!" and though they pinched me severely, I stuck to them, although my walk increased the pain every moment. At length I turned back and hobbled through the town to my mother. When I arrived there, a worse sorrow awaited me; I learned from my precious mother that father had drawn his money, but had deposited it away from home, probably with some crony of a tavern-keeper. He had treated himself, of course; the taste of liquor had revived an appetite which had ruled him, to our sorrow, all his life; and he was now "on the spree," and drinking up our little, but sole fortune [some of it was afterwards recovered]. We were very sorrowful, of course. By the time I had to leave for my place of employment, against my morrow's work, my feet were so swollen I was forced to take my fine shoes in my hand and to limp to my quarters by a back street. Just at this humiliating point, God's mercy interposed in my behalf.

I stole into the premises by the back gate, and sat down on a pile of boards in the woodshed, with my back towards Yonge Street, overlooking the orchard, now in full bloom, and fragrant as the "spicy breezes which blow soft o'er Ceylon's isle," and in full view of a glorious unclouded sunset. Presently two boys younger than I—Frederick Phipps and Willie Jones —came in from the Methodist Sunday-School, on which I, alas! had long turned my back. There were no library books, or even prizes, then distributed, but each of the boys had in his hand a religious tract, and they gave them up to me, who always dearly loved a book, especially if it contained a story, a composition which was now to lead to my salvation. One of the tracts was "The Life of Old Bridget,"—the other was "Important Questions Answered from Scripture." Old Bridget, an afflicted woman, the early part of whose life had been irreligious, had been led by the death of her pious husband, a baker, to reflection, repentance, and conversion. She afterwards became a cripple by rheumatism, and was obliged to carry on her late husband's business under great disadvantages to support herself, performing the labours of her trade on her knees instead of her feet. Nevertheless, religion made her resigned and extremely happy in the midst of all her afflictions. I thought—though young and healthy, I am not happy, but disappointed and miserable. How gladly would I give up for ever all that the world has to give, and accept of that poor woman's lot, if I could only be as happy as she was in hope of a heavenly life. That tract had so solemnized and softened me, that I did what I otherwise would not have done, if I had not read it, read the other tract. Let no one think that biographical tracts, with their pictures, are written and printed in vain. The "Questions" in the other tract related to our duty and sinfulness; our redemption and salvation by Jesus Christ; the nature and necessity of repentance and conversion, and the like. It deepened the impression made by the first tract. The other boys had left me alone, and I sat musing by myself. I had felt awakened and alarmed, almost every Sunday night, in returning from the preaching of John Ryerson, William Slater, Isaac Bateman Smith, David Culp, Henry Ryan, and David Youmans, in the Methodist Chapel. For, let people denounce "hell-fire" preaching as much as they like, it was always alarming sermons which aroused me the most. I almost always said to myself, while under the sermon, " I will be better ; I will repent and turn to God ;" but no sooner had I joined the men and boys in our rooms at Mr. Ketchum's, than their play and jokes drove away my resolution, and I said to myself, " Not to-night ; I will take another week of sinful pleasure, and I will surely turn to God, and begin a religious life next Sunday night." But, alas ! the following Sunday evening the same causes had the same effects, and I put off my repentance again. Thus did " procrastination prove the thief of time," and I had lost a whole year, and stood on the brink of ruin from day to day.

Although it will break the continuity of my story a little, and make it perhaps a little too long, I must relate one occurrence, for I can nowhere tell it so well. One Sunday afternoon, in 1823, I went to the old meeting-house, at what we now call the corner of King and Jordan streets (although there were no minor streets intersecting the block at the time, nor for several years after) accompanied by John Jones, sometimes a sort of evil genius to me. Some minister, whose looks did not impress themselves on my memory, preached. Another preacher was seated in the long, wide pulpit, who at the close of the sermon arose to give an exhortation—something which was then invariably given, if there was anybody to give it. I perceived that he had but one leg of bone and flesh— the other was of wood, and shod with iron—whom I did not then know, though I had heard of him, but afterwards knew him well, and learned to distinguish him as Thomas Harmon, the hero of Queenston Heights. The exhorter soon became very impassioned, stamping his wooden leg the while on the pulpit floor; and denounced hell and damnation, in no measured terms, against all impenitent sinners, in a most piteous voice; but he did not forget to press the weary and heavy laden to come to Christ, and welcome, then and there. His address impressed me so much, that I could scarcely conceal my intense emotion; at length he flung himself on the pulpit, and with hands stretched out and brought together, as if grasping after something, he cried out, with a voice quivering and vibrating with emotion, "Oh! ye hell-bound souls!" I felt as if I were just falling into perdition, and the man of God was grabbing after me! I quaked to my inmost soul, and left the house after the service very much solemnized. After we had passed out of hearing of the dispersing congregation, wishing to bring on some serious conversation with my companion, I remarked to Jones, "That was a good old man that exhorted." With an expression of ridicule and contempt, he burst out, "Ah! he's an old fool!" That scoffing utterance was enough to scatter all my soul-concern for that time, and the following week was passed in sin and folly like all the others, and from week to week for about three-quarters of a year.

But I must return to that Sunday night, in May,

1824, in the wood-shed with the tracts. I said to myself, "I will put off no longer; and whatever others may say or do, I will save my soul. That night I went alone and prayed; and prayed henceforth every day, not less than twice, but often three, four, five times, and even oftener in a day. But I think it will require another section before I have passed over the crisis which I always considered as my conversion.

No. XXXII.

MY LAST ACCEPTED DRAM.

IN my early days nearly every one drank a little, more or less, and the young as well as old. Professors of religion did not see the evil of giving and accepting treats, so long as it did not result in visible intoxication; and if it did once in a while result in that, it was considered an accident from miscalculation of the strength of the liquor, or their own "strength to mingle strong drink." I might say, in passing, that about the time of which I was writing I was sent by my master on a certain evening with a message to one of his neighbours, Elder D——, an old Scotch gentleman, and one of the elders of the newly-organized Presbyterian Church, with whom Rev. Mr. J——, an old Presbyterian minister from the country, very Scottish, was a guest. He was sometimes a guest at Mr. K.'s, but I suspect, for certain reasons, he preferred lodging at Elder D.'s. To deliver my message, I was shown into the room where the two Scotch seniors were in animated conversation. Vision was almost totally obscured with tobacco smoke, and the atmosphere was redolent with the fumes of hot whisky, while the punch-bowl sat between them on the table. They were not drunk, in the sense of drunkenness which then obtained:

> "They'd ta'en enough to make them canty,
> They were na' fu', but just had planty."

Judging from the fervour of their language, they might have been deeply engaged upon "the doctrines of grace."

But this is aside from the design of this story. Although I had never been taught to refuse a glass, from the moment I was resolved to save my soul I saw, intuitively, that drinking in any degree was incompatible with what was now my paramount purpose. The satisfaction produced by drink was not the sort of comfort my hungry and thirsty soul hankered after; yet in a moment of weakness and shame-facedness, I took a glass, to my deep sorrow and repentance.

Mr. Ketchum owned a small rough farm about three miles out of town, on the west side of Yonge Street, which, under the inspiration of the loyalty he cultivated, he called the "Wellington Farm." It was sown and planted under his own supervision; and a man, one Halliday, lived in the farm-house, who had the year before often worked with us in the establishment in town, where he and I were fellow-labourers and partial to each other. There was also a young man, Samuel Tivy by name, who had joined the Methodist

Church a few months before me, but "having no root in himself," he soon fell away. A short time after I set out, I spoke to him of my purposes; it touched him—he lifted up his voice and wept—confessed his faults, and the next Tuesday night he returned to class with me. Nevertheless, his persuasions led me to act, not only against my convictions, but also against my preferences. On the morning referred to, he and I were despatched to the Wellington Farm. I drove the horse and cart with a load of seed for the field, I think oats and potatoes; and Samuel drove a team of horses with a waggon containing a plough and harrow. We had luncheon with us, and the programme was, that he was to hold the plough, while I drove, and Halliday, perhaps, to plant the potatoes. My religious purpose was of recent origin, and, as yet, I had but little faith and courage, and especially I wished to conceal my change of mind from my late fellow-worker. When we arrived, he brought out his tin flask, and offered us a dram, and Tivy accepted it. My turn came next, but I hung back and refused, and would a thousand times had rather not accept, but Tivy urged the usual reasons assigned in that day, "A little will not hurt you," and Halliday looked so surprised, that I who had so often readily taken it with him should decline, that, fearing he would discover a secret which I had resolved to keep from him, I swallowed the poisonous bait. My meditations coming out had been of a religious character, and very tranquilizing; but presently the fumes of the liquor flew to my head and spoiled all my pious feelings. I kept away from the house and went on with my work in a very uncomfortable state of mind. At noon, I ate my luncheon of bread, and went out into the woods, where I tried to regain my communion with God. And I then and there formed the resolute purpose not to touch another glass of ardent spirits; and I received strength to keep my purpose, giving up whisky, rum, shrub, peppermint, beer, and cider, and because of its resemblance in looks to intoxicating drinks, I also eschewed the harmless spruce, or root beer, which the mistress used to brew every summer with the notion that it would "purify the blood." This was at least six years before the "Old pledge" was adopted, and ten, perhaps, before the formation of Teetotal Societies. The position I then took was an effectual and very necessary safeguard to me. It is likely this subject will fall in my way again. Religion, logically followed up, leads of itself to total abstinence; but without religion, it is very hard to persevere in the way of temperance.

I corrected my error, and spent a very happy week, almost wholly alone, carting manure from near where the little Episcopal Church now stands, opposite Mount Pleasant Cemetery, to the farm above mentioned. Deep and solemn were the thoughts revolving in the travailing heart of that uncouth young carter there, far from the haunts of polished society. What the travail issued in my next two sections will tell.

No. XXXIII.

HOW I CAME TO GO AMONG THE METHODISTS.

THE first person to whom I unfolded my purpose to serve God was my poor mother; and I did so at the first opportunity. I have said it was on a Sunday night I formed the deliberate purpose to lead a new life. The next day I was sent by my employer with the horse (faithful "Old Mink") and cart to do some errands through the town, such as I had to attend to nearly every day—namely, to call at the market, and several slaughter-houses, particularly that of Mr. Thomas Bright, at the corner of Ontario and Duke Streets, for whom Mr. Ketchum had a great regard, for what were called the "green" hides, in contradistinction to "dry" ones. But on my way to those places I must needs call at my mother's, who had then a temporary abode on the south-east corner of King and Sherbourne Streets, and avow my newly-formed purpose to my best earthly friend. She came out to the gate to meet me, and before we parted I said, "Mother, I am determined to set out and serve God and try to save my soul." It was like life from the dead to her poor withered heart. After referring to the cheering fact that Nathaniel, the next older than I, had taken up prayer at his bedside each night and morning, she said, "Well, John, your father is not a man to look after you; go and join the Methodists, you will find friends among them." I promised, and drove off with a resolute heart.

How I managed to get through that week among the wild men and boys in our large establishment, I can hardly tell; but I kept myself as much as I could apart from the rest, read my Bible and such grave sort of books as fell within my reach. I almost always had a book of some kind on my person and improved every leisure moment. There was one lad—not of our establishment, but often there—between whom and myself there was a great attachment, whom, because of that familiarity, I feared to meet, not feeling pluck enough to avow my purpose to my old companions, and I made several dodges to avoid meeting him; but a few days after it was unavoidable. I was walking by the side of the horse I was driving, whose heavy load prevented me driving rapidly away, when I saw my erstwhile friend bearing down upon me with eager pleasure in his countenance at the prospect of meeting me after our longer than usual separation; he rushed towards me with, "Well, John, how are you?" In answer, I said abruptly, "Well, Jem, I'm determined to reform my life, and try to save my soul." It seemed to afford him great pleasure, and he chimed in at once, "And so will I, John, try to be religious, too." Poor fellow! there was now a new tie between us, a tie which has never been severed.

But to return to the place where I lived. My serious reading was taken notice of, and some of the boys said, "John is becoming very religious." One of the hired girls, Margaret Magar, an obliging creature, for whom I had always a kindly feeling, one day when I was assisting her in doing something which she could not very well do alone, said, in a way to elicit my confidence, "John, have you any notion that you are going to die soon?" "Why, no; what makes you ask me that?" "Why, the boys think you must have some idea that you are going to die, or you would not be so serious, and be reading the Bible so much." I disclaimed any premonition of death, but said that I was resolved to try and be ready for death when it did come, as all are exposed to death. Not many months after, that young woman came and joined the society class to which I belonged; and when I travelled my first circuit her house was one of our stopping-places in our monthly rounds. She still survives, a venerable and much respected widow at the head of an affluent household, all of whom are members and supporters of our Church in the rising town of Alliston, now rejoicing in the name of Mrs. Fletcher.*

---

* Since the above was in print, Mrs. F. passed away in holy tranquility.

During that first week I was surprised into the last profane word I ever allowed myself to utter, the result of an evil habit. I was riding old Mink to pasture, barebacked, with nothing to hold or guide him but a halter, when, suddenly turning a corner, he was set upon and frightened by a dog, which angered me so, that I bestowed at least one word of abuse upon the cur, which I instantly felt defiled my mouth, and repented of, and, through the grace of God, never allowed myself to use again. Thus did I bid farewell to foul language forever.

The next Sunday I met my brother Nathaniel at our mother's, and with many tears stated my purpose to him, which he was prepared to approve, for he had started one or two weeks before me. He told me he had been at class-meeting, and asked me to accompany him the next Tuesday evening. We tried to improve that Sabbath in attending the meeting-house on King Street. The circuit preachers were absent at the second of the two famous camp meetings held in the Township of Ancaster, and we listened to exhorters, who declined entering the pulpit. The one for the morning was John Huston (from the country), afterwards a travelling preacher; and the one for the afternoon, "Willie Clarke," a gifted young Irishman, who, however did not wear his piety very threadbare, but many years after gave a son to the travelling ministry, a very devoted man, who died early.

To fulfil my engagement about going to class on

Tuesday evening, and yet not be observed by my fellow-boarders, I slipped out supperless when they went in to tea, turned up Newgate Street (now Adelaide) to Bay Street, till I saw my brother coming over the commons. We met and walked together to the class-leaders's (Mr. Patrick's) door. The class that evening was very small—nearly all the more lively and prominent members (and there were only about *thirty* in all,) were still absent at the camp meeting—perhaps eight or nine at the most. Mr. Doel "met" the class, and I was impressed and thrilled by everything I saw and heard. The manner in which they received my impassioned declaration of purpose—the testimonies of all—the psalms and hymns and spiritual songs by which they "taught and admonished" each other— were all touching and exciting to me. But I was most of all impressed by the way poor John Richards, himself a poor "Ready-to-halt," seized my hand after we had got out into the road, and exhorted me with tears never to imitate his early backsliding from his first love among the Baptists, when a boy in England. Though a man of sorrowful spirit, he was most blameless in life and conversation.

During the conversation which took place between John Richards and my brother (who were of the same trade, and well acquainted,) that evening in the road, I heard them speak in glowing terms of admiration of the deep piety and intense devotion of a young man, now absent with others at the camp-meeting, who had been a member of the Church about three months. When the opportunity offered I naturally clave to such a one, and met with the utmost condescension from him, though fully ten years older than myself. We lived hard by each other, and were destined, on the evenings when there were no meetings, and often after the society meetings were over, to go out of the town, either up Yonge Street or Dundas Street, and thence into the woods, sometimes in winter as well as summer, and for hours to pour out our souls to God in prayer, and to each other in Christian communion. Great was the benefit I received from that heavenly-minded young man. That was John Russell, whom I portrayed as an "Early Classmate," in the pages of my first work, "Past and Present."

For four weeks I met in class with dear William Patrick, without being formally received on trial (as the usage then was), or my name being inscribed upon the class-book. The quarterly love-feast was approaching, and the actual members received their tickets, without which they would not be permitted to enter. The love-feast as was most common then, was to be before the eleven o'clock service on Sunday morning; the doors to be opened at half-past eight, and closed at nine. The leader said to me, "John, you have no ticket of admission; but I will keep the door, and if you are there by the time I unlock it, I will let you in." I was there a full hour before the time, sitting upon a log not far off, employing the interval in reading my New Testament and Hymn-book, with which I had provided myself, and always carried on my person. (The Hymn-book I read consecutively through, as much by course as the Bible.) At length the leader approached down the road; I rose to my feet and went to meet him; he opened the door and let me in. When the speaking began I declared my purposes. At the close, the church door was opened for the admission of members, by the "preacher in charge," Rev. John Ryerson, giving an offer to any who "wished to join on trial," "to stand up." Nathaniel and I arose, the only ones who did, and our names were taken down, after an appeal had been made to the members, and we were accepted by show of hands, a usage which should never have been dropped. At the close of the love-feast, the Lord's Supper was administered, and we joined in the Holy Communion for the first time. That ever memorable and pregnant event occurred in June, 1824, *fifty-seven* years ago, when I lacked about two months of fifteen. A tie was then created, which, thank God, has never yet been severed, and I trust it never shall.

We had no presiding elder, as was usually the case, that day, but dear old Father Youmans acted as elder, it being what was then called "only a temporary quarterly."

No. XXXIV.

THE CRISIS I HAVE ALWAYS CALLED CONVERSION; AND WHEN, WHERE, AND HOW IT TOOK PLACE.

I FORMED the purpose to seek and serve God in the month of May, 1824; went to class-meeting a fortnight or so after; and about four weeks after that attended a love-feast, and was received on trial for membership in the Church. I found a happy difference between a religious and an irreligious life. My meditations of God were sweet; and sweet were the "drawings from above." Sometimes I thought I had a true Christian experience, and even professed it; at least others might have understood me so. But then I had feelings and thoughts of a different kind. I felt at times a great sense of darkness and depression, and I could scarcely tell why. I had heard that death was pleasant to the thought of a Christian; but "through fear of death, I was still subject to bondage." I said, "If it be so with me, indeed, why am I thus?" I read several extraordinary experiences, in which the subjects spoke ot seeing heaven open, and Christ upon the cross. That I had not seen, and concluded I was not converted. I foolishly sought for evidences or grounds of hope in my own inward experiences, and found none. Next I began to look out of myself, but not, as I should have done—to Christ by the eye of faith—but with the eye of the body, for signs and wonders, and portents in the sky; and resolved to accept of nothing short of that, that I might have a thrilling experience to relate. To gain it, I wept, and groaned, and fasted, till my countenance became haggard, and my eyes were swollen in my head, insomuch so that those around me noticed it. I became disappointed, dissatisfied, and even vexed and grieved with God, because he did not hear my cries. I was inclined to lay the blame on Him.

I used to remain to the Sunday noon class, as well as go to the one on Tuesday nights. It had a very inefficient leader (James Hunter, no great credit to the cause), and was, therefore, usually met by the preacher who had occupied the pulpit immediately before. On one of these occasions, when the Rev. John Ryerson was both preacher and leader, I complained—with a burdened heart, and with floods of briny tears—that "I *had* '*asked*,' and *had not* '*received;* I *had* '*sought*,' and *had not* '*found*,'" as if charging God with promise-breaking. The leader reminded me of Saul of Tarsus, who was three days in distress of soul, and thus tried to comfort me; yet little comfort did I accept; I thought if I could but get far enough away from the haunts of men, where I could use my voice in supplication to its utmost extent, it might ease my agony of soul. After dinner, if indeed I took any, I passed up Yonge Street, and about where Elm Street is now I turned westward into the woods, and getting into a thicket behind a tree, I fell on my knees and began to pray and cry, yea scream! while the tears streamed down my cheeks till my throat ached with pain, but no comfort came. While I was thus employed, a familiar voice accosted me; it was that of my childhood's friend, Edward Glennon, accompanied by a number of lads and young men. They had been seeking amusement abroad during the Sabbath hours, and hearing my cries they had come towards the place. Edward said, "John, what are you doing there?" "Ned, I am doing what you ought to be doing—asking God to have mercy on my soul." "Well," said he, "you need not pray so loud." Rising from my knees, I said, "I will go where I can pray as loud as I like," and rushed still farther into the thicket. But I returned to the chapel at night as sad as I left in the morning. I heard that Neddy said, "John Carroll had been a good fellow," he was "sorry he had turned hypocrite."

But gradually I became more calm, and wisely determined not to prescribe a way to God; and looked for comfort in the ordinary means. Sometimes I thought I found the promises sweet, but still it was a question. Have I *received* the pardon which I know Christ purchased by His blood? Often and often did I repeat the verse which says:—

> " 'Tis a point I long to know;
> Oft it causes anxious thought;
> Do I love the Lord or no?
> Am I His or am I not?"

The day of deliverance, however, was near. The month of August had come, and with it Conference. Our circuit preachers, Revds. John Ryerson and William Slater, were away. A supply was provided for the York pulpit for that day from a neighbouring circuit—the "New Settlements," embracing nine or ten townships to the north-west of the town—as it proved a junior, who had been travelling the previous year under the direction of the presiding elder. I had gone, as usual, to the chapel timely, before the hour of preaching, and after kneeling had seated myself on one of the short seats to the right of the pulpit, where the male members generally sat, facing the sisters on the other side, and was occupied, as was my wont, in reading my Testament, or hymn-book, when a stranger in the garb of a preacher (with dark frock coat of some thin coarse material, and a broad-leafed hat in his hand) passed before me, groping his way up the pulpit stairs. He was medium-sized, rather coarse-featured, with coarse brown hair, freckled both on face and hands, with a meekly, stooping carriage. He kneeled a while in silent prayer, and then rose and commenced the service. His manner was solemn and subdued, but he read well, and his voice was strong, clear, and flexible, and very pleasant to hear. By the way he held the book to his face, it was evident he was very short-sighted; and his accent was slightly Irish. His prayer lifted us heaven-ward at once, and the poor seeking boy among the rest. His text, Gal. iii. 13, " Christ hath redeemed us from the curse of the law, being made a curse for us," was fundamental, and graciously timely for me. I thought it was the ablest sermon I had ever heard; or rather, I thought not then of the sermon as a performance, but of its theme or subject. I forgot my sorrows and perplexities. Indeed, I thought not of any kind of introspection—I was looking outward and upward; and, without knowing it, "looking unto Jesus." I was, unconsciously believing upon Him with my heart unto righteousness; and thinking that if I had a thousand souls, I could cast them all upon Him. I had an encouraging story to tell in class; and went home and to Sunday-School, oh! so very happy.

That evening the stranger preached again, with equal sweetness and power. His morning sermon was on the work done *for* us; in the evening, it was the work to be wrought *in* us, from the words, "Except ye be converted, and become as children, ye can in no case enter the kingdom of heaven." Matt. xviii. 3. His description of a convert so exactly tallied with what I felt, that I said to myself, "Sure enough, I AM converted!" In the morning I received the witness of God's spirit; after the evening sermon, I had the witness of my own spirit. How truly did I now go on my way rejoicing!

I afterwards heard that it was the Rev. Rowley Heyland, who had been thus made the instrument of leading me to Christ. He was ever afterwards my favourite preacher, of all those in the Connexion. I loved the very ground upon which he walked. And had Rowley Heyland been as studious as he might have been; more attentive to his person and the minor proprieties; and if he had never become committed to the management of property acquired by marriage, he would have had few equals and no superiors. As it was, all his life, and it was a long one, he preached, from time to time, with the Holy Ghost sent down from heaven. It was characterized, ever and anon, by what the old preachers used to call "shocks of power."

A few weeks after my conversion, through the effect of a sermon by Father Youmans, I received a further blessing—a persuasion that God had cleansed my inmost heart. What I experienced in those days prepared me to receive the testimony of Scripture relative to God's speaking to holy men of old. With Paul, I truly felt that God had "revealed his Son in me." I assuredly "tasted the good word of God," and "felt the powers of the world to come." When I arose in the morning, it seemed as if all creation was praising the Fountain of Beneficence; and when I laid my head on my pillow at night, it would have delighted me if I had possessed the assurance that I should never open my eyes on this material creation more. Surely it is proof of the supernatural and the divine that an uncouth, unlettered boy was so illuminated and so blessed!

> " Should all the plans that men devise,
>   Assault my faith with treacherous art,
> I'd call them vanity and lies,
>   And bind thy Gospel to my heart!"

No XXXV.

WHAT MODICUMS* OF KNOWLEDGE I POSSESSED AT FIFTEEN, AND HOW I HAD STUMBLED INTO THEIR POSSESSION.

I SPEAK mainly in this section of such kinds of knowledge as belong to what is usually called education or learning. But as there can be no knowledge where there is no mind, no intellect, to hold it (for an imbecile, an idiot, can have no knowledge) therefore a retrospective inquiry into the process by which knowledge has dribbled into a young mind will naturally involve, to some extent at least, the discovery of its gradual development.

I have said in other parts of this book that the

---

* The hypercritical, watching for evidences of the old itinerant's illiteracy, may say, "Modicums is Latin, and its plural is modica." Well, may not extraneous words become so domesticated, as to conform to English modes of inflection. I suppose Shakespeare knew English, if he did not know Latin. He says:—

"What modicums of wit he utters."

faculties of attention and memory in me showed themselves very early by comparing notes with others; I now think, earlier than in most children. It was noticed at home, that I took learning easy, and that it was a pity that I could not have opportunities for a liberal education. About 1820, when I was ten or eleven years of age, some respectable people occupied for a time an unfinished upper part of a house belonging to my brother Thomas, on their way to settle beyond Lake Simcoe. A lady of that company, then a young married woman, Mrs. Charles Partridge, informed me, full fifty years afterwards, that my paternal-hearted brother, Thomas (of course, unknown to me) had spoken to them of his little brother John's readiness to take learning, and his own regret of his inability to furnish him with the means of gaining such an acquisition as he had a capacity for receiving.

But I am proceeding too fast. I began with the intention of trying to recall the first little glimmerings of light which shone in on the morning twilight of my infant mind. I must have become acquainted with the meaning of words earlier than most children. I can remember, that during the excitement and alarm attendant on the inroads of the American Indians at the house of Mr. Lawrence at the Cross Roads, mentioned elsewhere, in 1813, when I could not have been more than four years old, that when Mrs. Cassidy knocked away the fusee pointed at the breast of the wounded Corporal Smith lying on the floor, and exclaimed, "Don't murder the man in the house!" that, from my defect of hearing, which must have shown itself thus early, I thought she said, "Man of the house," and instantly thought "he is not the man of the house—Mr. Lawrence is the man of the house." So early had I picked up the meaning of a colloquialism, which, I suspect, children of that age do not usually know how to apply.

I think I knew how to repeat the days of the week, consecutively, about the age of five, and soon after the months of the year. Soon after that, I began to learn to count; but I think I had not attained to the ability to count a hundred till some time later still. Beyond the number ten, I think it was not so much a matter of arbitrary memory as of reasoning and reflection. Reflection taught me, that after ten, it was merely a repetition of the same process, the two, three, four, five, and so on, being repeated again. After a while it dawned upon me, that twenty, thirty, forty, fifty, sixty, seventy, eighty, and ninety were a development of one, two, three, etc.; or twos, threes, and fours of tens.

I learned my letters at home without a teacher, perhaps, with some assistance from my next older brothers; although I am sure it was the prompting of curiosity which led me to seek to find out; and by myself I learned to combine the letters and spell out a sentence in the New Testament, or among the hymns at the back of it. I was not six years old when I could perform this exploit, of which I was very proud.

Just about this time a hawker came to the door with trifles of various kinds to sell, and for "a York shilling," as seven-pence halfpenny was then called, we purchased a very small primer, which among other little matters, gave the length of the several months in a little rhyme to help the memory, thus:—

> "Thirty days hath September,
> April, June, and November;
> All the rest have thirty-one,
> Excepting February alone,
> Which claimeth just eight and a score;
> But in every leap year we give it one more."

This I immediately learned, and thenceforth was able to determine the length of any given month; and to this day I have no other way of determining.

The following winter, there being no school handy for us little ones, Mrs. Glennon, the Doctor's widow, who lived in the other end of the same house as the one in which we lived, who had received a fair education when young, and who had ample necessity for anything she could make, was persuaded to set up a school in her own place, and commenced with a good many little children and growing girls—indeed some of the latter were young women for size—and four of our family were sent to her school; but I now suspect, I derived no benefit from that first attempt in the scholastic line. Our teacher had no experience or tact in teaching. And she was totally without skill or authority to govern a school. She never could govern her own children, three at least of whom were in that school. She was a very small person, and the big boys and girls treated her with contempt, and none so much so as her own eldest daughter, Theresa, a very hoydenish girl. One day "Trase" became utterly unmanageable, and set her mother at defiance. Indeed, the latter confessed she "could do nothing with her." Upon this, a stout, strong, young woman, by the name of Ann Skinner, a step-daughter of the late Mr. Senclair, long of the Don Mills, sympathizing with Mrs. Glennon (for the school was now wholly demoralized) offered her services to punish Theresa, and received permission, and commenced operations with a will. But the refractory girl had no disposition to submit patiently. Besides what she lacked in strength, she made up in natural fighting qualities. So that it soon became a rough and tumble battle through the room, over benches, tables, and chairs, and on to the bed, which stood in the corner, the curtains of which (duly emblazoned with Bluebeard and his wives) were pulled down. It ended in a sort of drawn battle, Theresa getting a pretty thorough slapping and Miss Skinner getting a punch in the eye which left it painful and inflamed, and I suspect blackened in the end—a pity for the young lady, for she was a very comely person, and not undeserving. She afterwards married Mr. John Hayes, the "Jack Hayes" of the young men's nomenclature.

The reader will expect to hear that an academy

conducted on such eclectic principles could hardly sustain itself long, and that it soon collapsed, thus giving me a long college vacation; which was no great interruption of my improvement, as the reader will surmise, when I tell him I was taught, in spelling the word Aaron, instead of saying "double a-r-o-n," to say "big A, little a, r-o-n—Aaron." Reverence at least was taught by our Roman Catholic preceptress, which was to bow our heads when we pronounced the name of Christ.

I went no more to school until "our boys" had returned from the war, which school opened the summer I was six years old. It was taught by the Mr. Barber I have already mentioned, the husband of Miss Kendrake, the granddaughter of Lord Rodney. This school also was set up at my parents' solicitation. Mr. Barber was a slender person, who had lost some of the fingers from one hand, which constituted a justification of his natural indisposition to work. Before the school enterprise, he had been, I think, a sort of auxiliary of George Carey, who ran a sort of stage from York to Niagara, that I think was hauled off when the war closed. Barber wanted employment; he had some little education, and a school was needed in our section of the town for those who did not attend the District Grammar School, which was mostly appropriated by the descendants of the Family Compact. "Old Judd" taught a school in the east end of King Street; but a school was required to succeed one which had been taught by an old gentleman by the name of Bennett, held near the junction of Richmond and Yonge Streets, in his own residence, who for some reason had given up. Mr. Barber opened near the same spot, in a longish, low room, painted red, with a long front window, which building had been used by a person known as "Old Goff," as saddle and harness-maker's shop, who, I think, about that time went to "the shades" by drink, as nearly every fourth or fifth person did in those days. The property around that corner had belonged to a Mr. Chesney, a man of some substance, who died and left a wife, known for a time as the Widow Chesney, during whose widowhood things were going to wreck. But about the time it came much under our notice, a bachelor Scotchman, by the name of Drummond, came to the place, courted and married the widow and the property; set up his business of carpenter, joiner, and builder, and put the whole premises in a thorough state of repair. He lived and died a man of respectability and substance.

There was a large school made up of young people of various ages, from toddling infancy, almost up to adult years. Five of our family went there, including Tom, a great favourite among the young ladies for his good looks and gallant ways, who was trying to remedy the hiatus in his school studies created by his two years' service in the "Flying Artillery." Mr. Ketchum sent four pupils, Miss Love, his step-daughter; Miss Polly, his own eldest daughter, (then very beautiful);

Miss Fidelia, afterwards Mrs. (Rev. James) Harris; and William, then simply known as "Sonny Ketchum." Hiram Street, son of Mr. Timothy Street, afterwards the founder of Streetsville, a buckish boy of sixteen or seventeen, was there all the way from the Niargara River. A very popular young fellow, not much older, by the name of John Cameron, attended there, who went from home for a time, learned to drink, came back a sot, and died in a cart, about the age of twenty or twenty-five, in which he was being conveyed from the street, where he was picked up in a state of destitution, to the hospital. Allan Jeffrey was there, a very fine lad in disposition and looks, who lived where Yorkville now stands, his father's the only house in the place.

I was a great favourite with the teacher, and was never punished by him except once, when my little brother, our unfailing companion—Ned Glennon—and myself, had the misfortune to underestimate the strength of one of Mr. Drummond's broad boards, on which we were "teetering," which broke beneath our weight. Mr. Drummond complained, and we were feruled on our right hands. The others cried, but I boasted that I never winced. I suspect the master favoured me. That was my only punishment during the whole of my school-life anywhere.

I learned to read and spell, and was at the head of the second class. I seldom missed a word in those days, which was more than I could say in after years. Spelling well is the fruits of drill, which must be gone into thoroughly, early and long. But, alas! interruptions came, and I found it hard to surmount the effects.

Early in the autumn we had a great spelling match between our school and Mr. Judd's. It was a regular challenge, I think, from Mr. Judd, whose strong point was spelling, duly prepared for, and came off on a certain sunny day. We assembled at the Red School House,—were duly drilled,—charged as to how we were to behave, marshalled, and marched in procession down the road which formed the boundary between the town and the adjacent farms, which we now know as Richmond and Duchess Streets, till we reached the corner of Duchess and Ontario Streets, but that we did not do continuously; for, if I remember right, at Sherbourne Street we made a detour northwards into what we now call Queen, went down that street to Ontario, when we turned south, to a sort of avenue, or bower, formed by parallel rows of cherry-trees on the northern corner of the Ridout property, the use of which was granted to the schools for the spelling match, a spot which is yet without houses. Only the first class on each side was brought into action, which some of the best spellers in the lower classes regretted. Furthermore, that class itself was winnowed to leave out doubtful ones. But, as far as our side was concerned, the selections were not all judicious; a girl by the name of Betsey Hardy, who had afterwards a not very enviable history, was, through the master's partiality retained, and by her frequent failures brought us defeat. Besides, Mr. Barber was hardly the man to cope with such a determined old pedagogue as Judd. They took turns in giving out spellings, and what word failed on one side passed to the other, while all the failures were duly registered according to a system agreed on before hand; but where there was any difference of opinion, Barber had not pertinacity enough for Judd, and acknowledged our defeat. Many of the gentry of our little capital came to witness the display; and in the end, the scholars were rewarded or consoled by a treat of luscious peaches, and, if I rember right, cakes as well. That was the first of the only two school treats in which I remember to have been a participant. That was nearly sixty-five years ago.

While attending that school, I first heard the project of a Sunday-school from the lips of its first Missionary in Canada, the Rev. Thaddeus Osgood, who addressed us, and offered the first prayer I ever heard, by both of which I was solemnized and wept, hiding myself behind others to conceal my emotion and tears. The projected Sunday-school did not come into operation for four or five years to come.

The winter came. The school closed,[*] and my schooling was interrupted, during which I pretty nearly lost all I had gained; albeit I did con over the Testament from time to time, and a copy of Dr. Watts' "Divine and Moral Songs for Children," which consti-

[*] As an easy employment, our teacher adopted that of Bailiff.

tuted almost my only reading book. Often did I pore over—

> "The voice of the sluggard,
> I hear him complain," &c. ;

> "Let dogs delight to bark and bite,
> For God hath made them so," &c.

which, with others of a similar character, left no ill impression on my infant mind and heart. Once I received more commendation than I deserved, by helping out my mother and brother William in some discussion of theirs on the subject of our Lord's resurrection, by turning to a chapter on the subject which I had been spelling out by myself, and which, if tested, I fear was the only one I could have read intelligibly. I was then in the neighbourhood of eight years old. It was about that time I used to hear read the songs about Robinhood already referred to, but which I could scarcely say I was able to read myself, though I did afterwards.

The only schooling I received for nearly or quite two years thereafter was one fortnight, in which I took an older brother's place in Mr. Judd's school. His academy was conducted in the "Old Yellow House," quite an institution in its day. For a long time, there was the concession of a small lot on the corner of Ontario and King Streets for a market, though not built on for a long period after the time to which I refer. The yellow house came next eastward of the vacant lot, on

King Street. Who built and owned the house originally I know not; I know, however, it was owned and occupied for a dwelling by Dr. Stoyles after his second marriage (to Mrs. Matthews). It had at one time been one of the most pretentious houses in the infant town. It was only a story and a half in height, with dormer windows in the roof, and one if not two bay windows below, facing King Street. It covered a good deal of ground both below and above. How it had come so early to be a hack for all purposes, I know not; but for many years the lower front rooms were rented for school purposes, and the upstair's apartments were rented as residences for the poor. For a long time it bore the name of being haunted; and one room, I know, which was used as "black hole" to confine refractory pupils in was dreaded for that reason by such hapless urchins as had the misfortune to be doomed to solitary confinement therein.* The wood, when there was any, was stored and chopped there. I say, when there was any, for there was sometimes a famine of that indispensable article; and then the scholars were turned out to gather fuel, consisting of roots and limbs of trees, old knots, and bits of bark, to be picked in plenty in the Park, which began on the east side of Parliament Street, and, which, despite all the poaching by townspeople, was down to a much later period, covered with trees and logs.

* Eight or nine years after, a Methodist Society class met in that room.

Mr. Judd's method of teaching was characterized by the spelling, which was a large element in the exercises, being conducted in chorus, the good spellers leading, and the learners following, and all at the top of their voices, thus: l-e-g-e-r, leger; d-e, legerde; m-a-i-n; legerdemain. "The noise was as the sound of many waters," and could be heard for a great distance around. It suited the teacher well enough, for he was quite deaf; and it was fun for the children. And a great deal of this sort of drill made them ready spellers of, at least, all the words in the text book.

There was a stout boy at that school who gained an undesirable notoriety in after years. His name was William (usually called "Bill") Bastedo, some relative of Mr. Joseph Rogers, who had come from his country-home to learn the hat-making business; and it was thought desirable for him to receive schooling early, before he settled down to his trade. He was a kind of silent, diffident lad, and other boys, for a time, rather put upon him; but his temper proved to be hot when roused, and when he resorted to blows, (school boys' usual method of settling difficulties) then he proved to be possessed of unusual muscular strength and striking power. I remember he awed us all one day: a lad a head taller than himself, was asked a civil question by Bill, and gave an impertinent answer, upon which Bastedo, by a blow under the ear laid him flat on his face. This discovery was a misfortune to my hero, who thenceforth became a buffer and engaged in battles innumerable, in one of which encounters he broke a man's jaw. All sorts of dissipation followed in the train of this *penchant* for fighting, and issued in the waste of more than half his life. But the grace of God is greater than the strength of the pugilist. I was told, some seven or ten years ago, by a young relative of his that "Old Bill" was still alive, and had become a Christian and a Methodist, for which I felt thankful to God.

The following summer, that is in 1817, a large school was conducted in the same place by a new teacher, and I suspect a more competent one than any I have mentioned, a Mr. Castles, a Scotchman, not large, but determined enough to hold the biggest and most rebelliously inclined boy in subjection. Some of his "trainings" of those big ones, I remember. Our master boarded with Mr. Ketchum, who, I think I heard, received lessons from him out of hours. Mr. Castles was not an unkind man, and I confess I loved him, and believed I was a favourite with him. He was the first teacher I had known to pray with his school, which he did sometimes,—perhaps on Monday mornings. Saturday afternoons he taught the Church of England Catechism, to all whose parents desired it. Unhappily, my parents did not desire me to learn it, under the supposition, that all that related to "baptism," and "godfathers and godmothers" was inapplicable to me and my brothers, as we had never been baptized, much less had we ever had a godfather or godmother.

18

But I have deeply regretted the omission, since I have been able to understand how important and valuable it would have been to know that formulary, and especially to have committed to memory the Ten Commandments and the Apostles' Creed. The result of the omission was, I had to commit them to memory after I began to prepare for the ministry.

Before I dismiss the subject of "my schools and school-masters," to use a phrase of Hugh Miller's, I must not forget, in the interests of correct history, to tell that up to my ninth year, I never attended a school where geography (at least with maps) and grammar were taught; "the three Rs" constituted the curriculum, and the first R, so far, was all that I had learned. American books were largely used; for we had then no national ones of our own, nor for long afterwards. Webster's was our spelling-book, which displaced old English Dilworth, with his n-a, na; t-i, nati; on-nation. Something at which my "Britisher" father was furious, denouncing the tion *shuns*, in no moderate terms. The American Selections also largely displaced the noble English Reader of Lindley Murray as a reading-book. Selections to read and declaim on special occasions, from one or other of these books, constituted all the elocutionary training given, which did not leave any of us very finished elocutionists.

With the close of Castle's school, in the winter of 1817-18, at the age of nine and a half, my school-going almost wholly ended, until at the age of seventeen, I started anew and pursued a course on my own account. True, about the age of eleven, Mr. James Bigelow, a famous teacher before that, set me a few copies, taught me how to hold my pen, and showed me how to make the letters of the MS. alphabet. Also, did I not go one month, a little later to Mr. Appleton, a fierce English pedagogue, who never learned himself to place his aspirates aright; (he taught in Market Lane) and learned something of the first four rules of arithmetic. Furthermore, I was about as long, a year later, in Mr. Spragg's Central School, perhaps a little longer. But I never could "get the hang" of the Lancastrian system, employed therein. Drill and parade seldom do much for children; there must be more personal contact with the teacher's mind; and the child must have time to think out his lessons.

That was my last schooling for a long time, except what I learned at the Sunday-school, where, in those days, we did spell as well as read; and we learned much relative to the meaning of words, in which latter, by a kind of intuition, I excelled all of my own age. But then I was behind in spelling, and my teacher, Mr. Patrick, would not allow me to move down when I failed in that respect, on the ground, that "John," unlike the rest, "had to work instead of going to school." I thought out the etymology of many of the words I was taught to define afterwards, while at work by myself in the bush. · I have spoken of what books were accessible there. In town the year before my conversion, I read the whole of Cervantes' Don Quixote, and thought it the prince of story-books!

I might have continued to go to night-school, after I returned to town and got a place; but I was so far behind in school learning, that I was ashamed to be pitted against other boys, who had possessed greater advantages; albeit, I had read more books, and had quite as much general information as they. It was religion which stimulated my mind afresh and overcame this false shame, and it was a subsequent desire for the ministry, as I shall have to tell, which put me upon regular study.

Thus, when I was converted at fifteen, I could read pretty well, scrawl my name, and, by counting my fingers, do a sum in simple addition. I had a good many facts of history in my head; yet as I knew nothing of geography and chronology, they were in a pitiful jumble; and my blunders in story-telling, which then obtained as an amusement among boys, in which Arabian-like accomplishment I was conceded to excel, have seemed very ludicrous to myself since I became better informed—only that the remembrance has often covered my face with blushes. Oh! ignorance, what a humiliator thou art!

No. XXXVI.

MY BOYISH THOUGHTS OF A BUSINESS FOR LIFE, AND THE ONE I FINALLY CHOSE.

THROUGH the lowly situation of my friends and the sordid influence of my surroundings, I cannot say that I ever seriously thought of a liberal, or a learned profession, until it was too late to secure so elevated a prize. True, when I was very young, and off and on, till I was converted, my father's and brothers' war stories, and my own war experiences, made me sigh for the profession of arms; my idea being to begin as a common soldier, and to rise from the ranks to, of course, a command! That project, however, never advanced the first step towards realization.

I was noted, they said, from a child for arguing my own case, whenever my views were crossed, or I found myself in any disagreement with others; on which account they used to call me "the lawyer," and to say

I would do well in the legal profession. But, certainly, there was no serious thought of our moving in that direction, and if we seriously intended it, to all human appearance, the object was impossible of achievement to us. It would not have been a popular profession with us or our friends, if practicable, as a general opinion among us was that all lawyers were rogues, and it was next to impossible for them to be otherwise than such.

But one other liberal profession did once open to me in a form that was practicable; but I myself turned from it for want of interest. Just about the time the break-up in our family took place in the spring of 1822, when I was revolving the matter of going out to my brother in the bush, a physician, a near neighbour, who had observed my industrious habits, and that I had been brought up among horses, and furthermore, was told by mother that I had a good capacity for learning and was fond of books, if not of study, proposed to her, that I should come and live in his family, groom his horse, do his errands, and attend his office in his absence; and that he would furnish me with books, and teach me all that he knew himself—both preparatory and professional, and open my way into practice. Such a method was then not unusual. Students "studied with a doctor," as it was termed; went to New York, or some other distant place for lectures; came back and went before a board of medical examiners, and if approved, were licensed. Dr. McCaig, who made the proposal was not a haughty, stuck-up sort of man, but very plain and condescending, his practice being largely among the humbler classes, especially those of his own nationality —the Irish; and I have no doubt, that so far as non-pretentiousness was concerned, we would have got on together well enough; and yet, though largely the poor man's doctor, I have reason to believe he was well educated, both in general learning and that which related to his profession as the majority of physicians in his day, and better indeed, than a great many. He had the reputation of being very skillful. And had I then possessed the advanced views I held afterwards, I would have accepted his offer. But all my friends belonged to the operative classes in society, and any aspiration to anything higher, was like a desertion, if not a reflection, on them. We were all so narrow, as to think that *gentility* and *pride* were inseparable—a great instance of folly, but not the only one of which we were guilty. Besides, I had predilections for farming; and, just then, was all agog to go to the bush. By the choice I made, I escaped, especially as it was then conducted, one of the most slavish professions a human being could engage in. Besides, in not going to Dr. McCaig, I escaped something worse. He and his wife, I believe were Protestants, perhaps—as North of Ireland people often are—of Presbyterian proclivities; but whether, if I had gone with him (for he soon after went out on Yonge Street, near where Newtonbrook now stands), I would have come under those influences, which, two years after, led me to Christ, and four years after that again, into the ministry. Besides, not being converted, I would have stood a chance to go far in the opposite direction. If I had remained unconverted and continued to live in his family, I would have been almost sure to have become a drunkard, as so many in that noble profession (strange to say) have done; the Irish national beverage, whisky punch, was an institution with them; and I think I was informed, that poor McCaig's early death was largely due to drink. If true, it was a pity, for, from all I ever heard, he was a noble man. Alas! Alas! for the many mighty fallen! There is no telling what might have been, had I gone into medicine; but my good friend, Dr. James Brown, then of Peterboro', used to say to me, when he saw the energy and industry I put into the ministry, "Mr. Carroll, if you had been a doctor, you would have made a fortune."

A real aspiration of mine, of a semi-liberal kind, was more feasible, and might have been attained, if my friends had possessed discernment and reflection, or any energy been shown, or pains taken to plan for me, and then to carry their plans into execution—that was the career of *an artist*. I always had a quick eye for external appearances and a disposition to reproduce them. I very readily cut the profile of almost all visible objects in paper—especially, sheep, oxen, horses, dogs, and men; also, it was thought that I could draw them correctly on a slate, which I amused myself for hours in doing. And when that canvas was not wide enough I filled the great wide hearthstones with these rough cartoons; or the floor and walls of the house with crayon sketches in chalk. To sketch from nature seemed always to me one of the most desirable of accomplishments; and yet the opportunity of even attempting to learn it, did not occur till far on in life, when my engagements were too numerous to leave sufficient leisure for the necessary practice. As a trade, because of these tastes, I would have preferred that of painter to almost any other; only I did not like the idea of being suspended in midair painting the walls of a high house or a steeple. Otherwise, if I had once got into ordinary house and sign painting, it would have led to portraits and the finer parts of the art. But I never met the man to learn from, or the opening in any respect. I have in some measure indemnified myself for the loss, and gratified the graphic propensity in my mind by a great many pen-portraits and pictures of scenery as well as human persons. It would afford me pleasure now to furnish the letter-press for pictorial illustrations of books, and I have furnished some, but never done anything of that kind that paid me for my time.

Another fanciful attachment to an impracticable scheme, and one that would have been less beneficial to me than that of an artist was this. When I was about seven or eight years old, it was discovered, that while describing any scene between persons that I had witnessed, that I unconsciously personated the people I described; and that I had ready and accurate powers of mimicry. One of the first of these occurrences that I recollect was the appeal of "Mother Long," an affected old coloured neighbour, to Mr. Drummond, already mentioned, for assistance to get her "cross-grained little brat" (as she called him) of a son, John, free from the consequences of a case of *assault and battery* (or "salt and batry," as it used to be called,) brought against him by a Mr. Heward, who lived hard by, which struck them as so histrionic as to cause them great amusement, and they afterwards brought me forward to re-enact it for the amusement of visitors. These powers of mimicry often led those who knew me to say, that "John would make a good play-actor," and that I "ought to go on the stage." I always delighted in spectacular representations, and had I been trained, I might have made a *comic* actor at least. Whatever good elocutionary drill might have done me, play-acting would have ruined me as to morals and religion. Upon the whole, therefore, I have cause to be thankful, that no opening for following this bent occurred; albeit, I am sorry I never had the first lesson in elocution and declaiming in any school that I ever attended.

Having eliminated all the visionary schemes that flitted, for a short time before my fancy, I may say, I was shut up to some form of manual labour—either farming, to which I have said, I was partial—or a mechanical art. The prospect of a farmer's life, however, closed with my leaving my brother's; and I became a boy of all, or any work, about a tannery. When I was converted I was receiving the monthly wages of four dollars. At that wage I continued to work for one year after my becoming religious; and I now wish I had never sought any other relation; for my wages would have soon been increased, and would have gone on increasing every year as my strength and activity increased. And with increased wages, I might have done more for an old, infirm father and mother, and a blind brother whose only income was a pension of £20 ($80) a year; besides I might have saved something to educate myself. Many well-intentioned friends said I ought to learn a trade. Of these, the late Joshua Van Allen, a zealous young Methodist, then very influential in the junior circles of the York society, was especially forward and earnest. And as there was nothing so attainable as Mr. Ketchum's business, through my mother, between whom and him there was a great mutual respect, I applied and was accepted to learn the tanning and currying trade; and gave up the horse and cart, the hayfork and shovel; and took up the "flesher" and "worker," and in due time the "scouring brush," and "currying knife;" but then as I was supposed to be learning a business, I had to keep on at the wages I received when only fourteen; now I was sixteen and on to seventeen and over. The whole matter was against my convictions for all this time, there was not an hour I did not revolve in my mind the Christian ministry as a life-work. But that must be relegated to a separate article.

No. XXXVII.

A SUMMARY AND CONNECTION OF THE FORGOING STORIES.

I RELINQUISHED the idea of a continuous narrative—first intended, and even drawn up far beyond the period of my boyhood, for reasons assigned in the preface; in doing which, I have probably failed in leaving a correct succession of the events that transpired in my young life for the first fifteen years of my existence. To supply this lack to such as might be inclined to complain of it, I now furnish a digest and summary of the pen-pictures above exhibited, briefly supplying some omissions. Those who do not need any such presentation may skip this section.

The reader is hereby reminded that I was born of parents of unequal ages, a father of about sixty, and a mother about forty, the eleventh child, and the last but one, who was born half an hour after me, whom I have survived more than sixty years. I only just escaped being born in Fredericton, the capital of **New Brunswick**, to be brought into the world on Saltkill's Island in Passimmaquady, Bay of Fundy, N.B. A few days after my birth I removed across the Province line to Campo Bello Island within the State of Maine, U.S. At three weeks old, we went by a sailing vessel to New York; thence by a sloop up the Hudson to Albany; next in a springless lumber-waggon over, or through (literally through) execrable roads to Youngstown on the Niagara River. Then ferried across to Queenstown, U.C., where we remained till the following spring.

Lived about two years in the Niagara Country, mostly on the Ten Mile Creek—partly at the "Lower Ten," and partly at the "Upper Ten." Just as we were about to leave that region, somewhere near the Twelve, I lost by a cruel death my best and ablest brother, Joseph. Then, in sad desolation as a family, we proceeded by a toilsome journey to the Grand River country, where we lived in two several places— at Fairchild's Creek, and on an Indian farm belonging to Chief Davis, on the river bank in the heart of the Indian country.

In 1813, father joined the army, and trailed us out to Niagara, where we witnessed the battle, a fortnight after our arrival there. Mother and we, her four youngest children, escaped out of the town during the action, and fled to the Cross Roads, four miles away, and took up our abode at the house of Mr. George

Lawrence, where we remained a good part of the summer, until we were disturbed by an onset of American Indians. Upon which, we fled towards the interior, suffering great fatigue and hunger by the way—passing through the Black Swamp road, and spent the early part of autumn in the vicinity of the "Upper Ten" Mile Creek and the Twelve.

Our next removal was to Burlington Bay, where we lived, or existed—first in an unfinished house, then in a hole in the ground at the Heights, and next in a loft in what is now the centre of Hamilton City. With the removal of the army, we went to Queenston, where, for a time, we were a united family again, living over the military blacksmith's shop.

Early in the summer of 1814, father, mother, and the four youngest children, coasted around the Lake to York; where, after a short interval in and near the fort, we took up our abode in the town, in which we remained till the close of the war.

That town was the base of the family's operations so long as we held together as a family of any sort. My several places of abode after the war, till I went to the bush in 1821, were the corner of George and Duchess Streets; Duke Street, a short time; the corner of Bay and Richmond; near the corner of Richmond and John Streets; Adelaide, near York; and Duke, once more. And after returning from the bush, at Mr. Ketchum's, corner of Yonge and Adelaide, till my conversion and afterwards.

* A friend suggests that I may not live to produce the volumes promised to succeed this; and in that case the more important part of the story of my life will remain untold. In the event of my passing away, the reader may be told, that I began to exhort about one year and a half after my conversion; a short time after which, I left my business and spent about two years at school, and in teaching, during which period I exercised my gifts in public constantly—went out as a supply on a Circuit before I was nineteen, four years after my conversion—and have spent all the time since, fifty-three years, in some form or another, in the Christian ministry.

THE END.

BEN OWEN.

BEN OWEN

A Lancashire Story.

BY

JENNIE PERRETT.

"He that does good deeds here, waits at a table
Where angels are his fellow-servitors."

TORONTO:
WILLIAM BRIGGS,
78 & 80 King Street East.

1882.

CONTENTS.

CHAPTER.		PAGE
I.	Kept in	7
II.	Ben's Home	18
III.	An Evening Visit	25
IV.	Sam'l Hornby's General Shop	35
V.	A Bitter Disappointment	43
VI.	The Strangers	50
VII.	Mr. Henry Ashford's Refusal	57
VIII.	A Painful Discovery	62
IX.	In the Works	70
X.	New Year's Eve	79
IX.	At Liberty	87

BEN OWEN.

CHAPTER I.

KEPT IN.

THE heat had been intense all the day, for more than a week no rain had fallen; the grass in the fields, and along the roadside, was brown and scorched, the thirsty flowers in the gardens drooped upon their stems, only the tall sunflowers held their heads erect, and looked proudly up to the blue, cloudless sky.

The church clock of the village of Ashleigh had just struck four when a slight breeze arose, stirring gently the branches of the trees in the playground of the village school, and the birds that had been venturesome enough to build their nests there, peeped cautiously and expectantly around.

The breeze *might* mean that rain was coming, or it

might not; anyhow it was a new topic for conversation; there had been nothing but the heat to chatter about for some days past; so the birds chirped and twittered away, and the most weatherwise amongst them watched a tiny, white, fleecy-looking cloud passing along the sky.

Some one else as well as the watchful little songsters saw the first signs of the coming shower. A tall, stalwart man, who had been walking through the dusty lanes, and now came slowly up the street where there was no shade or shelter from the sun's burning rays, looked up, and as he saw the cloud, a grim smile of satisfaction passed over his hard, stern face. And a little girl who stood at the open door of the school, watching a butterfly with bright, coloured wings, saw the same tiny cloud, but it was no longer alone, others larger and darker were spreading themselves rapidly over the sky.

The child left her post, and hastened across the room.

"What is it, Nancy?" asked the schoolmaster kindly; "you may stand at the door a few minutes longer."

"Please, Mester Deane, it's comin'," said the child.

"What is coming, Nancy?"

"Please, sir, th' rain's comin'."

The schoolmaster went to the door, and looked up at the dark clouds.

"Yes, Nancy, you are right," he said, "we shall hav a heavy shower, and then the air will be cooler."

Mr. Deane rejoiced at the thought, for he had found the intense heat very trying.

It had certainly affected the children's conduct; they had been restless, fidgety, inattentive, and sleepy the whole of the day. More than one little head had fallen weariedly upon the desk, the book or pen had dropped from the tired hand, and certain unmistakable sounds had borne witness to the fact that for a time at least sleep had conquered any desire for knowledge.

Mr. Deane had not attempted to awaken the sleepers, he put the cushion from his chair under a little girl's curly head, and he placed another wearied child in a small recess near his own desk.

More than once he thought of dismissing his scholars early in the afternoon, and giving them an additional hour's instruction another day.

But the schoolmaster was a quiet, methodical man; with him each hour of the day had its allotted amount of work, and he shrank nervously from any deviation from the existing school routine.

Therefore, instead of closing before the appointed time, he exerted himself to the utmost to make the afternoon lessons as pleasant as he possibly could, and exercised an unusual amount of patience on behalf of his scholars.

They were troublesome and unruly, these children; almost unconsciously they had taken up the idea that a schoolmaster was a tyrant whom they were bound to outwit, and cheat, and conquer if they possibly could.

Some of them would have rebelled openly had they dared, or if they could have gained anything by so doing, at being obliged to attend a school at all. They were not so entirely to blame for this, as any one unacquainted with the facts of the case might have supposed them to be.

For the children knew what Her Majesty's Inspector who visited Ashleigh at certain times did not know, how some of the parents grudged the few pence weekly for "th' school wage." And also how they grudged still more the precious hours which bore no fruit, so far as they in their shortsightedness could see. The children knew, too, how they were kept at home on the faintest pretext of an excuse to help with the work of the household.

Still, parents and children had sense enough to know that it was useless fighting against the laws of the country. The Government had taken all children from collieries, factories, and workshops of every description into its own hands, and was fully prepared to carry out all it had undertaken.

But, if the Ashleigh children could not unsettle the Government, they could, *and they did,* make one of its representatives, in the form of the schoolmaster, very uncomfortable at times.

The village was a few miles away from busy, noisy Manchester, and some of the oldest inhabitants of Ashleigh could remember the time when the houses on the high road to the city were few and far between.

But the houses were very numerous now, and in the village itself whole rows of workmen's cottages had been built during the last few years for the accommodation of families who worked at the Ashleigh Calico-print Works.

To these Works, the calico woven in the cotton mills was brought, here it was bleached, and passed from the men working in the "dyehouse," "steaming" and "raising rooms," to the women and girls who did the "plaiting" and "folding," the "sewing" and the "marking."

When it left the warehouse placed in immense bales on large lurries it was no longer plain calico, but print of all colours and various patterns.

Some of the bales went direct to the Manchester market, and from thence all over the United Kingdom; and some went to Liverpool, and from thence across the broad Atlantic, and away to far distant lands.

The Print Works found employment not only for men and women, but also for children.

At the age of ten they could enter as "half-timers," working one part of the day, and attending the school the other part. Working among men and women, many of whom had not "the fear of God before their eyes," seeing and hearing much that was wrong; was it any wonder that the children soon lost the innocence of childhood, and that their finer feelings were dulled and blunted ?

Mr. Deane endeavoured to bear these facts in mind in all his dealings with his scholars. And on this hot summer afternoon, wearied as he felt, not one impatient word escaped his lips, and when he saw the gathering clouds he resolved to dismiss the children at once, so that they might reach their homes before the rain came. So he rang the bell, and gave the word of command, "All books closed."

At that very moment a little boy sitting on one of the back seats took a hard, green apple from his pocket, and deliberately threw it at a boy who was sitting on a form in front of him.

The apple went too far, it missed the boy, and hit the master instead.

Mr. Deane's pale face flushed; some of the children laughed, and looked round at one another, and then stared at the master, wondering what he would do.

They were not left to wonder long. Mr. Deane looked gravely at them, and said quickly, but firmly, "How many times have I forbidden you to throw anything across the schoolroom? Only a week ago one of the windows was broken by a ball, and the other day a little girl was hurt by an old knife thrown by a thoughtless boy; now, children, I ask you who has thrown this apple?"

All were silent for a few moments, then little Nancy's voice was heard.

"Please, Sir," she said, "yo' dunnot need to think as onybody throwed it *at yo'*, yon apple were na meant for yo'."

"I don't think it was, Nancy, it was intended to hit some one else, and I hope the boy or girl who threw it will at once tell me the truth. I would rather have a dozen apples thrown, and every window broken, than that one of you should tell me a lie!"

There was silence again, only broken by the ticking of the clock, and the patter of some raindrops on the stone step at the door; then came a dull, heavy sound like thunder in the distance.

A pale-faced lad about thirteen years of age started as he heard the sound; the master looked steadily at him, the boy *felt* rather than *saw* the look; his face flushed crimson, and his eyes sought the ground.

Naturally unsuspicious though he was, Mr. Deane felt certain that the lad had some knowledge of the point in question, and he was grieved at the thought; he liked the boy, and up to the present time had always found him truthful and obedient. He waited a little while, hoping that he would speak, then he said, "Ben Owen, did you throw that apple?"

The boy looked up then. "No, Sir," he replied.

But his eyes dropped again as soon as he had spoken, and the bright colour rushed to his face.

Mr. Deane was grieved and puzzled, and the children began to look impatiently towards the door.

"Ben Owen," asked the master, "can you tell me who did throw the apple?"

The boy raised his head, an earnest, beseeching look in his blue eyes.

"Did you hear my question?"

"Yes, Sir."

"Am I right in believing you know who threw that apple?"

"Yes, Sir."

"Who was it then?"

"Please, Sir, I canna tell yo'!"

"Very well, if you cannot, or rather you *will not*, tell me, you will be kept in after the others have left. Mind, children," added Mr. Deane, "I do not wish to encourage you to tell tales of one another, but I am determined that this dangerous practice of throwing things across the schoolroom shall be put an end to."

When the school was dismissed, a few boys lingered near the door, and Ben Owen went back to his own seat.

"Ben Owen," said the master, "I will leave you three sums to work while I am away, numbers ninety-one, ninety-two, and ninety-three; I will return presently. Run away home, boys," he added, as he locked the schoolroom door, and walked quickly away.

Ben Owen took from his desk his slate and book; as regarded his task he would rather have had a page of history or poetry to learn. He was not quick at figures, and the three sums given him meant for him an hour's hard work.

An hour's work! And his head ached and throbbed *now*; he had been up since five o'clock, in the Print Works by six, in the hot schoolroom all the afternoon;

he had behaved well himself, and had done his best in his quiet way to persuade the boys in his class to behave well too.

As he thought of this his mouth quivered, and he leaned his head upon his hands; there was no tormenting schoolfellow near to call him "a cry baby," the hot, burning tears fell fast now.

They fell upon his slate, rubbing out the figures he had just made. He pushed back his hair from his forehead; such beautiful hair it was, as fair and curly as that of any dainty drawing-room pet.

"I'm a brave soldier, I am," said Ben half aloud, as he commenced his sum again; "it is na such as me as will win th' prize. Th' Great Master did na stop to think about Himself when He were on earth, He had a world of trouble and died a shameful death for us, but we think we mun ha' no trouble, we're noan so ready to take up our cross and follow Him."

The rain was falling fast now, the wind had risen, the peals of thunder were long and loud, and the flashes of lightning bright and vivid.

The boy all alone in the large schoolroom looked up to the window nearest to him, and a bright smile passed over his face.

"It's a real storm an' no mistake," he said, "an' I'm glad now I've done as I have, poor little Jimmy is so feart of thunder, he would ha' shrieked if he'd been here alone, an' I'm noan feart mysen; it's all of God, whether it be thunder, or hail and tempest, or th' still small voice."

Ben applied himself with redoubled energy to his task.

Half an hour passed away; the storm was at its height now, the rain falling in torrents.

"It does na' stop," said Ben; "there's a mighty sight of water *outside*, I wish there were but a gill-pot full in here, I'm real dry, I am; what with th' heat an' th' dust I feel pretty near choking."

On the floor, by Mr. Deane's seat, just where it had fallen, lay the apple, the innocent cause of all the trouble.

The boy's eyes brightened as they rested on it; green and sour, and uninviting as it looked, it was only too tempting to the thirsty lad. He left his seat, and stooped to pick it up; he held it for a moment in his hands, and then dropped it as suddenly as if it were a burning coal.

"It's like as if th' heat had turned my brain," he exclaimed, "Lord Jesus forgive me, I were na' thinking rightly what I were going to do, I conna *steal!*

"No, I conna, by th' Great Master's help I will na steal," he said, as the tempter whispered to him that the apple no longer belonged to any one, no one wanted it, it would never be thought of again.

"Yon apple's not mine, an' I will ha' nowt to do wi' it," exclaimed Ben.

And praying for grace to resist the temptation, thirsty and wearied though he was, he finished his task, and sat quietly waiting for the schoolmaster's return. More than an hour had passed away before he heard the sound of the key in the lock, and saw Mr. Deane coming towards him. Ben rose from his seat, and gave the slate to the master.

"The answers are correct," said Mr. Deane, as he handed back the slate, and looked earnestly at the boy's face.

Very tired the pale face looked now, the features worn and thin, there were lines about the mouth that told their own story of the boy's powers of endurance being tried to the extreme point at times.

But there was no trace of sullenness there, no resentment.

"Ben," said Mr. Deane, "I must have been away an hour and a half, I never intended to stay so long, but after I reached my house and was waiting for a cup of tea (it does not sound very manly, Ben, and you need not tell any one), I almost fainted."

"Yo' did, Sir? Ay, but yo' are noan strong enough for such like work as yo' have here, we're a rough lot here; I reckon they are a deal smoother spoken, softer mannered sort o' folks, where yo' come from. I'm sorry, Sir, as I couldna' feel it reet to tell yo' what yo' axed me, but I knew him as had throwed yon apple would ha' had to be kept in, an' I could na' think of letting a little chap who's feart of his own shadder, bide here alone; yo' will forgive me, will yo' not, Sir?"

"I will, my lad," replied the master, as he turned his steps homeward again.

B

CHAPTER II.

BEN'S HOME.

THE cottage in which Ben lived stood alone, near the church.

To this cottage, sixteen years before, Ben's father, an industrous, steady young man, had brought his bride. Four years of quiet happiness passed by, then the messenger who visits the homes of rich and poor alike came to the cottage, and called away the kind husband, the loving father.

Ben was a baby then, a year old, and became the joy and delight of his widowed mother's heart.

The widow was not left wholly unprovided for. Her husband had saved a little money, and had bought the cottage in which they lived.

Mrs. Owen commenced again her former business of dressmaking, and earned sufficient to keep her child and herself in comparative comfort.

When Ben was six years of age, his mother became the wife of a man named Bell, the night-watchman at the Print Works.

Those who knew Bell best, knew how utterly unsuited he was in every way to Mary Owen, and with true northern frankness did not hesitate to tell her so: they reminded her that he was not a godly man, and that he was considered selfish and miserly.

Mrs. Owen listened quietly to these objections; as to being selfish, she said, well, all men grew more or less selfish who always lived alone, and who had only their own comfort to study.

As to being miserly, she granted John Bell took great care of his money, still it was better he should do that than squander it at the public-house as so many did.

And as to his not being a religious man, well, he did not drink, nor swear, nor gamble, nor quarrel with his neighbours; and when once they were married she knew she should be able to persuade him to attend Church with her; she would win him away from his love of gold, and teach him to "set his affections on things above."

"Tha' art makin' a mistake, Mary Owen," said old James Wynnatt, one of the oldest inhabitants of the village, "tha' art goin' to be onequally yoked, an there's never no good comes o' that: yon chap's ways are not thy ways; if I'd twenty darters John Bell should na' ha' ony one o' them, that he should na'."

"Mary's made up her moind, oim thinkin', an' hoo'll noan listen to thee, James," said the good man's wife, "hoo'll do her own."

She " did her own ;" that is to say, she refused to listen to her friends, and had her own way.

After her second marriage she still lived on in her old home. Her friends surmised, and rightly too, that the days of her widowhood, sad though they were, had yet been brighter and happier than those which followed.

But whatever disappointments and troubles befell Mary, she never complained of them, she kept her own counsel.

She had her boy, her fair-haired darling, she could not be utterly miserable so long as he was spared to her.

And she worked away more industriously than ever at her business, for, though John Bell earned good wages, and had few personal expenses, yet he only gave his wife a few shillings weekly for housekeeping.

So Mary had to supplement the small sum from her own earnings, and she also put by some money weekly for a special purpose.

The kind, loving mother wanted to keep her only child at home, and at school, longer than was customary in Ashleigh, and then apprentice him to some business.

She had her own hopes and ambitions, this quiet-looking woman, who rose early, and sat up late, and kept her home so scrupulously clean and tidy, and who was never heard to murmur or repine.

Mary Bell not only hoped, and planned, but she

sought help where alone true help is to be found; by exercise of faith in a crucified Redeemer she sought and found forgiveness for her sins, and rejoiced in the love of God.

And, as the mother Hannah took her child to the Temple, and "lent him to the Lord," so Mary took her boy in faith and prayer to the Saviour; and He who said, "Suffer little children to come unto me, and forbid them not," heard and answered the mother's prayers, and before Mary passed away from earth she had the happiness of knowing that her child, young as he was, was a true follower of Christ.

Ben was nine years old when he lost his mother; how keenly he felt her death he alone knew.

It was sudden, and unexpected. For some weeks Mary had not been well, but she was one who would never complain about any ailment until compelled to do so; she put down some work one day intending to finish it the next, but ere the sun set on the following day she had reached the city where "there is no more pain, neither sorrow, nor sighing."

Some said John Bell did not feel his wife's death at all. He certainly felt it, in so far as it affected his own personal comfort; but if he had ever had any real, true affection for her he would have shown more regard to her wishes than he did, when he entered her boy at ten years of age as a half-timer at the Works.

Ben knew his mother's wishes, and pleaded earnestly with his stepfather to let him go to school at least another year or two.

"Tha' wilt go to th' school half the day until tha' art fourteen," replied John Bell, "what more dost tha' want? Dost tha' want to be one o' th' gentry, or a larned man same as th' parson? Tha' dost try to mince thee words foine same as he does!"

"I should like something different from yon Works," replied Ben; and, almost unintentionally, he gave utterance to the longings of his heart, "I should like when I'm a man to be a missionary."

"Tha' would loike to be a missioner? That comes o' church goin', an' meetin' goin', and Bible readin'; now look here, young Ben, oi'll ha' no more o' such loike nonsense; let them go to furrin' parts as 'ave got no carakter to get work in their own country, an honest man does na' need to leave his own land."

"But missionaries go to do good."

"Let em bide whom oi say, an' as for thee, tha' wilt go to th' Works, an' earn thysen a carakter same as oi did."

So that question was settled.

Ben offered no further opposition to his father's wishes, and John Bell rejoiced that he had, as he considered so easily, and so effectually, settled the question of the boy's future life.

Had he known the thoughts and plans passing through the young mind; had he heard the earnest prayers the boy offered, that if it were the Lord's will he might one day realize his heart's desire, John Bell might not have felt so elated. He had his own schemes with regard to the future, and for the present the wages the boy earned weekly purchased his food and clothing.

For the food was plain, and poor as to quality, and as to quantity, Ben had not the amount of nourishment a growing child required; often he rose from the table at meal times only half satisfied, yet unwilling to ask for more.

Sometimes he would look longingly at the loaf on the table, and John Bell, seeing the look, would cut him another piece of bread, and tell him at the same time that if he himself ate as greedily as Ben did they would both soon be " in th' Union."

The poor boy, who was not greedy, but was painfully sensitive, would make some stammering apology, and resolve to eat less for the future.

Then, Ben's clothing certainly could not have been very costly, a common suit for week days, and a better one for Sundays, and these of the cheapest and plainest material.

And those who knew how neatly and carefully the boy had been dressed during his mother's lifetime, made remarks about his present appearance which were anything but complimentary to John Bell.

But Bell had decidedly too good an opinion of himself to trouble greatly about the opinion of others.

He visited no one, and no one visited him; a more unsociable man could scarcely be found.

He allowed Ben to go to church, though he boasted

of the fact that he had never been there himself since the day of his wife's funeral.

Sometimes he would give Ben permission to read to him, and on these occasions would either sit in dogged silence, or give utterance to sneers and contemptuous remarks. He was a man of one idea, of one fixed purpose, he meant to save and to make money, he was determined to die a rich man.

Other men as poor as he had made fortunes for themselves: why should not he succeed as they had done? To this end he worked, and pinched, and saved, and each year the sum in the savings bank became larger, and the man's life and sympathies grew narrower, and his heart became harder.

He did not hesitate, in order to add to his gains, to take advantage of the widow, the poor, and the fatherless. In his case "the love of money" was indeed "the root of all evil."

CHAPTER III

AN EVENING VISIT.

BEN found his father standing at the door when he reached his home after the long afternoon he had spent at school.

"A minute longer an' oi should ha' been off," said John Bell. "Tha' hast been kept in, oi hear; it's not for me to say if tha' desarved it or not, but th' Government says we are boun' to uphold th' skoomesters, so happen oi owt to thrash thee, but as 'tis th' first offence oi dunnot want to be too hard on thee, tha' wilt ha' to go bowt thee tea, an' think on as it does na happen again, lad."

"Shall I bring your supper?" asked Ben.

"Ay, tha' con bring it at noine o'clock, it's wrapped up in yon hankercher, an' thine is on a plate in th' cupboard; come, Jess, we mun go."

Jess, the watchman's dog, looked up wistfully in Ben's pale face, and followed her master slowly, and apparently unwilling: the dog obeyed her master, but she *loved* the boy.

John Bell was not one who valued the affection of man or beast, or else he might have felt jealous of the preference Jess invariably showed for his stepson.

"It's better walkin' now nor it were this afternoon," muttered Bell; "what a graidely foo' yon skoomester mun be if he conna tackle sich a lad as Ben, he's ower quiet to gi' onybody mich trouble."

Ben closed the garden gate and entered the cottage, hung up his well-worn cap, put his books on the table, and sat down on a low rocking-chair. The room was clean and tidy, there had been a small fire lighted to boil the water for John Bell's tea, but it had been allowed to go out directly after, and the tiny kettle stood on the hob filled with cold water.

"I'm not so very hungry," said Ben, as if trying to convince himself, "but I am thirsty;" and taking a cup from the shelf he filled it with water and drank it eagerly. Then he washed his hands and face and sat down to learn his lessons. He did his best to fix his attention on his books, but he was sick and faint for want of food.

He opened the cupboard door and looked at the plate upon which his father had placed his supper.

A hard crust of bread, and a very small piece of cheese, about two mouthfuls altogether for a hungry boy.

"If I eat it now I shall be hungry again before I go to bed," said Ben thoughtfully, as he left the food untouched and sat down again. His tired eyes wandered round the room as if in search of some beloved object.

There was the chair near the window, his mother's favourite seat, and the table she used for her work; the book-shelves in the corner containing her modest library, her Bible, and "The Pilgrim's Progress," "Foxe's Book of Martyrs," and two or three hymn-books. The boy's thoughts went back to the time, the never-to-be-forgotten time, when he had his mother ever with him as his constant friend. He heard the gentle tones of her voice again as she read to him from the precious Book the sweet story of old, he saw her pleading with his stern stepfather to grant him some childish pleasure, or to forgive some childish offence; again he wandered with her through the fields and lanes, and filled his hands with daisies for her to weave into chains for him.

Again he sat by her side near the bright fire, when the snow lay white on the ground, and the bright-eyed robins came up boldly to the window-sill for the crumbs his mother never forgot to place there.

Once more he knelt at her knee, and offered up the prayers she had taught him, and heard her gentle whisper, "God bless you, my boy," the mother's hand again pushed back the curly locks from the boy's fair brow, he was clasped tightly in her arms, and felt her loving kisses on his face.

"Mother, mother," he cried, "oh, tell me that you will never leave me again."

"Ben, Ben," exclaimed a child's voice, "dunnot carry on so, I'm feart, I am." Ben opened his eyes, and saw the little schoolfellow on whose account he had been punished.

"Why, Jimmy," he exclaimed, "how long have you been here, how is it I did na' hear you?"

"I opened th' door an' comed in," replied Jimmy, "an' then I seed as tha' wert asleep, an' I waited a bit thinkin' tha' would waken up, but when tha' called out 'Mother, mother,' I were feart, I were, so I shrieked out a bit: see I've brought thee some cakes an' a tin can full o' tea. I told mother tha' had been kept in all along o' me, an' she said as she were sure tha' would ha' to go bowt thee tea, so when I knowed thy father were safe in th' Works I comed along, an' I ha' na' spilled a drop, no that I ha' na'," said the little fellow proudly.

"Your mother is real kind to think o' me," said Ben, as he poured the tea out into a cup.

"Nay, it's thee as is kind," exclaimed the child. "Mother said there were nor a lad in th' whole school as would ha' done as tha' did to-day. How is it tha' art different like from th' rest o' them, Ben?"

"I dunno as I'm so different," replied Ben, who was quietly enjoying the tea and cakes. "I try to say my words same as Mr. Deane an' Mr. Mervyn, but I'm noan a graidely talker for all that."

"It's not just the talkin', tha' dost na' fight nor swear nor knock th' little uns about same as th' other big uns do."

"No, I dunnot," said Ben, "because th' Bible tells

me I mun think of Christ, an' try to follow th' example He left us, an' tha' knows how kind an' gentle He was."

"Ay, it says in th' hymn-book, 'Gentle Jesus, meek an' mild.' Ben," added the child, looking timidly around, "art na' tha' feart to bide here alone at neet?"

"Feart! Nay, Jimmy, why should I be? I am as safe here alone as in a room full o' people. Father goes away at six an' I take him his supper at nine, then I come back an' go to bed, an' never see him again until six in th' mornin'!"

"Does he sleep most o' th' day?" asked Jimmy, wonderingly.

"He sleeps in the forenoon mostly, an' sometimes he goes out a bit before tea for a walk."

"He went out this arternoon, mother seed him go up th' street just before t' rain came; how it did come down, Ben, an' th' thunder an' th' lightnin'. Oh! I did wish as I'd never throwed yon apple. I meant it to hit Charlie Wills, I did, he'd been teasin' me all th' arternoon, an' I thowt I'd give him a real stinger on th' side o' his head, an' then I were real feart arter when I thowt I'd ha' to be kept in all alone; it were mean o' me to let Mr. Deane keep thee in instead though, that it were."

"I think tha' should tell Mr. Deane th' truth about it, not for my sake," said Ben, gently, "but because it's right an' pleasing to God when we tell th' truth, an' tha' does na' need to be feart o' Mr. Deane, he's as kind as he can be."

"Ay, he is," said Jimmy, "how long has he been here now, Ben?"

"Three months."

"I'll tell him in th' mornin' I will."

"Tha' had better tell him now."

"What, to-neet, Ben?"

"Why not?"

"It would be troublin' him."

"Not so, Mr. Deane would na' think it a trouble he's been noan so well to-day, an' happen he'd sleep all th' better for knowin' a little lad had found courage to tell him th' truth."

"Wilt tha' come wi' me?" asked Jimmy.

"Ay, I'll come, we'd best go reet off at once."

The little hand Jimmy placed in Ben's friendly grasp trembled.

"Come along," said Ben, cheerily, "haven't I told thee tha' dost na' need to fear?"

"Tha' wilt knock at th' door an' ax for him," whispered Jimmy.

"Ay, sure I will," replied his friend.

Mr. Deane himself opened the door in answer to Ben's gentle knock.

There stood the two boys, Ben pale and tired, Jimmy trembling and tearful. The schoolmaster looked at them inquiringly.

"What is the matter with Jimmy," he said, "has any one hurt him?"

"Tell him," sobbed the child, clinging more closely to Ben, "I conna."

"Come in, boys," said Mr. Deane, leading the way to his pleasant sitting-room; "now tell me all about it," he added, as he closed the door.

"Jimmy wants to tell yo' as he throwed yon apple at school to-day, he wants to be a good boy, an' always speak th' truth," said Ben.

The ice was fairly broken now, and venturing to look up in Mr. Deane's kind face, Jimmy saw how needless his fears had been.

"I throwed it at Charlie Wills," said the child, whose tongue was loosened now, "he'd been teasin' me for ever so long, pullin' faces at me, an' callin' me crybaby; an' I forgot all as yo' said about throwin' things in th' school-room, an' then I were so feart o' bein' kept in I dare na' tell yo', but Ben said I mun tell yo' the truth."

"Ben was right," said Mr. Deane, "never be afraid to speak the truth, Jimmy; whatever it may cost you, or however hard it may seem, still, never hide the truth; I am thankful to find I have a boy in my school who not only tries to be good and upright himself, but also endeavours to help and teach others."

Just then the door opened, and an old lady came quietly into the room. Such a beautiful old lady Ben thought as he looked at her.

She wore a black dress, not a silk, but of some soft, shiny material, and a small grey shawl upon her shoulders, and a white net cap with pale lavender ribbons.

She would always have worn black ribbons in her snow-white cap in memory of her precious dead, had she not yielded to the wishes of her only son, with whom she lived, who begged her not to dress herself entirely in mourning.

She spoke kindly to the boys, and smiled approvingly when her son told her briefly their errand.

"You will never be sorry for what you have done to-night," she said to Jimmy; then noticing Ben's wearied look she turned to him and said, "You ought to be in bed and asleep, my boy, you look so tired."

"I am tired," replied Ben, "but I must take my father's supper to him before I go to bed."

"Does your father work at night then?"

"He's watchman at the Works, ma'am, he's there from six at night to six in th' mornin'."

"Is your name Ben Owen?"

"Yes, ma'am."

"Ah! then I heard about you to-day at old James Wynnatt's. You see I am only beginning to know some of the people now, Ben, we have not been here long, and I have been very busy since we came. Good night, my boy, and remember, Ben, if I can help you at any time I will."

Thanking her for her kindness, the boys hurried away, Jimmy ready for any amount of conversation, Ben more quiet and thoughtful than ever.

"Wasn't they kind, Ben? An' isn't schoolmaster's mother like a pictur', an' flowers all o'er th' carpet, an a big chimbley glass, an' a sight o' books, did'st tha' not see it all?"

"Yes, I saw it all," replied Ben, to whose imagination the room had seemed like a leaf out of a story-book; the pretty paper on the walls, the plain but tastefully arranged furniture, the white curtains looped with bows of coloured ribbon, the books and ornaments, the sweet summer flowers on the table and mantelpiece; all the nameless, little refinements; Ben was conscious of all these.

But to the motherless boy, the sweetest and the fairest of all had been the sight of Mrs. Deane, her motherly presence, and her kind words.

He recalled each glance of the loving eyes that had shed so many tears, but had not forgotten how to smile upon the young, and his heart beat faster when he remembered her promise of help.

How Mrs. Deane could befriend him he could not tell, he did not stop to question, but rejoiced at the remembrance of her promise.

He took his father's supper to the Works, and on his way home called to thank Jimmy's mother for the tea so kindly sent.

It was too dark to attempt to learn his lessons, and he had only a very small piece of candle ("enough to last him a week," his father had told him the day before), so he resolved to rise an hour earlier the next morning.

He ate his supper standing by the window, and

talking to a lark in a tiny cage. His father had brought the lark home a year ago, and had kept him a prisoner ever since.

Ben had begged and pleaded for the bird's freedom far more earnestly than he ever had done for any favour for himself, but John Bell only laughed at him.

So the boy, thwarted and defeated in his kind purposes, did all in his power to make the poor little songster's captivity less painful.

There were two cupboards in the room, in one some of the food was kept, in the other John Bell kept his lantern, and a few books and papers.

The second shelf in the cupboard was given to Ben.

Here he kept a slate, his old copy-books, and some of the toys his mother gave him when a child.

One of these toys was a small money-box in the shape of a house, and this Ben kept far back in the darkest corner of the cupboard.

Any one opening the door, and not stopping to look carefully, would never have noticed the little box, but Ben knew exactly where it was, and before he went to bed he climbed upon a chair and carefully reached it down. He emptied its contents on the table, and lighted the candle just for a minute while he counted the money.

"Only one more," he said, "then I shall ha' enough."

He put the money back again, and replaced the box, blew out the candle, and went to his lonely little bed, confiding himself first to the all-watchful care of Him "who neither slumbers nor sleeps."

CHAPTER IV.

SAM'L HORNBY'S GENERAL SHOP.

"MAY I go as far as Eastfield to-night, father?" asked Ben the following afternoon.

"Ay, tha' con go," replied John Bell ungraciously, "it's a good three miles to Eastfield, an' three back agen makes six, there's nothin' like trampin' along country roads for wearin' out shoe leather, an' tha' wilt come whom as hungry as a hunter!"

"I shall na' want more supper than I have other nights," said Ben quietly.

"More supper! No, oi should think not, we should very soon be in th' Union if tha' started eatin' more nor tha' dost now."

And John Bell, having found as he thought sufficient cause for grumbling, grumbled away until it was time for him to start off to his work.

Eastfield was a queer little place, half village and half town, three miles away from Ashleigh.

There were no large Print Works there, but there were two cotton factories. There was not much intercourse between the two places.

The Eastfield people trooped over once a year to the annual fair, "th' wakes" at Ashleigh, and the Ashleigh people returned the compliment by attending "th' wakes" at Eastfield, and that was about all. Each of the two places had its own shops, and co-operative stores, therefore each was independent of the other as regarded business transactions.

Little Ben Owen had at this time a private business transaction pending at Eastfield.

There was a shop there known to all the boys in the neighbourhood, the like of which was certainly not to be found in Ben's native village.

The proprietor of this renowned establishment designated it modestly as "A General Shop," but, as he did not deal in soap, candles, treacle, or blacking, and various other useful articles which are always to be met with in a genuine *bonâ-fide* " General Shop," this designation might prove rather misleading.

A curious collection of useful and ornamental articles Samuel Hornby (or "Sam'l" as his neighbours called him) always kept in stock.

He had ironmongery of every description, from bedsteads, and bright, shining fenders and fireirons, to small, clasp-handled knives, and pennyworths of brass-headed nails and tin-tacks. Crockeryware of all kinds was also to be met with here; jugs and mugs of all sizes hung on nails around the shop and warehouse adjoining, while dinner and tea services of various colours, and most remarkable patterns, were placed safely row above row on high shelves.

Here the hawker could replenish his stock of note paper and envelopes, thimbles, buttons, hooks and eyes, paltry jewellery and picture frames; and here, too, the thrifty housewife could buy needles by the hundred, and reels of cotton at so much per dozen, at a lower price than at the draper's.

No wonder Sam'l's shop was a popular institution, and Sam'l himself a successful and prosperous man.

Sharp and shrewd, he made but few mistakes in buying or selling.

He made a sad mistake once, though!

It was after a trip to Blackpool, where Sam'l and some of his friends went one Whit Monday, and where they enjoyed themselves greatly.

During the few hours they spent there they managed to have a drive, a donkey-ride to South Shore, a walk through the town, and along the promenade and pier; and in memory of their visit they were photographed by a travelling photographer.

Nor was this all.

They dined at an eating-house, and had tea and shrimps in a damp arbour, they had a bathe in the sea, and a row in a small boat, in which they struggled bravely through all the earlier stages of sea-sickness, and presented themselves afterwards with pale, sickly faces at a chemist's shop.

The chemist was a humane man, and seeing at once that in their present state of feeling any attempts at conversation would not be pleasant, he kindly refrained from asking them many questions, but quickly mixed some powders in soda water glasses, and handed them the mixture with an air of quiet sympathy.

"He were precious sharp a mixin' up yon fizzin' stuff," observed one of the party, as they left the shop.

"It's noan th' first toime as he's seen pasty-faced looking foaks," replied Sam'l, "he knows by this toime pretty well what to do; them little boats ought to be put down, they didn't ought to be allowed to upset people's feelin's in this way."

But Sam'l soon forgot his vexation, and sat down for a little rest. While resting he listened with delight to the music played by a German band, and to the songs sung by some negro minstrels. Sam'l seated himself about half-way between the two rival representatives of the musical world.

One of his friends suggested that they should go nearer the one or the other, in order that they might hear more distinctly, and more fully appreciate the merits of the performance.

"Tha' con go reet in th' front o' th' minsters, or reet in th' front o' th' Prussians, oi shall bide where oi am," replied Sam'l, "an' get all oi con for my money, oi dunno' come to Blackpool every day." So Sam'l remained where he was. It might have been more than slightly trying to a musical, or highly sensitive ear, to hear "Die Wacht am Rhein" vainly trying to assert the supremacy over "Ring, Ring the Banjo;" but to Sam'l it was delightful; and with praiseworthy impartiality he bestowed the same remuneration on the grinning black-faced man in the coloured cotton suit and grey hat, who collected on behalf of the minstrels, as he did on the solemn-faced German who asked for a small donation for the band.

"Tha' does na' need to think as oi'm deceived by thee black face," he said to the minstrel, as he placed some coppers in his grey hat; "oi come fro' Eastfield i' Lancashire, an' we're noan sich foos there as not to know a nigger when we see one!"

"Tha' art th' genuine article," he said to the astonished German, "but oi'm feart tha' wilt do thysen some harm some day if tha' blows yon trumpet so hard."

It was soon after this memorable visit that Sam'l made a rash, and as it proved, an unfortunate speculation.

His quick, observant eyes had seen in the market at Blackpool, a number of pretty china cups bearing this inscription, "A present from Blackpool for a good boy."

The idea suggested itself to Sam'l's enterprising spirit why should he not have china mugs for sale similar to these, only with the name Eastfield substituted for Blackpool?

He wrote off at once to the Potteries to order fifty.

A reply came by return of post to say that an order could not be executed for a smaller number than a hundred and fifty.

"Then send a hundred an' fifty, an' look sharp about it," wrote back Sam'l.

In a wonderful short space of time the goods arrived.

Sam'l carefully unpacked the large crate; not one of the precious mugs was broken, nor, so far as he could tell, even cracked.

He rubbed and polished each one separately with a corner of his large apron (a very useful article was Sam'l's apron, it answered the purpose of teacloth, duster, and pocket-handkerchief, and occasionally did duty as a table-cloth), and then placed them in rows in his window.

He made room there for as many as he possibly could, even taking down a timepiece, a set of lustres, and some figures under glass shades which had been a source of wonder and admiration to the juveniles of Eastfield for many months.

"No fear that they'll sell," said Sam'l to himself as he looked at his window, "oi shall ha' to order more."

But he never did order any more, simply because he found himself unable to dispose of those he had. Whether it was because the boys at Eastfield (and there were plenty of them, of all ages and sizes) could not truthfully be said to belong to the class for whom the mugs were intended; or whether the boys themselves showed a lamentable want of taste by persuading their parents to bestow upon them as rewards for good conduct, other gifts, such as balls, tops, knives, kites, etc., certain it is that the mugs remained on hand, greatly to Sam'l's annoyance.

The village schoolmistress bought nine, and gave them away to the most docile and diligent of her pupils.

"Have yo' no cups for good girls as well as good boys, Sam'l?" asked a motherly-looking woman one day when she was making several purchases at the shop.

"Nay, oi never gave th' lassies a thowt," replied Sam'l.

"Well, oi'm surprised," said the good woman, "tha' knows oi've three girls, an' oi would ha' bowt them each a gill-pot like yon, for they're real pretty."

"Then why no ha' them?" exclaimed Sam'l, "what does it matter if it says boy or girl? Th' tea ull taste all the same, an' little uns like yourn conna read, yo' know."

"Martha Ann can read a bit," said the mother, with a slightly injured air.

"They sell a sight o' cups like these at th' seaside," said Sam'l to another customer the same day.

"Oi know they do," replied the party addressed, "but Eastfield is na' th' seaside, an' children would na' set as mich store by them there mugs same as they would if they'd comed fro' Blackpool and Southport."

In vain Sam'l spoke about the beauty and utility of the mugs; he invariably offered them for approval to any strangers passing through the village, who happened to find their way to his shop.

Perhaps they did not care to be troubled with such breakable articles as china cups, or they may not have admired Eastfield sufficiently to wish to carry away a memento of it; anyhow they always declined the purchase.

In his anxiety to dispose of his large order, Sam'l even offered the unfortunate mugs at a little more than cost price, at so much per dozen, but all in vain. He sold about twenty of them, kept a few on a shelf in the shop, and packed the remainder away in his warehouse, "a livin' moniment of my folly in imitatin' waterin' places," Sam'l would sometimes say.

CHAPTER V.

A BITTER DISAPPOINTMENT.

IT was after seven o'clock when Ben reached Eastfield; and Sam'l was busy in his shop.

Ben waited until several customers had been attended to, and then stated his business.

"A cage tha' says," said Sam'l, "oi ha' a graidely lot o' cages, lad, what sort were it?"

"A wicker cage," replied Ben, "a good sized un, yo' said it were two an' six but you would let me ha' it for two shillin'!"

"Ay so oi did now oi think on't; well dost tha' want to tak it wi' thee now?"

"Nay, I ha' only getten one an' eleven pence, but I thowt I'd come an' make sure that as th' cage were na' gone, I shall soon ha' another penny, an' then I'll come again, good night, an' thank yo'."

"Here, stop," exclaimed Sam'l, "hast getten th' money wi' thee?"

"No," replied Ben.

"Tha should ha' browt it, oi would ha' letten thee ha' th' cage, an' ha' trusted to thee bringing me th' other penny, tha' looks honest."

"I am honest," replied the lad, "an' no fear but I'll come soon an' fetch th' cage away."

"I shall soon ha' it now," said Ben to himself as he walked homewards, "an' the lark will be a sight better off in yon than in th' little cage. I wish father would let it go free, it seems to long to fly away, an' beats itself against th' bars of th' cage till I'm sure it must be hurt sometimes; an' when it sings it seems to be beggin' an' prayin' for its liberty."

A year ago John Bell had greatly astonished Ben by telling him that he had resolved to give him a penny every other Saturday for pocket-money. Not a very large sum certainly, not half the amount other boys of Ben's age spent weekly in marbles and sweets, but small as it was it was a great surprise to Ben, who knew his father's love of money.

"A penny every other week, Ben, makes two an' tuppence a year," said his father, "think o' that, Ben; think o' all as con be done wi' two an' tuppence; why there's mony a mon i' Manchester ridin' i' his carriage as did na' ha' more nor two an' tuppence to start wi' i' life."

Ben spent the first three pennies he saved in purchasing some daisy roots, which he planted on his mother's grave.

He then began to save his money again, intending

to buy some more plants for the same purpose early in the spring.

But when the spring came, Ben had resolved to spend his mony on something else. "Mother loved th' birds," he said, " an' she would ha' grieved to see th' poor lark frettin' itself in its little cage, she'd be far better pleased if I spent th' money on th' poor bird."

That very week a boy passed the cottage, carrying in his hand a good-sized wicker cage.

"What might yo' give for that?" asked Ben.

"I gave one an' sixpence at Sam'l Hornby's o'er at Eastfield, but he has some a deal bigger for two shillin' an' two an' six, but this is big enough for a throstle."

"It's cruel to keep 'em," said Ben.

"To keep what," asked the lad, " th' cages?"

"No, th' birds."

"Not it, they're as well off in th' cages as flyin' all o'er the country."

"Happen yo' think as yo' would be as well off in th' prison as yo' are out," said Ben.

"Nay, oi dunnot."

"Well, th' cage is a prison for th' bird, an' what stone walls would be for thee th' bars of th' cage are for th' bird."

"They conna feel th' same as us."

"Conna they? I'm noan so sure o' that, there's a power o' things in th' world we know very little about, happen we'll be wiser some day, but I'm sure an' certain for my own part as everything that has life can feel."

"Oi dunnot clem my bird," said the lad sullenly.

"They dunnot clem folks in th' prison, they give 'em their vittles reg'lar; but there's not many as likes goin' there for all that. It isna' enough for th' bird to ha' a bit o' seed to eat, an' a drop o' water to drink, it wants its nest an' th' sunshine, it wants to watch th' dew fall, an' see th' sunset, it wants to hear what th' winds are whisperin' about to th' trees, and see th' flowers grow. Ah! there's a sight o' things a bird must miss when he's shut up in a cage."

From that time Ben's decision was made.

The first two shillings he could save should be given for a better cage for the captive lark. For this purpose he saved his tiny hoard of pocket-money, and went over to Eastfield, and inspected Sam'l Hornby's assortment of cages.

Now he had only to wait until Saterday, when he would receive another penny, then he would have the sum required.

The time would soon be here now, only another day before Saturday.

On the Friday evening he took down from its hiding-place his little box, and opened it.

Alas for poor Ben!

What a bitter disappointment for the boy's tender, loving heart! The money was gone, the whole of it!

Poor disappointed Ben!

He stood by the table gazing absently at the empty box; he climbed upon a chair, and searched among the books, papers, and toys in the cupboard, all in vain.

No stray pennies had found their way out of the box, and hidden themselves elsewhere.

"Father has taken them," said Ben, " he might ha, told me first."

He closed the cupboard door, and sat down on the low rocking-chair on which his mother had sat and nursed him when he was a little child. He thought of his mother then, and a hard lump rose in his throat.

He laid his head upon the table, and remained perfectly still for a few minutes; then he rose, and with trembling hands took from the shelf his mother's Bible.

"She said it were always a comfort to her an' it has been to me. I'll read some of her favourite verses."

He turned to the twenty-third Psalm.

" The Lord is my Shepherd, I shall not want."

" No, I shall not want," he exclaimed, " The Lord will take care of me."

Then he read many of the precious promises written in the New Testament.

" There's one grander an' greater than any other, in Revelations," he said : then, having found the verse he sought, he read, " Him that overcometh will I make a pillar in the temple of my God, and he shall go no more out, and I will write upon him the name of my God, and the name of the city of my God, which is New Jerusalem, which cometh down out of heaven from my God, and I will write upon him my new name."

Then he read the twenty-first verse of the same chapter, "To him that overcometh will I grant to sit with me in my throne, even as I also overcame, and am set down with my Father in His throne."

"To him that overcometh," repeated Ben, as he closed the Book; "that means there's a battle to fight, a victory to win; Lord Jesus, give me grace and strength to conquer, and oh, bless my father, for Christ's sake."

John Bell made no remark about the money when Ben took his supper to the Works that evening, but the next day he put a penny on the table.

"That's for thee," he said, "an' oi'm real pleased, Ben, to see as tha' does na' squander thee money same as some lads: oi put another penny to them as tha' had saved, an' oi've put it in th' Savings Bank in thy name."

"Thank yo'," replied Ben, "but I'd set my heart on buyin' a bigger cage for th' lark. I can get one for two shillin'."

"Th' bird's reet enough where it is," said his father impatiently; "tha' dost getten sich fancies, Ben, oi never seed such a queer lad in my life."

No more pennies found their way into the little money-box in the cupboard.

Ben went to Mrs. Deane, and asked her if she could kindly take care of his pocket-money for him.

"There's plenty in th' village as would do that an' more for me if I axed 'em, but they might talk about it," said the boy.

"I understand," said Mrs. Deane, "I will take care of anything you bring me, Ben, but will not say a word about it."

Not even to this kind friend did Ben tell the story of his disappointment, he bore it patiently and uncomplainingly.

Only through the bright summer's days, when the lark seemed to droop and pine in its tiny cage, Ben would think of his two shillings in the Savings Bank, and turning to the bird would say, "I ha' na' th' power to set thee free, but tha' should ha' had a better home than that, if I could but ha' spent my money as I wished."

And Sam'l Hornby, in his shop at Eastfield, wondered what had become of the boy, who had seemed so wishful to purchase the wicker cage.

CHAPTER VI.

THE STRANGERS.

THE bright summer days were over, the leaves had changed their colours, and fallen from the trees, and were blown hither and thither by the cold autumnal winds.

The summer had been unusually hot, and it was foretold that the coming winter would be very severe.

Prudent housewives as they heard this looked over their stock of blankets, and winter clothing, and bought as many warm garments as they could afford, in order to be well prepared to meet the cold weather.

Anxious, careworn women, whose husbands spent the greater part of their earnings at the public-house, and who knew by past experience how much easier it is to meet the home wants in the summer than in the winter, sighed, as they thought of the cold days and the long dark nights, towards which they were hastening.

"Coals will be dear an' food will be dear, it's to be

hoped we'll be able to keep out of th' Union," said John Bell.

Ben had grown accustomed to his father's imaginary picture of their residence in "th' Union;" he had cried "wolf" so often that Ben was not to be easily frightened now.

He only wished that his father would buy him a warmer suit, and allow him to have a small fire in the evenings, for the nights were chilly, and Ben himself was far from well.

"If tha' art cold tha' con come to th' Works to me an' Jess, it's warm enough there," said John Bell, in answer to the boy's request.

But Ben did not care to be in the Works longer than he was obliged to be, so he made no further complaint about the cold.

When once December had fairly set in, his father would have a fire lighted each morning, and kept in the whole of the day; a poor, miserable apology for a fire certainly, still it would be better than none at all.

"What a bad cough tha' hast got, Ben," said old Mrs. Wynnatt, as the boy was passing her door one Saturday afternoon, "come in, lad, come in."

Ben went in, and took a seat near the large, bright fire.

"It looks comfortable here," he said.

"It is comfortable," said Mrs. Wynnatt, "we ha' a many mercies to be thankful for, Ben."

"That we ha'," said old James, from his seat in the

chimney-corner; "there's somebody knockin' at th door," he added, turning to his wife.

"Nay, it were but th' wind," she replied.

"Th' wind dunnot gi' double knocks at doors i' that way," said the old man.

"Perhaps it's father looking for me," said Ben, and he jumped up, and opened the door.

Two men stood outside, strangers to Ben, two men in warm overcoats, and round felt hats.

Old James caught sight of them.

"Come in," he said, "come in out of th' rain."

"Thank you," said one of the strangers as they stepped inside the clean, warm kitchen, and wiped their feet upon the mat.

"Could you tell me where we could get lodgings?" asked the other stranger.

"Lodgings," exclaimed old James, "what, in th village?"

"Yes," replied the stranger with a smile, "is my request a remarkable one?"

"No one takes a house or lodgings in th' village unles they're boun' to work here."

"We might be here a week or two," said the stranger carelessly, "we have some business matters to attend to in Manchester, and some friends we want to look up, but we do not wish to stay in Manchester, we are accustomed to the country."

"It's considered healthy here, is it not?" inquired the other stranger.

"Healthy! ay, yes, it's healthy enough," replied old James.

"There's Mrs. Thorp's," said Mrs. Wynnatt, who was busy thinking about the lodgings, "she has two rooms she lets sometimes."

"We could manage with two rooms, though we should prefer three," said the younger of the two men. "Would you kindly tell us the way to Mrs. Thorp's, and we will make inquiries about her rooms?"

"I will show you th' house," said Ben, putting on his cap.

"Ay, do, Ben, that's a good lad, an' then come back an' h' a cup o' tea with us," said Mrs. Wynnatt.

"Thank yo', if father does na' mind, I will."

The strangers followed Ben down the lane, and into the village street. It was a dull November day, a damp day of mist and drizzling rain, and the children seemed one and all to have decided to spend their weekly holiday indoors.

Some of the fathers of the families had sauntered into the public-houses, and some were, to use their own expression, "cleanin' themselves," that is to say, having a wash, and changing their working clothes for their second-best suits, in which, after tea was over, they would go out shopping with their wives, or go and smoke a pipe and have a chat with a neighbour. Some were nursing the baby, or giving Tommy or Bobby "a ride to Banbury Cross," while the mothers got the four o'clock tea ready, for they kept early hours on Saturdays at Ashleigh.

So it happened that Ben and his two companions made their way to Mrs. Thorp's cottage without attracting much attention.

Joe Brown, the dirtiest and most neglected boy in the village, saw them, and rushed home to tell his mother that "Ben Owen were walkin' along o' some stranger chaps."

Martha Brown, who had the most unruly children, the most miserable home, and certainly the longest tongue, in the parish, ran out into the middle of the road, and was just in time to see the strangers' coat-tails disappear into Mrs. Thorp's house.

"They've gone to Mrs. Thorp's," exclaimed Martha, "happen they're relations o' hers; what were they loike, Joe?"

"Oi dunno'," replied Joe, moodily, "an' oi dunnot care, nother!"

Mrs. Thorp's husband was the gardener at "Ashleigh House," the residence of Mr. Ashford, the owner of the Print Works.

Mr. Ashford intended to build a cottage for James Thorp in a field behind his house, but until this was done James was to live rent free in one of the houses in the village street.

James' wife was "noan Lancashire," the Ashleigh people were wont to say. She came from the south of England, and was a quiet, retiring woman.

Ben Owen's mother had been her only intimate friend in the place; to every one else she was "Mrs. Thorp," civil and obliging, but nothing more.

She had only two children, Jimmy, Ben's little friend, and a little girl. Her family being so small, and her husband away at his work all the day, she liked to let two of her rooms when she could.

But "apartments" were not greatly in request at Ashleigh; sometimes a respectable workman would occupy Mrs. Thorp's rooms while waiting to obtain a suitable house, but for the greater part of the year they were unoccupied.

This was the case now; and after hearing the reasons the strangers gave for their stay in the village, she showed them her parlour and spare bed-room, made all the necessary arrangements about terms, and, leaving them upstairs unpacking the carpet bags they had with them, she went down to the kitchen, where she had left Ben talking to Jimmy.

"They are going to stay for a week at least, Ben," said Mrs. Thorp; "don't hurry away, stay and have tea with us, my husband will be home directly. He said only yesterday that he never got sight of you now."

Jimmy and his sister Susy added their entreaties to their mother's invitation, but Ben thanked them, and told them he had promised to go back to old James Wynnatt's, if his father would allow him.

John Bell readily gave the desired permission, and Ben walked quickly back to the old man's cottage. The tea was ready on a small, round table, drawn close to the fire. The bread was home-made, and so were the currant-cakes, and the hot muffins.

Ben thought of tea-time at home, the stale, hard

crusts with their thin scraping of butter, and the poor, weak mixture which was supposed to be tea.

The boy often wondered how his father bore the many privations of their daily life.

If he gave Ben only the plainest and the poorest fare, the boy was just enough to acknowledge that he did not purchase luxuries for himself.

To get and to save was the end and aim of the money-lover's existence.

"An' so th' strangers have gone to Mrs. Thorp's," said old James, as he handed Ben his tea.

"Yes, they've taken th' rooms for a week at least," replied Ben; "they axed a sight o' questions as we went there."

"Did they now?"

"Yes, they axed if Mr. Ashford were at home now, or away. They said some one had told 'em as th' Print Works belonged to a Mr. Ashford, who were away for a month or two at once sometimes, on account of his health, an' they axed me my name, an' where I lived, an' where my father worked?"

"Did'st tha' hear their names?"

"Grant; they said they were cousins."

"They're uncommonly loike one another, oi should ha' took 'em for brothers," said Mrs. Wynnatt.

"I showed 'em th' church," said Ben, "an' told 'em what time th' services began."

"That were reet, lad," said old James approvingly; "if they're God-fearing men they'll find their way to His house to worship Him."

CHAPTER VII.

MR. HENRY ASHFORD'S REFUSAL.

SUNDAY was the happiest day in the week to Ben: he always went twice to the Sunday-school, and twice to church, and was one of the most attentive listeners to Mr. Mervyn's faithful sermons.

Mrs. Deane would often look across from her seat by her son's side, to the corner where the boy sat, and, as she noticed the eagerness with which he listened to the truths of the Gospel, she thought of the hopes and plans he had confided to her.

Ben had told her that he longed above everything else in the world to try to teach others about Jesus.

"If I conna be made learned enough to go abroad an' teach th' heathen about th' Saviour, still I might happen get learning enough to work in some o' th' streets an' lanes o' th' cities. Some left their fishermen's nets, an' some th' plough, an' some their business, to work for th' Great Master. I dunnot think He'd despise me because I'm but a poor lad," Ben had said to her.

"No, my boy," was Mrs. Deane's reply, "the Saviour would never despise your willing services; if it be His will that you should work for Him, a way will be opened. Remember always that the Lord knows best."

The boy's longings and desires for future usefulness, did not so engross his mind as to cause him to neglect the opportunities to work for Christ that day by day presented themselves.

He was ever ready to show kindness to any one whom he could in any way befriend; he bore patiently the taunts and jeers of his schoolfellows and work-mates; and refrained from murmuring at the many hardships of his lot in life.

The two strangers who had taken Mrs. Thorp's apartments did not make their appearance at church on the Sunday.

Ben saw them walking about the village in the afternoon, and pointed them out to his father.

"Oi wonder who they con be," said John Bell; "does Mester Deane know owt about 'em, Ben?"

"Mr. Deane!" exclaimed the boy, "no, how should he know anything?"

"Nay, oi conna tell, lad, oi thowt happen he moight, he's lookin' a deal better is Mester Deane since he comed here."

"He is better," replied Ben, "he is stronger than he was."

This was really the case; Mr. Deane's health had certainly improved, he said himself that he felt stronger than he had done for years.

His work in the school was not so hard a task as it had been at first, the children were not so rebellious. Some of them felt perhaps that it was useless fighting against a master who was quietly resolved to be obeyed, but the majority of them had learned to love Mr. Deane, and did not find it difficult to obey him.

The first week in November passed away, and then the second, and the two strangers still stayed on at Mrs. Thorp's.

Sometimes they went away for a day or two, and then returned.

They stopped Ben one morning on his way home to breakfast, and asked him if he thought they could obtain an order to see the Works before they left the village.

"There's no orders given as I knows on," replied the boy: "no one is allowed to go through th' Works unless they're friends o' Mr. Ashford's."

"Is Mr. Ashford still away?" asked the younger of the two men.

"Yes, he's still away. Mr. Henry Ashford is at home, he comes to th' Works every day."

"Mr. Henry Ashford is the son?"

"Yes, th' eldest son. Mr. Lionel does na' live here, he's in th' army."

"Then I think we must ask Mr. Henry Ashford's

permission," and bidding Ben good morning the two men went on their way.

That same morning a note was brought to Mr. Henry Ashford as he sat at his desk in his father's office. He read it carefully through, and smiled.

"No, no, Mr. Robert Grant," he said, "we cannot tell what your business may be, and, therefore, certainly cannot write out an order for you and your cousin to view the Print Works. My father's word is law here, and if we broke our rules for one we might break them for twenty strangers." And, taking a sheet of note-paper from his desk, Mr. Henry replied briefly, "The Works are not allowed to be viewed by strangers; this is our rule." The answer was given to one of the clerks, who carried it to the outer office, where the elder of the two strangers was standing.

"This reply is from Mr. Henry Ashford himself I presume?" said Mr. Robert Grant.

"From Mr. Henry himself," replied the clerk.

"Thank you," said Mr. Grant, "my cousin and I would like to have seen the Works before leaving the neighbourhood, but it does not signify."

Mr. Robert Grant and his cousin spent the remainder of the day away from the village, and when they returned in the evening they told Mrs. Thorp they thought they should remain a week or two longer if convenient to her.

Mrs. Thorpe raised no objections; they paid for their rooms regularly, and did not keep late hours, or disturb her in any way

They were respectably dressed, and appeared to have plenty of money.

"They don't belong to th' gentry, an' they don't belong to th' workin' class," said John Bell, "but they're civil-spoken men for all that; if they'd axed me oi could ha' telled them they'd noan get leave to go o'er th' Works, th' master's more particular now nor ever he were sin' he's getten th' new machinery in; besides, there's things in th' colour shop an dyehouse it would na' do for every one to see; there's trade secrets here same as elsewhere; there's nobbut one or two as ha' worked there as knows all th' processes."

"Oi know as mich as onybody," said old James Wynnatt, who was listening to Bell, "boy an' man, I've worked there all my life."

"Ay, no doubt tha' knows as mich as onybody," replied John Bell, "take care tha' dost na' tell thee wife; there's nowt con be kept quiet when once a woman knows it."

"Dost think so," said old James; "th' Good Book tells me it were nor a woman as betrayed th' Lord an' th' Saviour into th' hands of the chief priests and captains for thirty pieces o' silver, an' it were a woman as browt th' alabaster box o' ointment, an' poured it on th' Saviour's head; an' it were th' women as followed Him from Galilee ministering unto Him; an' it wore th' women as were at th' sepulchre early in th' mornin'. Nay, nay, John Bell, they're noan so bad, tha' dost na' need to think or speak lightly o' th' women foaks."

CHAPTER VIII.

A PAINFUL DISCOVERY.

NOVEMBER was drawing to a close, and Ben's cough grew worse each day.

Mrs. Deane sent him some medicine, and gave him some flannel vests, and warm stockings.

And John Bell, miser though he was, took pity on the boy so far as to allow a fire to be lighted and kept in each evening.

One afternoon Mr. Deane asked Ben to go to his house for a book he wanted.

The nearest way from the school was across a field at the end of the playground.

A gate at the other side of the field opened into the lane where the schoolmaster lived.

It was a quiet spot, only a few houses had been built there.

There were fine tall trees on either side of the road, and on summer evenings "Low Lane," as it was called, was a favourite walk for the children and lovers from the village.

There were no children, and no lovers in the lane on this November afternoon, but to his surprise, just as he reached the gate, Ben saw his father, Mr. Robert Grant, and his cousin, walking slowly along the lane.

The boy did not wish to speak to any of the party just then, he wanted to hurry on to Mr. Deane's house, so he drew back from the gate, and stood near the wall that separated the field from the road.

On came the three men talking eagerly. Ben thought at first they were quarrelling, and hoped that they would not decide to return home the very way that he had come, or look over the stone wall and discover him standing there.

On they came, nearer and nearer. Now the boy could tell from the tones of their voices that they were not quarrelling as he had feared at first, but arguing, or discussing some question very earnestly.

"Twenty pounds," he heard Mr. Robert Grant say, "it's really too high a figure, my good man."

"Please yoursen," was John Bell's sullen reply, "it's not my business."

"Don't speak so loud," said the younger of the two Grants cautiously.

Ben drew a long breath and looked round.

Yes, they had gone now; he waited a few moments, then opened the gate and hastened away up the lane.

Mrs. Deane gave him the book he had been sent for.

"Did you come across the field?" she asked

"Yes, ma'am," replied the boy.

"Don't go back that way, then," said his kind friend, "the grass is so wet."

So Ben returned by the lane. He saw nothing, however, of his father or the two Grants, and John Bell made no reference at tea-time to his afternoon's walk, and Ben asked no questions.

Only as he sat alone by the fire, at night, he wondered what business transactions his father could possibly have with Mrs. Thorp's lodgers.

What was the money for?

Had the two strangers got into debt, and borrowed, or wished to borrow, money from John Bell, who in return required the sum of twenty pounds as interest?

No, that was too wild and silly a notion, and Ben laughed at himself for having entertained it for a moment.

Besides, how should they know, even supposing them to be in pecuniary difficulties, that the night-watchman at the Print Works had saved money?

The next afternoon, when school was over, Jimmy Thorp showed Ben a sixpence.

"It's moine," said the little fellow, "th' lodgers gived it me, they've gone away to-day for good."

"Have they really?" asked Ben.

"Yes, they shook hands with mother, an' said good-bye quite perlite," said Jimmy, who was evidently greatly impressed.

"Mother says she wishes oi'd learn to speak same as they do," he continued, "she's goin' to give me a shillin' when I don't say toime an' moine."

"But time and mine instead," said Ben, who knew Mrs. Thorp's dislike to the Lancashire dialect.

"Ben," said his father, as he started off to the Works that evening, "oi'll noan tak' th' dog to-neet."

"Not take Jess!" exclaimed Ben.

"Not tak' Jess," repeated Bell, "th' dog's moine, oi con tak' it or leave it if oi choose."

"Of course," said Ben, wondering in his own mind what new whim or caprice this could be.

Even Jess looked puzzled, but was very well pleased to remain at home with Ben.

"He'd ha' thowt it queer or else oi would ha' told him not to ha' browt my supper," said Bell to himself as he walked along.

The person referred to was Ben, and why on this occasion his father should trouble about what he thought, seeing that at other times he cared nothing for his opinion, Bell only knew.

Ben had finished learning his lessons, and was reading a book Mrs. Deane had lent him, when he heard a knock at the door.

"Who's comin' now?" he said.

He opened the door, and to his surprise saw his little friend Jimmy, almost breathless from haste and excitement, and with tears running down his rosy cheeks.

"What is the matter?" asked Ben.

"Oh, please, Ben," panted the child, "mother says wilt tha' go to Leyton for th' doctor?"

E

" The doctor ?   Who is ill ?"

" Susy, she's real bad, an' father's gone off to-day, he will na' be back before th' mornin'; it could na' ha' happened worse, mother says, th' lodgers gone an' all, they'd ha' fetched the doctor."

" I'll fetch him," said Ben, getting ready at once; " who said he'd gone to Leyton ? "

" Th' housekeeper," replied Jimmy, " oi went to his house an' she said he'd gone to Leyton Lodge to dine an' spend th' evenin'; them were her words; they dunnot ha' their dinner afore seven, tha' knows."

" No," said Ben, " but th' doctor will na' be long comin' when once I've seed him. Run back, Jimmy, an' tell mother not to fret, we'll soon ha' Susy well again, please God."

The nearest way to Leyton was past Mr. Deane's house.

With Jess by his side Ben hurried on; his cough was very troublesome sometimes; now and then he was obliged to stop for a few moments, in order to get his breath.

It was a rough, windy night, and it was bad walking along the roads after the heavy rains.

" Th' doctor will ha' his trap an' drive me back wi' him," said Ben; " two miles will na' seem far when one's ridin'."

Scarcely had the thought passed through the boy's mind when he heard the sound of wheels.

" Happen some one else ha' sent for th' doctor," he said, and stood still to see the conveyance pass.

"I'll shout out if it's him, an' tell him about Susy," he thought.

But the conveyance did not pass the spot where the boy stood, holding Jess tightly by the collar, for the dog was apt to be rather too demonstrative sometimes to strangers.

Instead of passing, the conveyance drew up at the side of the road, and two men got down from it.

"I have paid your master for the trap, and here is a shilling for yourself," said a voice which Ben recognized instantly as Mr. Robert Grant's.

"Thank yo', Sir," replied the driver, "it's a good step to the village, oi'll drive yo' on wi' pleasure."

"No, thank you," said Mr. Robert Grant, "we prefer to walk after our long drive."

"There," Ben heard him say as the conveyance drove back towards Leyton again, "I hope you are satisfied, my dear brother; our appointment with our mutual friend is at half-past twelve, and here we are at nine o'clock in these delightful lanes."

"Better too soon than too late," replied the younger Grant, "if we were five minutes late, Bell would think we had turned faint-hearted. Let us walk back a few yards and then turn into the Eastfield road."

Poor Ben! There he stood, still holding Jess by the collar, fearing he knew not what if the two men should find him there and know that he had overheard their words,—words spoken so rapidly and quietly Ben wondered that he had overheard them.

But the boy's sense of hearing was wonderfully quick, and he had recognized Grant's voice at once.

It was too dark to see many yards ahead, so Ben waited until he thought he had allowed the two men sufficient time to get into the Eastfield road: then he hastened on.

He reached Leyton Lodge and asked for Dr. Eliot.

When the doctor heard Ben's errand, he prepared to return with him immediately.

A kind, good, and clever man was Dr. Eliot, respected by all who knew him.

Seated by his side in the dog-cart, Ben thought anxiously about the discovery he had made of the return of the two Grants.

What was their business with his father?

What appointment had they made with him or he with them.

Only one answer to these questions presented itself to the boy's agitated mind.

His father must have consented to admit them into the Works on condition that they paid him a sum of money.

His father must have been tempted, bribed, to commit an act so base, so treacherous, that Ben's pale face flushed crimson at the mere thought of it.

Should he be in time, could he do anything, to prevent their accomplishing their purpose?

"What a bad cough you have, Ben," said the doctor,

"you ought not to be out these wet, cold nights; I shall have you laid up next."

"I hope not, Sir," replied Ben, but he shivered as he spoke, and Dr. Eliot bade him wrap his rug tightly round him.

It was as much from nervous agitation as from cold that the boy was trembling, but the doctor did not know this.

"Get away home and to bed, my lad," he said, as they stopped at Mrs. Thorp's door, "and keep out of the night air until your cough is better.'

CHAPTER IX.

IN THE WORKS.

WITH trembling hands Ben unlocked the cottage door, and not waiting even to strike a light, he groped his way to the cupboard and took out his father's supper.

Jess stood at the gate, prepared to follow him to the Works and home again as faithfully as she had followed him to and from Leyton.

"Nay, nay, Jess," said the boy, "tha' must bide here," and he sent the good dog back into the cottage, and locked the door.

Jess whined piteously, but Ben went on his way as though he heard it not.

"I mun stop there," he said to himself, "I mun stop there, but *how?*"

He rang a bell at a small side gate near the large ones leading into the yard.

He heard his father open a door, and walk across the yard.

"Who's there?" he asked.

"It's Ben, father," said the lad.

Bell unfastened a bolt on the small gate by which he admitted himself, the large ones were not unlocked before morning for the workpeople.

The small gate closed itself with a spring, and could not be opened from the outside without a key.

Ben noticed his father did not stop to fasten the bolt after admitting him, evidently he expected him to return home very soon.

Lately Ben had always taken his father's supper to the Works, and Bell found the boy's short visits a pleasant relief to the monotony of his duties.

In his own hard, stern way, the watchman cared more for Ben than he ever had done for any one else.

"Tha' art late," he said, as they entered a little room on the first floor where he sat to eat his supper, "where hast tha' been?"

"I'm very late, I know," replied Ben. "Jimmy Thorp came to ask me to fetch th' doctor fro' Leyton Lodge, little Susy were very ill an' James Thorp away; I went as fast as ever I could, an' th' doctor drove me back, but I'm very late for all that."

"It's strikin' ten now," said Bell, with his mouth full of bread and cheese, "tha' mun be off sharp. How yon door bangs in one o' th' rooms, oi mun stop that."

Taking up his lantern the watchman slowly climbed the stairs.

Ben was too much accustomed to his father's unceremonious conduct to offer any remonstrance at being left alone in the dark. Besides, could anything have served his purpose better?

He had been wondering how he could contrive to remain all night in the Works; now an opportunity had presented itself.

In a moment he rushed from the room and went as quickly as he could down a long passage.

He had no difficulty in finding his way about in the dark, he knew the Works so well.

There was a door at the end of the passage down which he hastened, which opened in a room where large baskets, or "skips" as they are called, were kept. As quick as thought Ben slipped behind a row of the skips, and crouched down on the floor.

"So Ben's gone," said John Bell, when he returned to the little room, and his half-finished supper; "well it isna th' first toime as he's found his way out in th' dark, an' it were toime he were gone, oi'll fasten th' bolt now," and taking his lantern in his hand, Bell crossed the yard, and bolted the gate.

Ben heard his footsteps in the yard, and heard him return and lock the door.

What should he do now?

Go back to his father, and beg, implore, and entreat him to allow no stranger's foot to cross the threshold of the door?

And what if his father laughed him to scorn? Or, ndignant at the accusation, refused to listen to him?

What if, after all, his father were innocent of all this; what if it were but some dreadful dream, some vision of his disordered imagination ? Ben was no coward, but he shrank from the thought of accusing his father of acting in so mean and despicable a manner.

Better that he should stay quietly where he was, and when daylight drew near he would seek his father, and tell him why he had remained in the Works all night, to save him if he could from that which was sinful.

He would tell him, too, how ill he felt, and ask his permission to rest for a day or two.

Poor Ben, his whole frame trembled, and his brain seemed to be in a perfect whirl.

"Lord help me," he said.

He tried to clothe his thoughts and longings in other words, but words failed him.

"Lord help me," he murmured again.

The large clock struck eleven, and soon afterwards Ben heard his father coming down the passage that led to the room where he was.

He crouched down behind the skips, and remained still and quiet on the floor. He heard his father's heavy footstep as he crossed the room, and, fearful lest his cough should come on, and betray his hiding-place, he took from his pocket a lozenge he had had given him, and as quietly as possible put it in his mouth. In doing this, however, his arm rubbed against one of the skips, making a slight noise.

"Rats," said John Bell, "oi mun ax for some more poison for 'em."

With his lantern in one hand, and his watchman's staff in the other, he walked through the room and out of the other door.

Then the thought entered Ben's mind, what if his father should lock the doors at the end of the passages leading to the long-room where he was hiding!

He groped his way to the nearest door, the one by which his father had entered, and went cautiously along the passage.

No, there was no door locked there. Ben could, if he wished, return to the little room in which Bell took his supper.

A fit of coughing came on, long and violent, and Ben crept back to the long-room and skips again.

The watchman away up in the rooms where the silent machinery stood never heard the sound.

He only heard the splash of the rain against the windows, and the wind rising and moaning around the building.

The clock struck twelve, and Ben, who was listening to every sound, heard his father descend the stairs, and unlock the door by which he went in and out.

"He's goin' to th' engine-house now," said Ben, for his father had told him the times at which he went to attend to the fires.

Then Ben left the long-room, and the skips, and went nearer to the door, and listened.

The clock struck the quarter, and his father had not returned.

Then the half-hour, and Ben heard the gate opened and closed again, and footsteps coming quietly and cautiously towards the door.

Could Ben reach the door first, and bolt and bar them out?

The thought came too late, for as the boy rushed onwards he heard the three men quietly enter, and the door fastened once more.

But a moment's reflection showed him that had he carried out his purpose Bell would still have found his way in; for he had all the keys with him, and, rather than have been baffled and thwarted in his purpose at the very outset, he would have smashed one of the lower windows, and obtained admittance in that way.

"Has't browt money?" Ben heard his father ask, as the three men entered the little room.

"Seeing is believing," said Robert Grant, taking out his pocket-book.

"Four fivers," said Bell; "now to work, oi'll see yo' dunnot leave wi'out settlin' up wi' me."

"We'll do nothing shabby, depend upon it," said the other Grant (Will, his brother called him); "we might have to ask a favour again some time."

"Come on, then," said Bell, "let's waste no more toime, yo' mun be clear out o' here in two hours. What is to be first, th' new machines?"

"Yes, we may as well have a look at those," said

Mr. Robert Grant, taking in his hand the lantern Bell had lighted for him; my brother will not want one," he added, "he has his note-book to attend to."

The three men went up the stairs, the two with the lanterns walking first, Will Grant with his pencil and note-book in his hand the last.

Ben's mind was fully made up now.

"Lord help me," he prayed again.

Then, only waiting until he heard his father close the door of the room he and the two men had entered, he went quietly up the stairs. He opened the door and stood face to face with the three men. The two Grants looked at each other but said not a word; but the watchman put down his lantern, and seized the trembling boy in his strong grasp.

The broad-shouldered man, with his heavy brow, and dark, angry eyes, was not a pleasant sight to look upon just then.

"Art tha' alone?" cried Bell.

"Ay, alone," said Ben, faintly.

"Dost tha' know why they're here?" asked the father, pointing towards the two men.

"I know all," said Ben. "Father," he gasped, "they have bribed you, tempted you, but it is not too late, you have not touched their money, only let 'em go their way, an' I'll not breathe to any one."

"Tha' wilt breathe no word as it is," exclaimed Bell, almost mad with passion, "swear tha' wilt na' say one word o' what tha' hast seen an' heard, or oi'll put it out o' thee power to speak; th' dead tell no tales."

"Nay, nay, gently," interposed Mr. Robert Grant, "tell the boy he shall have a good present out of the money you receive if he promises to hold his tongue. We are doing no harm here, my boy," he added.

Ben heard not a word he said, he felt his strength failing him fast, his face was as white as death, and his eyes sought his father's face.

His brain was dizzy; he seemed to hear his father's threat repeated again and again, and he found himself wondering *how* he would kill him! With one blow? Or would he throw him into the deep pond—"the lodge," as it was called—at the other side of the Works?

There would be a hue and cry made for him, and if his body were found there the people would only conclude that he had fallen in by accident; others had met with death in the treacherous lodge, and why not Ben?

"Lord help me," he said again.

John Bell relaxed his hold of the boy, and stood watching him, no sign of pity or forbearance on his stern, hard face; all the man's evil passions were roused within him.

"Swear!" he exclaimed.

Ben bowed his head a moment, and his pale lips moved as if in prayer.

Then he looked up, and Bell saw the unutterable horror expressed in the boy's white face, but he saw no yielding fear.

"Wilt tha' swear?" he said again.

"I conna swear," said Ben; "it's only reet as th' master should know as there's traitors here; if I live I'll tell him, unless yo' will bid 'em go."

Not pausing to listen to the remonstrances of the two Grants, mad with anger, blinded with passion, John Bell raised his hand and struck at the boy.

Ben saw his hand raised, and moved aside to ward off the blow if possible, but his strength was almost gone; he reeled and fell backwards on the floor, hitting his head as he did so against an iron wheel.

"Come," whispered Will Grant, hoarsely. "Come Robert, the lad may be dead."

Self-preservation was a very powerful instinct in Robert Grant's mind, and without pausing even to look at Ben, he took up his lantern and walked towards the door.

John Bell followed the two men down the stairs, and out into the cold night air; mechanically he unlocked the door, and unfastened the gate.

Both the men spoke to him, but he never noticed or answered their remarks, or raised any objections to their sudden departure.

He bolted the gate, and locked the door again, climbed the stairs, and entered the room, where lay on the floor, white and still, the boy who had chosen rather to suffer death than to commit sin.

CHAPTER X.

NEW YEAR'S EVE.

AT first John Bell believed that Ben was dead; he thought that the shock and fright had killed him. But as he bent down over the quiet form, he heard him breathing, very faintly, very feebly, it is true, but still life had not left him.

Bell took off his coat, and made a pillow of it for the boy's head.

As he did so, he saw how in falling he had given his head a severe blow.

There was a deep cut above the left eye, a broad gash made by a sharp point projecting from the wheel against which Ben had knocked himself.

Bell shuddered as he tied his handkerchief over the wound.

Then he got some water, and bathed the boy's face and hands.

Still there was no sign of any return to consciousness, and all Bell's fears came back again.

"Oi mun get him to th' cottage an' to bed," he said at last.

There was a man who lived near the Works who could undertake the watchman's duties, if he would.

To his house Bell hastened, and succeeded in arousing him at once.

"Wilt tha' go to th' Works for me," he said. "Ben is ill, an' oi mun go whom."

"Ben ill! Ah, oi'll go," replied the man; "leave th' keys here."

Back to the Works Bell went with rapid steps. He wrapped his coat round the still unconscious boy.

Even then, unnerved and excited as he was, the man's habitual caution did not forsake him.

He stooped down, and by the light of his lantern looked carefully on the floor where the boy had fallen. No, there were no tell-tale marks there, and Bell breathed more freely again.

He carried the boy in his arms to the cottage where Martin, who had promised to be his substitute, lived.

He put the keys on the step and knocked at the door.

"Th' keys are on th' step," he shouted, and was gone before Martin, who was slow in speech and slow at work, could reply.

The cottage was soon reached, the key taken from Ben's pocket, and the door unlocked.

Jess made a piteous moan as Bell placed the boy on the old-fashioned chintz-covered sofa that stood in the front room.

Then Bell went for the doctor; he told him Ben had had a fall and hurt his head.

"Poor lad," said Dr. Eliot, "he is not in a state of health to stand any severe shock. I'll come at once, Bell; I was just going to bed; I only left Mrs. Thorp's half-an-hour ago."

Bell watched by the poor lad's side until daybreak and then went to Mr. Deane.

"They're two chaps as 'ave come into some property, an' they've some reason or other fur wantin' to know all th' ins an' outs o' calico-printin'; they were nettled at Mr. Henry's refusin' to let 'em go o'er th' Works, an' they made a bet wi' some o' their friends i' Manchester as they would go i' spite o' him; oi've heard Ben read how Judas sold his Master fur thirty pieces o' silver; oi sold moine fur four bank-notes! Yo' con tell on me, Mr. Deane; but as yo' are a mon an' a Christian, wait while Ben is better, oi should go mad if oi were took from him just now."

"I shall not betray your confidence," said Mr. Deane; "rest assured you shall remain with Ben."

"And your mother, will she come an' see him? He thinks a sight on her."

"Yes, she will come; I had better tell her how Ben got the blow."

"Ay, tell her, tell her, hoo's not one to chatter," replied Bell, forgetting in his anxiety for Ben his distrust of a woman's power to keep a secret.

It was a nasty blow the doctor said, when he came

F

the second time to see the boy, but there was not much fear but that he would recover from its effects; only, and the doctor looked very grave now, the boy seemed to be so very weak, only the night before he had been pained to hear what a bad cough he had.

"If it's nobbut weakness hinders him getting better, there's a sight o' things money can buy to mak' foaks strong," exclaimed Bell; "see here, doctor, Ben con ha' onything as ud do him good, oi've money saved an' oi'll spend it all to get him well."

The first week in December passed, then the second, and still Ben lay in a state of unconsciousness. Now and then he seemed to rally, and Bell's hopes rose high, only to die away again as the boy relapsed into unconsciousness.

There was no delirium; he never called for his dead mother, or imagined she was with him, or spoke of the past; he simply lay on his little bed, "slippin' away fro' life," old Mrs. Wynnatt said.

The third week came, and then Ben slowly returned to consciousness again. He opened his eyes one afternoon, and saw his father standing at the foot of the bed intently watching him.

"Father," he said, "how is Susy?"

"Susy!" repeated Bell; "who is Susy?"

"Mrs. Thorp's little girl, I fetched th' doctor, yo' know," gasped Ben.

"Oh! Susy Thorp, she ails nothin', it were a fit, she were cuttin' a tooth, th' doctor soon had her round again. Ben," continued Bell, going nearer to the boy, "Ben, dost tha' moind now all as 'appened, them two scamps as bribed me, an' how tha' camed, an' oi threatened oi'd kill thee an' oi hit out at thee an' tha' fell an' knocked thysen ?"

"I knocked mysen, did I ?" said the boy, wonderingly. "Ay, I know all th' rest."

"Con yo' ever forgive me, Ben ?"

"Forgive yo' ?"

And the boy looked up into the man's worn, haggard face; he took his hand and pressed it to his lips. "It's all reet between thee an' me, father, say no more about that."

For several days after Ben seemed really better, but the doctor only shook his head when Bell declared the lad would soon be well again. The patient himself appeared to think that he was slowly but surely recovering.

"When I'm better," he said, on Christmas Day to Mrs. Deane, who was sitting beside him, "father is goin' to church with me."

The doctor was in the room, and heard the remark. As he shook hands with Mrs. Deane, he said, "Try if you can gently tell the poor boy that there is little or no hope of his recovery. Should he grow suddenly worse he may be alarmed."

"Ben," said the old lady, quietly, when they were alone together, "would you grieve very much if you knew you would never be better here on earth again?"

The boy looked earnestly at her. "There's father," he said; "all I want to do for him, and th' work I want to do for th' dear Lord?"

"The Lord will take care of your father, Ben, and of the work too, He will send forth other labourers if it please Him to call you home to Himself."

"I'm *young to die*," said the boy; "an' oh! if I'd had health an' strength I'd ha' loved to work for Christ; but if it's His will for me to go, then I'll noan murmur."

He seemed better all that week, but the next week he grew worse again, weaker and weaker day by day.

John Bell told Mr. Ashford of the boy's critical state, and that the second doctor called in only confirmed Dr. Eliot's opinion that the boy might pass away any moment.

"He has no stamina, no constitution to fall back upon," said the medical men.

"And you want to be released from your duties in order to be at home with him," said Mr. Ashford kindly; "stay with him by all means, I will find a substitute for your work."

All that medical skill could suggest was done for Ben, but no human means could save the boy's young life.

The last day of the old year came, and still Ben lingered.

"I thought I should see th' old year out,' he said. "Father, I mun be th' first to wish yo' a happy New

Year; I'll wish it yo' now, lest I should be asleep when it comes."

"There'll be no happy years for me, Ben, if tha' goes," sobbed Bell.

"There'll be *peace*," said the boy. "Th' peace th' world conna give nor take away. Father, mind, yo' promised me yo' would seek it."

"Oi will, lad, oi will," replied Bell.

"What shall I read to you, Ben?" asked Mrs. Deane that evening.

"Read in the Revelation," said Ben, "about him that overcometh."

"Th' reward's too great for me, Lord," they heard him whisper as his friend closed the book; a crown, an' a seat on th' throne, an' a new name! I've done nothin' for Thee, Lord!"

Then he opened his eyes, and looked round the room.

Mr. Deane and his mother, John Bell, and old Mrs. Wynatt, were all there. "How good you've all been," said Ben; "do I hear th' bells ringin'?"

No, the bells were not ringing, they told him.

"Is this dyin'?" he asked. "*I'm noan feart.*"

There was another pause; then he said, "Mother, are yo' callin' me? I'm comin' now, mother!"

Then all was still and silent for a time.

Then the church bells rang out, welcoming the new year.

But the boy in the little cottage heard them not.

He had gone to the city where time is not counted by weeks and months and years.

"For a thousand years in Thy sight are but as yesterday when it is past, and as a watch in the night."

CHAPTER XL.

AT LIBERTY.

JOHN BELL kept faithfully the promises he had made to Ben. He attended the services of the church, and read the Bible daily; he prayed earnestly, and yet failed for a time to find the peace of which Ben had spoken.

He was sitting alone in the cottage one afternoon, thinking of the boy who had found this peace, and who had been "faithful even unto death."

He thought of the lad's patience, his gentleness and forbearance, and he thought of his own coldness and harshness.

The man's wrong-doing had been great, but his repentance was true and sincere. "Oi'd gi' all th' money oi ha' in th' bank, an' all oi ha' invested, oi'd gi' it gladly, freely, only to ha' Ben here again," he exclaimed.

Then he thought of the home the boy had gone to,

the bright and happy home the Saviour had prepared for him.

"He said he were '*noan feart*' to go, that were because he loved th' Saviour," said Bell. "Why did he love Him so?"

He took up Ben's little Bible, and turned to the story of the Cross. He read it over and over again.

"Oi see it now," he said at last. "Christ died for us because He loved us, an' all he axes us to do is to love Him an' try to do His will."

The next day he found his way to Mr. Deane.

"Oi comed to tell yo' oi believe in Him," he said.

"Believe in whom?" asked Mr. Deane.

"Him as died on th' cross for th' sins of th' whole world, for *my* sins; oi believe He's forgiven me, though oi can *never forgive mysen*."

The next day he went to the parsonage and asked for "th' parson."

"What can I do for you, my friend?" asked Mr. Mervyn, kindly.

"Thank yo', Sir," replied Bell, "yo' 'ave done what yo' could for me. There's a bit o' money here," he added, placing a small canvas bag on the table, "an' yo' can gi' it to th' poor, or to th' missioners, or what yo' think best. Him as is gone would ha' been a missioner if he'd lived; *he wor one while he did live;* he missioned to me same as no one else in th' world ever did. Oi could ha' made his life a deal brighter, Sir, if oi had na' loved my money so; but I conna undo th' past. Yo' shall ha' some more money fro me another day, Sir;" and before Mr. Mervyn could express his happiness at the change in the man's feelings, or his thanks for the unexpected gift of ten pounds, he had gone.

The spring came with all its promises of new life and beauty.

One bright, warm afternoon, John Bell closed his cottage door, and went, as he often did, into the quiet churchyard.

In his hand he held a wicker cage containing the lark.

He had remembered Ben's wish, and had bought a larger cage for the bird.

He walked slowly through the churchyard until he came to the boy's grave.

What a quiet, peaceful spot it was!

The bright sunlight passed in and out through the boughs of the trees, and a bird on a hawthorn tree sang clearly and sweetly, but yet softly, as though it feared to disturb the sleeper's rest.

"Ben, little Ben," said the tall, strong man, as he knelt beside the grave where pink and white daisies and sweet-scented violets grew, "Ben, oi've found th' peace th' telled me on, an' it were all thy doing, Ben."

And the strong man's tears fell fast.

Then, rising, he opened the door of the wicker cage.

"Him as is gone," he said to the lark, "loved for all things livin' to be free an' happy, he could na' abide to keep birds and sich loike caged up, he grieved to see thee frettin' in thy cage, but oi could na' turn thee out in th' cold winter. But it's spring toime now, an' tha' con build thysen a nest," he added, as he took the lark tenderly out of the cage.

The bird fluttered gently over the surface of the ground, then paused as if to rest.

"It's lame or hurt it's wing," exclaimed Bell.

But it was not lamed or hurt, it was only overjoyed to find itself free once more.

It rose again, higher, higher it soared this time.

Then it came back again, but only for a moment.

It flew suddenly from the ground; higher, higher it rose, and soared up to, and beyond, the trees, to where the white clouds drifted over the sunny sky; and, as it rose higher, and yet higher, it filled the air with song.

Printed at the Guardian Office, Toronto.

OUR PUBLICATIONS.

Works by Rev. John Carroll, D.D.

CASE AND HIS COTEMPORARIES. A Biographical History of Methodism in Canada. 5 vols., cloth, $4.90.

METHODIST BAPTISM. Limp cloth, 15 cents.

FATHER CORSON. Being the Life of the late Rev. Robert Corson. 12mo., cloth, 90 cents

THE EXPOSITION EXPOUNDED, DEFENDED, AND SUPPLEMENTED. Limp cloth, 40 cents.

SCHOOL OF THE PROPHETS; OR, FATHER MCROREY'S CLASS AND SQUIRE FIRSTMAN'S KITCHEN FIRE. A Book for Methodists. 264 pages, cloth, 80 cents.

THOUGHTS AND CONCLUSIONS OF A MAN OF YEARS, CONCERNING CHURCHES AND CHURCH CONNECTION. Paper, 5 cents.

Works by W. M. Punshon, D.D., LL.D.

LECTURES AND SERMONS. Printed on thick superfine paper, 378 pages, with a fine steel portrait, and strongly bound in extra fine cloth, $1.

THE PRODIGAL SON, FOUR DISCOURSES ON. 87 pages. Paper cover, 25 cents; cloth, 35 cents.

THE PULPIT AND THE PEW: THEIR DUTIES TO EACH OTHER AND TO GOD. Two Addresses. Paper cover, 10 cents; cloth, 45 cents.

TABOR; OR, THE CLASS-MEETING. A Plea and an Appeal. Paper, 5 cents each; 30 cents per dozen.

CANADA AND ITS RELIGIOUS PROSPECTS. Paper, 5 cents.

MEMORIAL SERMONS. Containing a Sermon, each, by Drs. Punshon, Gervase Smith, J. W. Lindsay, and A. P. Lowrey. Paper, 25 cents; cloth, 35 cents.

Works by Rev. J. Jackson Wray.

NESTLETON MAGNA, A STORY OF YORKSHIRE METHODISM. Illustrated. 12mo., cloth, $1.

MATTHEW MELLOWDEW, A STORY WITH MORE HEROES THAN ONE. Illustrated. 12mo., cloth, $1.

PAUL MEGGITT'S DELUSION. Illustrated. 12mo., cloth, $1.

OUR PUBLICATIONS.

Works by Rev. W. H. Withrow, M.A.

GREAT PREACHERS. Cloth, 60 cents.
KING'S MESSENGER; OR, LAWRENCE TEMPLE'S PROBATION. Cloth, 75 cents.
METHODIST WORTHIES. Cloth, 60 cents.
NEVILLE TRUEMAN, THE PIONEER PREACHER. Cloth, 75 cents.
ROMANCE OF MISSIONS. Cloth, 60 cents.
THE LIQUOR TRAFFIC. Paper, 5 cents.
PROHIBITION, THE DUTY OF THE HOUR. Paper, 5 cents.
IS ALCOHOL FOOD? Paper, 5 cents.
THE BIBLE AND THE TEMPERANCE QUESTION. Paper, 10 cents.
THE PHYSIOLOGICAL EFFECTS OF ALCOHOL. Paper, 10 cents.
INTEMPERANCE; ITS EVILS AND THEIR REMEDIES. Paper, 15 cents.

In Press,
POPULAR HISTORY OF CANADA. 600 pp., 8vo. Five steel engravings and 100 woodcuts.

Works by John Ashworth.

STRANGE TALES FROM HUMBLE LIFE. First Series, cloth, $1.
STRANGE TALES FROM HUMBLE LIFE. Second Series, cloth, 45 cents.

Works by Rev. J. Cynddylan Jones.

STUDIES IN MATTHEW. 12mo., cloth, $1.25.
STUDIES IN THE ACTS. 12mo., cloth, $1.50.

In preparation by the same Author.
STUDIES IN THE GOSPEL ACCORDING TO ST. JOHN.

THE BIBLE AND METHODIST HYMN BOOK COMBINED. The sheets of the Bible are printed in ruby type, and have been imported from England especially for this purpose, as well as the paper on which the Hymns are printed. 32mo., full morocco circuit, gilt edges, $3.50.

Also a
BIBLE AND METHODIST HYMN BOOK. Larger size and type than the above. The Bible is printed in minion type, and the Hymns in brevier on English paper. Crown 8vo., morocco circuit, gilt edges, $5.00. Levant morocco, kid lined, gilt edges, $6.00.

WESLEY'S DOCTRINAL STANDARDS. Part I. The Sermons, with Introductions, Analysis, and Notes. By Rev. N. Burwash, S.T.D., Prof. of Theology in the University of Victoria College, Cobourg. Large 8vo., cloth, 536 pages, $2.50.

OUR PUBLICATIONS.

TOWARD THE SUNRISE. Being Sketches of Travel in Europe and the East. With a Memorial Sketch of the Rev. Wm. Morley Punshon, LL.D. By the Rev. Hugh Johnston, M.A., B.D. 472 pages, with numerous Illustrations. Elegantly bound in extra English cloth, with black and gold stamping on side and back, $1.25.

At the request of many friends, Mr. Johnston has been induced to greatly enlarge the admirable Letters of Travel with which the readers of the *Guardian* were greatly delighted during the early part of this year. And he has added a more full and adequate memorial of Dr. Punshon than any which has elsewhere appeared.

ARROWS IN THE HEART OF THE KING'S ENEMIES; OR, ATHEISTIC ERRORS OF THE DAY REFUTED, AND THE DOCTRINE OF A PERSONAL GOD VINDICATED. By the Rev. Alexander W. McLeod, D.D., at one time editor of the *Wesleyan*, Halifax, N.S., now a minister of the M.E. Church, Baltimore, U.S. 12mo, cloth, 128 pages, 45 cents.

SPIRITUAL STRUGGLES OF A ROMAN CATHOLIC. An Autobiographical Sketch. By Louis N. Beaudry, with an introduction by Rev. B Hawley, D.D. With steel portrait. Cloth, $1.00.

THE RELIGION OF LIFE; OR, CHRIST AND NICODEMUS. By John G. Manly. Cloth, 50 cents.

CYCLOPÆDIA OF METHODISM IN CANADA. Containing Historical, Educational, and Statistical Information, dating from the beginning of the work in the several Provinces in the Dominion of Canada. By Rev. George H. Cornish. With artotype portrait. 8vo., cloth, $4.50; sheep, $5.

LOYALISTS OF AMERICA AND THEIR TIMES. By Rev. Egerton Ryerson, LL.D. 2 vols., large 8vo., with portrait. Cloth, $5; half morocco, $7.

COMPANION TO THE REVISED NEW TESTAMENT. By Alex. Roberts, D.D.; and an American Revisor. Paper, 30 cents; cloth, 65 cents.

LIFE OF HON. JUDGE WILMOT. By Rev. J. Lathern. With artotype portrait 12mo., cloth, 75 cents.

LIFE OF J. B. MORROW. By Rev. A. W. Nicolson. 75 cents.

LIFE OF GIDEON OUSELEY. By Rev. William Arthur, M.A. Cloth, $1.

OLD CHRISTIANITY AGAINST PAPAL NOVELTIES. By Gideon Ouseley. Illustrated. Cloth, $1.

A SUMMER IN PRAIRIE-LAND. By Rev. Alexander Sutherland, D.D. Illustrated. 12mo., paper, 40 cents; cloth, 70 cents.

LIFE AND TIMES OF ANSON GREEN, D.D. Written by himself. 12mo., cloth, with portrait, $1.

VOICES FROM THE THRONE; OR, GOD'S CALLS TO FAITH AND OBEDIENCE. By Rev. J. C. Seymour. Cloth, 50 cents.

THE GUIDING ANGEL. By Kate Murray. 18mo., cloth, 30 cents.

OUR PUBLICATIONS.

APPLIED LOGIC. By S. S. Nelles, LL.D. Cloth, 75 cents.
CHRISTIAN REWARDS. By Rev. J. S. Evans. Cloth, 50 cents.
CHRISTIAN PERFECTION. By Rev. J. Wesley. Paper, 10 cents; cloth, 20 cents.
THE CLASS-LEADER: HIS WORK AND HOW TO DO IT. By J. Atkinson, M.A. Cloth, 60 cents.
CONVERSATIONS ON BAPTISM. By Rev. A. Langford. Cloth, 30 cents.
CATECHISM OF BAPTISM. By D. D. Currie. Cloth, 50 cents.
SERMONS ON CHRISTIAN LIFE. By the Rev. C. W. Hawkins. 12mo., cloth, $1.
MEMORIALS OF MR. AND MRS. JACKSON. With steel portrait. Cloth, 75 cents.
CIRCUIT REGISTER. $1.50.
WEEKLY OFFERING BOOK. $1.50.
DISCIPLINE OF THE METHODIST CHURCH OF CANADA. 60 cents.
METHODIST HYMN-BOOK. In various sizes and styles of binding. Prices from 30 cents upwards.
METHODIST CATECHISMS. No. I, per dozen, 25 cents. No. II, per dozen, 60 cents. No. III, per dozen, 75 cents.
SUNDAY-SCHOOL RECORD BOOK. $1.25.
SUNDAY-SCHOOL MINUTE BOOK. Designed by Thomas Wallis. 60c.
SUNDAY-SCHOOL REGISTER. 50 cents.
SECRETARY'S MINUTE BOOK. 50 cents.
LIBRARIAN'S ACCOUNT BOOK. 50 cents.

MUSIC BOOKS.

	Per dozen.	Each.
SUNDAY-SCHOOL WAVE	$5 00	$0 50
SUNDAY-SCHOOL HARMONIUM	3 60	0 35
SUNDAY-SCHOOL ORGAN	5 00	0 50
SUNDAY-SCHOOL HARP	4 00	0 40
DOMINION SINGER (Harp and Organ)	9 00	0 90
METHODIST TUNE BOOK	10 00	1 00
CANADIAN CHURCH HARMONIST	10 00	1 00
SACRED HARMONY	8 00	0 75
COMPANION TO S. S. WAVE (words only)	1 20	0 15
COMPANION TO S. S. HARMONIUM	1 20	0 15
COMPANION TO S. S. ORGAN	1 75	0 20
COMPANION TO S. S. HARP	1 20	0 15
COMPANION TO DOMINION SINGER	3 00	0 30

All other leading Sunday-School Music Books in Stock.

WILLIAM BRIGGS,
78 & 80 King Street East, Toronto.

SUNDAY-SCHOOL LIBRARIES.

It will be to your advantage, if you want good, sound, Sunday-School Library Books, to write for lists. Our Libraries are cheap.

Dominion Libraries.

No. 1, 50 volumes, 16mo. ....$25 60 net.
No. 2, 100   "   18mo. .... 25 00 "

Little People's Picture Library.

50 volumes, 48mo..$10 00 net.

Acme Libraries.

No. 1, 50 volumes, 16mo. ....$25 00 net
No. 2, 50   "   16mo. .... 25 00 "

Excelsior Libraries.

No. 1, 50 volumes, 18mo. ....$15 00 net
No. 2, 40   "   18mo. .... 14 00 "
No. 3, 15   "   12mo. .... 9 00 "
No. 4, 15   "   12mo. .... 9 00 "

Model Libraries.

No. 1, 50 volumes, 16mo. ....$22 00 net
No. 2, 50   "   18mo. .... 16 50 "
No. 3, 50   "   16mo. .... 27 50 "

Economical Libraries.

No. A, 50 volumes, 12mo...........................$24 50 net.
No. B, 50   "   12mo. .... 29 50 "
No. C, 40   "   12mo. .... 18 50 "

Primary Library.

40 volumes, 18mo......................................$7 50 net.

The Olive Library.

40 large 16mo. volumes ....$25 00 net.

TORONTO SELECTED LIBRARIES.

No. 1, 100 volumes, 16mo.................................$25 00
No. 2, 100   "   16mo................................. 25 00
No. 5, 100   "   16mo................................. 25 00

All the above-mentioned Library Books contain many illustrations, are strongly bound, and put up in neat boxes ready for shipping. These Libraries are giving great satisfaction wherever sold.

Be sure to send for Lists of the Books contained in these Libraries, also of

SUNDAY-SCHOOL REQUISITES,

of which we have a large variety, to

WILLIAM BRIGGS,
78 & 80 King Street East, Toronto.

LIFE AND SPEECHES OF
HON. JOHN BRIGHT.
BY G. BARNETT SMITH,
Author of the Life of Hon. W. E. Gladstone.
Price, $2.75.

☞ *The English Edition sells at Twenty-four Shillings sterling.*

One large Crown 8vo. volume of 700 pages, with two fine steel portraits, one from the latest taken of Mr. Bright, the other from a painting made of him in early life.'

Every Parliamentary speech made by Mr. Bright, and every other one of his Public Addresses of importance is dealt with at length, and the finest and most important passages published in *extenso*. The biography is brought down to and includes the year 1881.

The London *Times* says:—"This work will be welcomed by a large number of readers. The author has taken great pains to make the work at once accurate and full. *He has evidently had access to private sources of information, for he gives accounts of Mr. Bright's personal life that it would otherwise not have been possible to give.* * * * He has followed his subject through all the steps of his career."

CHAMBERS' ENCYCLOPÆDIA,
Latest Edition, Cloth or Leather.

ENGLISH DICTIONARIES,
WEBSTER AND WORCESTER, UNABRIDGED, WITH NEW SUPPLEMENTS.

SOLE AGENT FOR CANADA FOR
Messrs. I. K. FUNK & Co.s PUBLICATIONS.

TEACHER'S EDITION OF THE REVISED NEW TESTAMENT. With an Index and Condensed Concordance, Harmony of the Gospels, Maps, Parallel Passages in full. Tables and many other indispensable Helps. Prices, Postage Free:—Cloth boards, red edges, $1.50; sheep, $2.00; French Morocco, gilt edges, $4.50; Turkey morocco, limp, gilt edges, $5.50; Levant morocco, divinity circuit, kid lined, silk sewed, $10.00.

YOUNG'S BIBLE CONCORDANCE. 4to., 1,090 pages, heavy paper Author's revised edition. Cloth, $4.65* ; sheep, $5.50* ; French Morocco, $5.75.* (Also the American Book Exchange Edition. Cloth $2.40, net).

TALKS ABOUT JESUS, TO BOYS AND GIRLS. Illustrations for teachers. By over thirty of the most eminent preachers, such as Farrar, Stanley, Newton, Taylor, Crafts, Vincent, &c. It is an attractive story book for children at home, or for Sunday-school libraries, as there are numerous stories in the sermons. A beautifully illustrated book. 12mo., cloth, 400 pages. $1.50.

THROUGH THE PRISON TO THE THRONE. Illustrations of Life from the Biography of Joseph. By Rev. Joseph S. Van Dyke. 12mo., cloth, $1.15.

A CRITICAL AND EXEGETICAL COMMENTARY ON THE BOOK OF EXODUS, with a New Translation. By James G. Murphy, D.D., T.C.D., Professor of Hebrew, Belfast. With Preface by Rev. John Hall, D.D. Two parts, paper, each 50 cents.

CHRISTIAN SOCIOLOGY. By Dr. Stuckenberg. 12mo., cloth, 382 pp., heavy tinted paper, $1.75.

CLERGYMEN'S AND STUDENTS' HEALTH ; OR, THE TRUE WAY TO ENJOY LIFE. By W. M. Cornell, M.D. 12mo., cloth, 300 pp., $1.15.

DRILL BOOK IN VOCAL CULTURE AND GESTURE. By Professor E. P. Thwing. Fifth edition. 12mo., manilla, 115 pp., 25c.*

FULTON'S REPLIES TO BEECHER, FARRAR AND INGERSOLL ON HELL. Three Sermons. One vol., 8vo., paper, 38 pp., 10c.*

GILEAD ; OR, THE VISION OF ALL SOULS' HOSPITAL. An Allegory. By Rev. J. Hyatt Smith, Member of Congress elect. 12mo., 360 pp , $1.15.

HANDBOOK OF ILLUSTRATIONS. [By Rev. E. P. Thwing First Series. Third edition. 25c*. Second Series, just issued, 25c.*

HOME ALTAR. By Dr. Deems. New edition. 12mo., Cloth, 281 pp , 90c.

THE HOMILIST. By David Thomas, D.D. Vol. XII., Editor's Series. Cloth, 12mo., 368 pp., heavy tinted paper, $1.50.

HOMILETIC ENCYCLOPÆDIA OF ILLUSTRATIONS IN THEOLOGY AND MORALS. A Handbook of Practical Divinity, and a Commentary on Holy Scripture. By Rev. R. A. Bertram. Royal 8vo., cloth, 892 pp., $4.50.

HOW TO PAY CHURCH DEBTS. By Sylvanus Stall. It is the only book on this subject. 12mo., 280 pp., tinted paper, $1.75.

GODET'S COMMENTARY ON THE GOSPEL OF ST. LUKE. With Preface and Notes. By John Hall, D.D. $2.80.

THESE SAYINGS OF MINE. By Jos. Parker, D.D. 8vo., cloth, heavy paper, $1.75.

THINGS NEW AND OLD. A Storehouse of Illustrations, Apologues, Adages, with their several applications, collected from the writings and sayings of the learned in all ages. By John Spencer. To which is added, "A Treasury of Similes," by Robert Cawdray. Royal 8vo., cloth, over 1,100 pp., $4.80.

STANDARD SERIES. CLASS A. Fifteen volumes by the most Eminent Authors. Nos. 1, 2, 5, 6, 7, 9, 10, 11, 20, 21, 32, 40, 41, 42, and 43 of Standard Series, bound in one vol. 4to., cloth, 670 pp., $3.50.

POPULAR HISTORY OF ENGLAND. By Charles Knight. 4to., 1,370 pp. Bound handsomely in cloth, 2 vols., $3.75.

☞ *Books marked with a * are sold net.*

Standard Series of cheap books bound in manilla. From Nos. 1 to 67, now ready. Prices vary.

☞ Send for Catalogue giving a complete list of our miscellaneous books.

All the latest leading books received and kept in stock as soon as published.

☞ *Our Stock is the largest in the Dominion in the following Departments, viz.* :—*Commentaries, Theology, Sermons, Lectures and Essays, History,* **Travels,** *Cyclopædias, Dictionaries, Poetry, Biography, Sunday-School* **Library** *and Prize Books, Sunday-School Cards and Tickets, Blank* **Books,** *Wall Maps, Mottoes,* **and** *every Description of Sunday-School Requisites, Music Books, Stationery, &c., &c.*

PERIODICALS.

PER YEAR—POSTAGE FREE.

CHRISTIAN GUARDIAN, Weekly. $2.00.

METHODIST MAGAZINE, 96 pages, Monthly. Illustrated. $2.00.

SUNDAY-SCHOOL BANNER. 32 pages, 8vo., Monthly. Under six copies, 65 cents; over six copies, 60 cents.

CANADIAN SCHOLAR'S QUARTERLY. 8 cents.

QUARTERLY REVIEW SERVICE. By the year, 24 cents a dozen, or $2.00 per 100; per quarter, 6 cents a dozen; 50 cents per 100.

PLEASANT HOURS. 8 pages, 4to., semi-monthly. Single copies, 30 cents; less than 20 copies, 22 cents; over 500 copies, 20 cents.

BEREAN LEAVES. Monthly; 100 copies per month, $5.50.

SUNBEAM. Semi-monthly; Less than 20 copies, 15 cents; 20 copies and upwards, 12 cents.

WILLIAM BRIGGS,
78 & 80 King Street East, Toronto.

www.ingramcontent.com/pod-product-compliance
Lightning Source LLC
Chambersburg PA
CBHW030428300426
44112CB00009B/901